SURPRISED BY GRACE

A Journey Beyond Personal Enlightenment

By
Amber Terrell

TRUE LIGHT PUBLISHING
Boulder, Colorado

SURPRISED BY GRACE
A Journey Beyond Personal Enlightenment

Cover and page design: Michelle Lundquist
Back cover photo: Maitri Robbins
Printed and bound by Thomson-Shore using recycled, acid-free paper
Manufactured in the United States of America

ISBN: 0-9656670-0-6
Library of Congress Catalog Card Number: 97-90029

TRUE LIGHT PUBLISHING
P.O. Box 17734
Boulder, CO 80308- 0734

Phone (303) 447-2547
Fax (303) 443-4373

With deepest gratitude to all those who read and commented on the manuscript and offered their suggestions, encouragement and support, especially to John Small, Shivaya Ma Ruane, Silvine and Stewart Farnell, Shanti Einolander, Ramananda and Moksha Bartek, and Achala Gebhardt. A special thanks to all those instrumental in this book coming to print, especially Toby Terrell, Michelle Lundquist, Fred Kries, Kali Grace, Maitri Robbins and the entire staff at Satsang Foundation & Press, and most of all to Gangaji.

*for
Gangaji,
River
of
Grace*

TABLE OF CONTENTS

THE SEARCH

*W*hen I set out in earnest on the spiritual quest as a young college student in the late sixties, there were certain images in my mind of what enlightenment would look like. As an enlightened being I imagined I would be "me," only with all the unwanted aspects of my personality corrected. And, having access to the limitless intelligence of the universe, I would of course be brilliant. Best of all, my life would be transformed into a blissful existence, a heaven-on-earth of perfect health and perfect circumstances, totally apart and protected from the disgusting, violent, selfish world I perceived all around me.

After more than a quarter of a century had passed—consumed in intense practice of meditation and yoga, fasting, study, long retreats in foreign lands, and years of service to an Indian teacher—I began to wonder, why hadn't enlightenment happened? Why hadn't my personality been fixed? Why, by now, didn't my life look like I imagined it should look?

By the end of 1994 a deep discouragement had set in. Though many beautiful, even spectacular experiences had occurred from time to time, though I had learned how to quiet the mind and breath, though I had even experienced certain of the *siddhis* (yogic powers),* enlightenment had remained a dream, a concept, existing in the mind only. It became obvious that in spite of years of sincere effort, no real progress had been made. Clearly there was a missing piece in my spiritual repertoire. But what? I had done all my practices so devotedly, for so long.

Into that darkest and most frustrated hour of my spiritual quest came a transmission of Grace so powerful that the mind was stopped, the dream was shattered by Reality, all concepts of enlightenment were quickly burned to ashes, and layer after layer of false identification with mind was ruthlessly cut. This

1

transmission took the form of a teacher named Gangaji, and emanated purely and directly from the lineage of one of the most respected sages of this century, Sri Ramana Maharshi.

Gangaji appeared in my life in the Spring of 1995 bearing a lei of roses in one hand and a sword in the other. With the roses she welcomed me, placing them around my neck in a loving embrace; with the sword she severed my head. This severing was only excruciating when I tried to cling to my head, to "mind" as something real, as who I was. As this illusion weakened, through the most unimaginable Grace, I saw that both the sword and the roses were the same—simply aspects of her infinite Love.

Gradually she revealed this Love to be my own Love, my own Self—not individual self as perceived by the mind, but true self, beyond mind, what some call the Christ Self or the universal Self—the ever-present Beloved.

Every human being, whether consciously or unconsciously, hunts for this Beloved Self in a thousand mental, emotional, and sensory directions. This hunting goes on incessantly in both the material and spiritual market-places of the world, until finally, often by some encounter with a powerful reflection of Self in someone or something, one is *stopped*—floored, flattened, surrendered—and in the stillness of That, one sees what has been overlooked, sees what has always been present, sees *finally* all that has ever been longed for is in reality *who one has always been.*

In that seeing is the awakening from a dream.

Many people speculate on whether or not a human teacher is necessary for this awakening, and in the past few years this question has become a topic of heated debate. Some argue that the intimate teacher/student relationship, so treasured and honored in the mystical traditions of the past, is unnecessary or inappropriate in this new age of conscious living. After all, isn't the truth really within us?

Theoretically, of course, an outer teacher need not be necessary. What everyone is seeking is nearer than breath, nearer than a heartbeat. But the resolve and ruthlessness required to cut the habit of mind identification is rare. Subtle indeed are the ways in which the ego avoids annihilation, carefully preserving itself even under the guise of "spiritual practice."

In Arthur C. Clarke's famous story *2001, A Space Odyssey*, the HAL 9000 computer can be seen as a perfect metaphor for the human ego. In the story, HAL is designed to run all aspects of the space ship, including life-support systems. When the crew notices that HAL has begun to make errors, errors it is not willing to admit, they realize the computer will have to be disconnected and the ship piloted via radio signals from HAL's twin computer back on earth. But HAL is not so easily disconnected. Its own preservation becomes more important than the service to mankind for which it has been designed. It begins to manipulate and destroy anything and anyone that threatens its existence, anything that might expose the lie of its betrayal.

The human ego operates in much the same way. *It* also is not so easily disconnected. Ego is pure illusion, created by the mistaken identification with mind and all its projections—mental, emotional, physical, and circumstantial—as who one is. Like HAL, it will put up a mighty defense to protect this illusion. Most people cannot see through the illusion, or the defense, long enough to really sever the habit of mental identification. It's like trusting HAL to sever its own misguided circuits.

This severing is traditionally the role of the guru, meaning literally, "dispeller of darkness." The guru is not only someone who has cut through the illusion, but one who reflects so purely this limitless reality which we all are that our own infinite Self can be seen reflected there. An indication that one has met one's true teacher is in this seeing of Self in the teacher, as in a spotless mirror.

This seeing is mysterious. It cannot be deserved. It cannot be bought. It cannot be explained or understood by the mind. The only word that comes close to describing it is *Grace*.

It is a mystery how this Grace may appear in one's life and penetrate the dream of separation. From the moment I first met Gangaji's eyes, Grace flooded every aspect of my life like a raging river floods the country-side, drowning everything in its wake, leaving no human-made structure intact, leaving nothing as it was. In the beginning this drowning caused much fear and struggling to arise. When everything one has identified with as "self" is being dissolved, there is a kind of death that is experienced. It has nothing to do with physical death. It is the death of the "personal," the death of separateness. It is the spiritual death spoken of in all the mystical traditions of the world, from St. John of the Cross, to the Vedic hymns of India, to the ecstatic poetry of the Sufis. It is a true death, a final death—a death of identification with all that can die and all that can be born. It is an awakening to eternity.

What a shock it has been to discover that enlightenment has nothing to do with the fulfillment of a personal wish list. Enlightenment is not personal at all. Ironically, it is the preoccupation with the personal, the clinging to mind and personality as who we are, that obscures the unbelievable Truth—enlightenment is already here, already who we are!

To all who have grown weary of the search, who feel a longing that burns deep within their heart, a longing which they know can never be satisfied through the usual avenues of career, relationship, and acquisition, or which remains unfulfilled after years of spiritual study and practice, I offer this account of a meeting with Grace, of a dissolving of the identification with the mind, of the end of a search and the end of a searcher.

1

Find the Searcher

"Like a lamp in a windless place that does not flicker"*— this is how the *Bhagavad Gita* describes the mind of an awakened being. Released from the pangs of anger, fear, and envy, such a soul remains at peace in the midst of the world, unmoved by the endless polarities of the "pairs of opposites"— pleasure/pain, gain/loss, arrogance/worthlessness, acceptance/rejection, happiness/sorrow, and on and on.*

All this philosophy I understood so well. But philosophy and understanding, I had finally come to realize, could not give me freedom.

I sat in the hall of the Unitarian Church in Boulder, Colorado with several hundred others, waiting for the "satsang" to begin, wondering why I had come. There had definitely been hesitation when a friend had called and invited me that day. "Satsang means 'association with Truth,' " my friend had explained.

I felt resistance. It sounded Indian. I had given up on the wisdom of India. As beautiful as it sounded in theory, I had ceased to believe that its messages and practices could translate into any real benefit for a seeker's life in the West at the close of the twentieth century.

My friend went on to tell me that the satsang was being held by a woman named "Gangaji." That sounded Indian too. More resistance. Gangaji, she further clarified, is a student of her own teacher, an Indian master named H.W.L. Poonja, whom she calls Papaji. She had told me about Papaji before and had offered to lend me some of his tapes and books, but I had always responded without interest.

This particular night, however, happened to be April 26, 1995, the eve of my twenty-sixth anniversary of consciously beginning the spiritual quest, of being initiated into the sacred practices of the East. And I was deeply discouraged. The date was a reminder of how I'd wasted my youth and my life in an elusive search for enlightenment. I was just discouraged enough to let go of preconceived ideas and judgments, for one evening anyway, and be guided. I agreed to go to the satsang, and talked my husband, Toby, into coming with me.

By the time we arrived at the church, the meeting hall was nearly full. Most people were sitting on the floor, Indian style, with cushions or back-jacks. A few chairs had been set up in the back of the room, but they had already been taken. Finding a vacant spot on the floor about half-way back, I sat down and hugged my knees, cramped between a large man and a bench full of people along the wall. "I'm getting too old for this Indian stuff," I grumbled.

In the very front of the room sat a small couch on a slightly raised platform, flanked by a modest arrangement of flowers and two large pictures of Indian men. I figured these must be Gangaji's teachers, for I had seen the same two pictures hanging on the wall in my friend's house. One of these faces had always caught my attention. The eyes were strikingly beautiful, swimming with compassion and love, and with a haunting depth. I found out later it was a picture of Sri Ramana Maharshi, the teacher of Papaji.

A video camera and audio equipment were set up in the center of the room. Bright lamps for the video-taping were focused on the raised couch where Gangaji would apparently be sitting. The rest of the hall was dimly lit. I glanced around the room at the many faces of seekers present. Some looked tired and drawn, perhaps from the strain and frustration of years of searching and practice. Others seemed bright and open with the innocent joy of hope and expectation—like mine, twenty-six years ago.

That night, there was no expectation in my heart, not consciously anyway. Again the thought flashed through my mind, why had I come? To please my friend, perhaps? Though the outer "worldly" aspects of my life had been relatively comfortable for the past few years—a loving husband, a beautiful Arabian horse, work I enjoyed, and many wonderful friends—still a deep restlessness plagued me. It was a longing to be free from the "pairs of opposites," to be like the "lamp in a windless place," to live each moment in connection with the Infinite. It was a longing that would wake me up at four in the morning crying out to the universe, "Hey, I DON'T GET IT! I've done everything I can do, and still, I DON'T GET IT!"

A few weeks before, a desperate cry had gone out from my heart for some kind of help. I asked all the guides and masters who had ever listened to my prayers for a flesh and blood teacher, a living example of this freedom I yearned for. By now I had done enough searching and reading and practicing to be very specific about what I wanted—not a person in a book, not a monk, not an Indian, not a disembodied ascended master, not some far-away teacher on a distant continent. As grateful as I was for all the teachings and teachers who had guided me thus far, I knew what I needed now was a flesh and blood westerner, someone who was living the infinite, someone who was nearby, someone who was *just like me*.

When Gangaji walked into the room that night, something stopped deep inside with a kind of quiet shock. For one thing, she was *Western*, with blond hair and about my own age. My friend had neglected to tell me that this teacher with an Indian name was in fact American.

As Gangaji negotiated the narrow pathway that had been carefully marked out with masking tape through the cushions and back-jacks, I watched her with an unusual intensity and interest. As she sat down cross-legged on the couch, time seemed distorted for a moment and the room went into slow motion. Something about her seemed familiar, as if I'd known this person for a long, long time. No, it was more than that— curiously, she reminded me of myself.

Gangaji closed her eyes, as did everyone else, so I supposed that the evening would begin with a meditation. I closed my eyes too, but I couldn't settle down. My mind was all over the place and my heart was racing. Strangely, I sensed her presence in the depth of my soul, as if watching my failed efforts at meditation. This irritated me, embarrassed me, or perhaps more accurately, humbled me, because meditation was the one thing I thought I could do really well. After all, I'd been doing it for twenty-six years—to the day!

After about fifteen or twenty minutes Gangaji opened her eyes. Placing her palms together she said quietly, *Welcome to satsang.* Then she asked for those who had never met her before to raise their hands so she could greet them. I lifted my hand slightly. There were a lot of new people present and it seemed her eyes swept the room quickly. Thinking she hadn't seen me, I found myself raising my hand a little higher. I don't know why it was important that she see me. I didn't really think about it. It was just an impulse.

To my surprise, she glanced over in my direction again and chuckled softly, *Yes, I see you.* It was with the tone and feeling that a busy mother might use with an anxious child clamoring for her attention. Embarrassed, I quickly dropped my hand and noticed a strange burning sensation that flashed through my body.

Then Gangaji began to speak to the group of about four hundred, including an overflow crowd in an adjoining room hooked up by video monitor. She spoke very clearly and with a slight Southern accent.

> *You are most welcome to satsang. In satsang, very simply you at least hear that you are already completely, totally perfect. And I'm not speaking of your body, or your mind, or your emotions, or the circumstances of your life. Those are inherently imperfect, and will remain imperfect, perfectly so. [Smiling] Okay?*

My mind rebelled for a moment, "Wait a minute! This isn't how enlightenment is supposed to look. All problems are supposed to disappear. You have perfect health, don't you? All bad karma is dissolved. What does she mean, we're already perfect? How can we be perfect when so many aspects of our lives remain imperfect?" But these inner voices soon fell silent. For in the past few years of my discouragement, I had begun to question whether I really understood what enlightenment meant at all. And so, I listened.

You have taken on some cloak called body, circum-
stances, thoughts, emotions. No problem with that. What
can be the problem with a cloak? A set of clothes?

Inherently, no problem. Only if you identify that you <u>are</u>
those things, you begin to suffer. Because, you see, these
cloaks, these clothes, begin to disintegrate very quickly. And
if you identify yourself with something that obviously disin-
tegrates, there is great fear and unnecessary suffering and a
search for that which is permanent.

My mind was inherently very analytical. In college I had
pursued a degree in philosophy and religious studies, and after
graduation had traveled the world, studying the mystical traditions of East and West—both intellectually and experientially.
I felt I knew quite a lot about truth, and most of my friends
respected my philosophical viewpoints. I was not easily impressed with those who professed to know something about spir-
ituality, and usually became bored and critical after a few minutes. For this reason, in the past few years, I had rarely attended
lectures or gatherings of this kind.

But as I listened to Gangaji's words, they conveyed a quiet
authority and a ring of truth which riveted my attention as no
words had done in years. The analytical component of my
brain seemed to be turned down. In fact, I soon realized that
what was going "in" was not strictly from her words. Something
deeper was being transmitted that was penetrating right past my
mind.

This is very good. I'm glad that you have searched for
that. And now, STOP! [laughter] Find the searcher. And
you will see this is only an image, only an idea, based on the
mistaken identity that you are not That which is already
whole and complete and perfect and limitless.

What does that mean? Find the searcher. I'd never thought
of that. Again I noticed that she reminded me of myself. What
was it? The way she pressed her lips together, some of her ges-
tures? I couldn't pin it down.

This is the last public satsang for a while here in Boulder. Then I will be back for most of the summer. But, plenty of time. We have, hmmm, an hour, an hour and fifteen minutes. Plenty of time. You have spent millions of years to get to this moment of hearing and receiving the Truth. Let's hope it was time well spent.* [laughter again]

She seemed to be speaking directly to me. For at that moment, mysteriously, I felt the pressure of those millions of years weighing heavily upon my shoulders. I felt an excitement, too, something electric in the air, like something important was happening, but I had no idea what.

Gangaji picked up a letter someone had written to her and asked for the author to raise their hand, so she could see where they were sitting. In the letter the person was expressing a lot of personal problems. Gangaji quickly and directly cut to the heart of the matter, pointing out that this being who was aware of the problems had not been touched by them, was in fact unchanged, whether circumstances presented problems or joy. I was awed by this response and recognized the truth of it. I'd never heard anyone speak in such a direct and true manner before.

After reading a few more letters, Gangaji began to take questions from the audience. As I watched her interacting with people it was obvious that, like myself, they were receiving something more than just her words. This became even more apparent when one man asked her about his agitated mind. Gangaji didn't even answer him, but just looked into his eyes intently for some time. Finally the man smiled and I could see his whole face change, his whole bearing relax. Gangaji acknowledged the silent change by saying simply, *Yes, that's better.*

It was clear that some kind of transmission was emanating from her, unspoken, that could be received by the open heart and mind. Her central message seemed to be, "Stop. Be still." But it wasn't like I heard that and then "did" it. From the moment she'd walked into the room it seemed that a profound stillness had overtaken me—by surprise.

Sometimes Gangaji's response to a question appeared gentle and loving; sometimes she responded more harshly. Each response seemed exactly right for the questioner, stopping their complaining or their intellectualizing, and turning them away from the question, back to the questioner.

The utter directness of her manner revealed a ruthless unsentimental disposition which I found mildly unsettling. But as I watched her interacting with people I got the strange sense that I was *seeing* the Freedom I had longed for. Something in the stillness and confidence with which she spoke conveyed this. She *knew* what she was saying. You could feel it in her words. She knew from direct experience, not from something she'd memorized or read or heard.

About half-way through the evening I found myself wondering, could this be the teacher I had cried out for? Does the universe really answer prayers that quickly? I was awed just considering this possibility. As the evening progressed I realized I was feeling an intense, haunting love for her, and yet definitely also a strong fear of her. For in her eyes I sensed a vastness that could destroy everything I thought I understood, everything I thought I was.

All too soon, the evening was over. Gangaji put her palms together again and said, *Om Shanti*, which I understood to mean, "Peace to all."

As she walked from the room my eyes and heart followed her. A deep sense of gratitude welled up inside, and a longing which I did not understand in my mind. The group was asked to sit quietly for five minutes until Gangaji and the staff members who were helping with the information tables outside had a chance to leave the hall.

After a few minutes, people began to file slowly out of the room. As my husband pulled me to my feet, I was in a kind of daze. Something wasn't working right in my brain. Even though there was a lot of commotion going on all around me in the crowded room, everything seemed strangely quiet and unmoving.

When we reached the door I asked Toby to leave a substantial donation in the basket. Our friend noticed the large bill in Toby's hand and commented, "Just a couple of dollars is fine. Nobody leaves that much." But some deep inexplicable gratitude had seized me, and I found myself grabbing the bill from my husband's hand and making sure it reached its destination in the basket.

After satsang our friend invited us over to her house for tea. Achala was from Germany, and since Toby was studying German, they conversed easily together. We sat around Achala's dining room table, sipping hot tea; as she and Toby chatted away about all kinds of things, I sat silent, unable to speak. It wasn't like I was thinking about anything Gangaji had said. I wasn't thinking anything. There was just this unmoving, gigantic stillness engulfing me. I knew something inside me had been radically altered, but I had no idea what or how.

That night as I lay in bed my body still burned with a strange fire. I felt an intense longing to be in the presence of this woman I knew nothing about. She had said this would be her last public appearance in Boulder for a while. Where was she going? I had to know.

I picked up the literature Achala had given me containing Gangaji's schedule and discovered she was giving a week-long retreat starting in a few days in Estes Park, a mountain resort town northwest of Boulder. Instantly I wanted to go.

Early the next morning a phone call to Satsang Foundation & Press, the organization that supports Gangaji's activities, revealed that the retreat had been filled up for weeks and that the waiting list was over a hundred people long! Disappointed, I hung up the phone. Perusing the literature again I found that there would be another retreat in southern Colorado at the end of August. The thought flashed through my mind, "That's even better; it will give me more time to check out this teacher and her teachings before committing myself to a week-long retreat with her." But a strong voice that seemed to come from deep in my soul replied, *"That will be too late."*

The strength of that voice took me by surprise, and I spent the morning fighting it, arguing with it, reasoning with it. But by the afternoon, I found myself picking up the phone again and calling the Foundation, this time requesting that my name be added to the long waiting list for Estes Park.

Somewhere inside, I knew I was going. There was a sense of destiny about it, like I was being "called," a sense that my whole life up to this point had been waiting, preparing, longing for this meeting.

In the next couple of days I borrowed some videotaped satsangs from Achala and viewed them one after the other. I began to analyze Gangaji's words, compare them to other teachings I had studied, compare her to other teachers I had been with—most of whom were Indian. A critical attitude arose. I began to identify some of what she was saying as coming from a Buddhist perspective and found myself vacillating back and forth, one minute not wanting to go to the retreat, glad that I hadn't gotten in, and the next moment being aware of an inexplicable pull to be with Gangaji again. It made no sense whatsoever. And, in the days that followed, I began to make a conscious effort to forget about the retreat, Gangaji, the whole thing, and busy myself with other activities.

By Saturday I had successfully pushed the retreat into the background of my attention. Then, that night, the night before the retreat was to begin, the Foundation phoned me with news—due to a last minute cancellation, so last minute that no one above me on the waiting list could change their plans, I had been accepted onto the retreat.

2

THE YOGI'S STAFF

On Sunday morning Toby loaded my suitcase and down comforter into our mini-van and we set out for Estes Park, driving north on highway 36. Since we owned only one car at the time and Toby would need it while I was away, the plan was for him to drop me off at the retreat, then come back to pick me up eight days later.

Winding up a forested canyon, the road took us through some of the most beautiful scenery in Colorado. But I hardly noticed. A strange mixture of joy and foreboding tugged at my emotions. The whole thing began to seem a little crazy. I was being dropped off for an entire week with a bunch of people I knew nothing about and with a teacher I'd only just met. It made no sense to my mind. And yet there was also this inexplicable thrill deep in my soul, and a mysterious "knowing" that what would take place in the next few days would alter my life forever.

Toby sensed something strange too. "I feel like you're not coming back," he said. "Not the same, anyway."

We arrived at our destination in the early afternoon. Situated in a high mountain valley about forty miles from Boulder, Estes Park is a beautiful mountain resort area, famous for its lofty peaks and as the gateway to Rocky Mountain National Park. After check-in and registration, Toby found my room by following the directions given to us at the registration table. It was in the main lodge, right next to the satsang hall. No other belongings were in the room, so I assumed my roommate hadn't arrived yet. It was a large room with its own bath and a beautiful view of the mountains. There was one set of bunk beds by the door, and a double bed along the window. The bunks didn't look very comfortable and I preferred being by a window where I could have fresh air, so I asked Toby to put my suitcase and down comforter on the double bed. After seeing that I was comfortably situated he informed me that he had studying to do at home and needed to get right back. We said goodbye to each other and he left.

It felt very strange having him leave me there like that. In the nine years we'd been married we had never been apart as long as eight days before. However, having an image of myself as very independent, I pushed aside the feelings of aloneness. Looking over the retreat schedule I found that there were more than two hours before dinner—enough time to complete my usual evening routine of yoga and meditation. I took a shower, and then, as I was preparing to do some yoga postures on the floor, my roommate arrived.

I could see she was disturbed as she sized up the bed situation. Finally she informed me that she wouldn't be able to sleep in the bottom bunk, due to claustrophobia, and was concerned that the top bunk wouldn't hold her weight, for she was fairly heavy-set. It seemed I had no choice but to give her the double bed.

That evening Gangaji greeted us with a short satsang. There were about a hundred and fifty people present, most sitting on the floor. I picked out a spot by the side door, against the wall, in between a chair and a table with a big plant on it. I felt unsettled; in the hours since Toby had dropped me off, my apprehension about being in this place with all these strangers had heightened.

I don't remember much of what Gangaji said that first night, except:

> *To realize the Truth of your Being you must be naked, exposed, and willing to die.*

This struck me as a bizarre, outrageous thing to say. I hated being naked, carefully avoided exposure of any kind, and had no idea what she meant by "willing to die." And this very private, shy person had no intention of making any changes in those directions.

As I listened to her welcoming the group to the retreat I felt resistance rising by the minute—resistance to her, resistance to being there, resistance to this group of strangers. What was I doing, trying one more "spiritual thing"?

Judgments began to arise: these people probably haven't been practicing as long as I have; they are probably beginners, for whom a quiet retreat like this might bring some sense of peace. I had spent years on silent retreats in Asia and Europe, many of them four to six months in length. I not only knew how to quiet the mind with my meditation practice, but had been trained how to teach others to do this, and had taught the practice for years. I knew how to silence the breath to almost nil. I had even experienced certain of the *siddhis*, yogic powers. What was I doing on this beginners' retreat? What I really needed was something more advanced. What I really needed was to find the missing piece.

Meanwhile, Gangaji was suggesting that this time on the retreat was a time to "see what has not been seen," to recognize what it is you are trying to get, and what it is you are trying to stay away from. And then to STOP—stop all moving toward and all moving away. "Retreat is a time to stop."

I didn't understand that. There were a lot of things I stayed away from, *had* to stay away from. I was a private, stay-to-myself sort of person. For I sensed there was a purity deep within and that the outer world constantly presented so much possibility of pollution.

It was not much more than twenty minutes that Gangaji met with us that first night before dismissing us so that all might rest from their traveling, for many had come a long way to attend this retreat with Gangaji.

I went back to my room feeling anything but restful. Some deep inner turmoil was churning inside. As I climbed the little ladder to my top bunk I felt eight years old again. My sister and I had shared a bunk-bed long ago and I had always had the top one because she used to walk in her sleep.

I lay there trying to get comfortable and realized my body had developed a strange burning again. I thought, "Maybe I'm getting sick. Surely I have a fever." My roommate was asleep and snoring. I felt uncomfortable sharing a room with some-one I didn't know. At home I was used to having my own room, even separate from my husband. A profoundly reclusive nature was etched deep into this personality and it needed a tremendous amount of space.

After an hour went by with no sleep in sight, I began to cry. At first I was concerned that I might disturb my roommate and tried to cry quietly, stifling the tears. But her hefty snores remained undisturbed in spite of my sobs. Relieved of my con-cern I let the tears flow unchecked, sobbing into the early morning. I had no idea why I was crying. I just felt horrible, trapped, alone in a way I had never felt alone.

About halfway through the night a plan formed in my mind to escape. I would call my husband in the morning to come get me. There would probably be no refund of the retreat fee at this point and he'd probably be mad, but it was worth it. I was deeply uncomfortable and unhappy, probably sick, and I had to get out of there.

But as the morning light grew brighter, I felt easier—which made absolutely no sense. After sobbing the entire night I should have been exhausted, a zombie, an emotional disaster area. Instead, I felt cleansed, deeply cleansed, and much lighter. I decided to hold off on calling my husband.

In the satsang hall that morning I found the same spot available against the side wall as the night before and once again hunkered down under the plant, between the small table and a chair. The man sitting on the chair smiled at me in a friendly way, but the sense of being an outsider was still vivid. I was used to attending retreats with people I'd been with for years, grown up with, known like family. There was a sense of being lost, alone, of not knowing what was going on.

Someone announced before satsang that the hall would be available twenty-four hours a day for "sitting," but there was to be no yoga or reading or napping going on there. I won-dered what this "sitting" was. I had always used a mantra in my meditations. But by then I had learned that Gangaji taught no techniques, gave no mantras, encouraged no practices of any kind. I wondered, "Then what are all these people doing sitting there so silently? Doing nothing?" There was no opportunity to ask anyone about it because the retreat was being held in "conversational silence." No one was supposed to speak, unnecessarily, outside of satsang. And I was not about to ask any questions *in* satsang—not yet anyway.

By the time Gangaji arrived, snow had begun to fall outside the wide picture windows. The mountains looked ethereal, wrapped in white mist. Several people spoke about how thrilled they were to be present in satsang with Gangaji in such a beautiful place. I, on the other hand, sat there feeling like I'd been dropped in the midst of someone else's family at Christmas time, watching everyone else open their presents.

Gangaji began that morning like this:

> *So, how will we pass this time? There is a great benefit of being removed from the normal day to day routine. But I'm not speaking of that. I'm speaking about internally. How do you spend your time? What are you thinking about? Are you thinking about getting something, or losing something, or keeping something, or keeping something away? If you are, it's wasted energy.*

That's exactly what I was thinking. Keeping myself away— away from all these people I didn't know, away from all this spiritual jargon that seemed so foreign compared to the language I was used to, away from this teacher who spoke so grimly of being "naked, exposed and willing to die."

Gangaji continued:

> *That's the usual, of course. Whatever the focus, whether it's getting the next meal, or getting the next experience, that's the usual.*
>
> *So the opportunity of retreat, of a silent retreat, is first of all to see how you are spending your time, and then to stop. Just like that, with no more discussion.*

She began reading a letter.

> Beloved teacher: Last night I was breaking with anger,
> fear, despair. I saw addiction everywhere. I saw my whole
> life as nothing more than various patterns of addiction.

She stopped reading and looked up, zeroed in on the letter's author and gave the person a hard look. She picked up a nerf ball that someone had put on her couch and threw it at the person. Everyone laughed.

> *This is the addiction, right here. To make this state-*
> *ment: "I saw my whole life as nothing more than various pat-*
> *terns of addiction." You give that addiction up. Really, this*
> *deserves to be deleted, finished.*

To my amazement, Gangaji proceeded to rip off a section of the person's letter, wad it up in her fist and throw it behind her, while everyone laughed. The poor person must have been dying. Is this what she meant by "willing to die?" I knew I couldn't handle it and right away decided against writing her any letters.

Then Gangaji told a story from her master.

> *You know this story Papaji tells? He was walking in*
> *Rishikesh, and he met a very old yogi on the path, who had*
> *this magnificent staff he was walking with. And so they sat*
> *and talked and had a very nice meal together.*
>
> *Finally the yogi said, "You know, my teacher passed to*
> *me very many powers, many siddhis. The most powerful one*
> *was the siddhi, the power of immortality. And this staff gives*
> *me this power of immortality. But there was one that he*
> *could not pass to me, because he had not realized it, and it*
> *was the power of freedom, the truth of freedom."*
>
> *And the yogi said to Papaji, "I see in your eyes that you*
> *know this. You have this power. Can you pass it to me? I*
> *have been waiting for so long."*

Suddenly I was riveted by this story. I too had been waiting for so long, practicing for so long. I too had attained siddhis, but not freedom.

Papaji said, "Yes, I'm very happy to." And he reached for the man's staff and he broke it, and he threw it in the Ganga. He said, "Now you will die like all men, and in that realize <u>who</u> dies."

This really shocked me, and stopped something deep inside. I had understood enlightenment to be synonymous with relative perfection, with having powers. A previous teacher I'd been with had emphasized the need to achieve perfection of the physiology as the vehicle of consciousness, of the possibility of controlling karma and the forces of nature, and developing yogic powers—these powers being, in fact, the proof of one's level of consciousness. Whether I had understood him correctly or not is now irrelevant. But this idea of developing something, of perfecting myself in some way, was deeply rooted. I had worked at it for years. This story of Papaji and the yogi now suggested that powers and relative perfection meant nothing. One could have the greatest of powers, even immortality of the body, and still not have freedom. Something about this story rang true deep in my soul. I listened more carefully as Gangaji continued.

So, it is very useful to know how to calm the mind. But if this becomes some kind of power to keep away, or to avoid, then it is useless. And you break it. You throw it away.

You understand? If you then substitute having a quiet mind as your goal, break it. Throw it away. It's just another goal. You <u>will</u> realize a quiet mind—and you will still be searching for true freedom.

I swallowed a dry lump in my throat. The arrogance of the night before drained out of me. She was talking about *me*. I was that old yogi. I had learned how to quiet the mind, the breath, the body. I had studied the yogic powers. And still I was searching for true freedom.

From the beginning I have said to you, I am not teaching you yogic powers. There are places where you can go and learn yogic powers. And there's nothing wrong with that.

I'm not teaching you anything. I have come to invite you into the depth of your being. This cannot be taught, and it is not a yogic power. It is the willingness to give up all powers. The power to suffer, and the power to be happy. It's the willingness to have that be broken and tossed aside.

In spite of the pain of this revelation, in spite of a kind of hopelessness it brought up, in spite of all the resistance in the mind, there was a deep undeniable "knowing" that what she spoke was the Truth. The willingness she spoke of was the willingness to awaken from the dream, rather than continually trying to perfect the dream. It was a rude awakening. It was the willingness to toss aside all attempts at personal attainment and fulfillment.

I felt a "crack" somewhere deep inside as I became aware of this willingness. Something let go that had been held tightly before. It was as if, in that moment, Gangaji broke my yogi's staff. Her next words hit their mark like the arrow of an exquisite marksman. Slowly and deliberately, as if directly to me, she said:

Now, you who thought you were at the top are just like everyone else. Now, we begin. Now, you can know freedom. *

3

THE MISSING PIECE

*T*hat afternoon I sat on my meditation mat in my room, reading a book I'd found on my roommate's dresser. The book was by Gangaji's teacher, H. W. L. Poonja, affectionately known as Papaji. Written in question and answer format, it contained Papaji's answers to questions from seekers during satsang. I opened to the first section, which was called "What is Enlightenment?"

> Traditionally, there are two prescribed ways. One is inquiry, which is suitable to very few, very fit people; the other is yoga. Yoga is concentration, meditation, and practice.
>
> For inquiry you must be able to discern what is real from what is unreal.
>
> Studying, pilgrimages, and dips in the holy waters are not going to help you. To know all the sutras and holy knowledge, like a parrot, is no help. Nor will gifts, austerities, or charities help.
>
> The most important requirement is the burning desire for freedom. This desire alone is enough. If you have a burning desire for freedom, satsang will come.*

For some indiscernible reason these words caused me to burst into tears. My roommate came in just then and found me sobbing. She broke silence and inquired if she could help. I thanked her and shook my head no. There was just no simple way to explain to anyone the unraveling of twenty-six years—perhaps of twenty-six million years.

Ever since the morning satsang, my frustration level had been mounting. Frustration with myself, my path, everything I thought I knew, everything I thought I had attained.

My roommate asked if I had eaten any dinner. Once again, I shook my head no. I could see she was genuinely concerned about me, and it touched my heart. Looking into her eyes I saw a gentle, caring person, and suddenly felt very lucky to have this beautiful soul as my roommate. I found out later she was the one who arranged the flowers in the satsang hall and also the flowers in Gangaji's cabin.

After she left the room, I lay down on my top bunk and tried to sleep. Though I felt physically and mentally exhausted from not having slept the night before, sleep would still not come. Our room happened to be right next to the satsang hall and as I lay there I became aware of a powerful silence coming from the other side of the wall.

After a while I decided to do some yoga postures, thinking that it might relax me. As I rolled out my mat on the floor and began my exercises, the silence coming from the satsang hall became unbearably intense—as if pulling on me.

I had experienced the power of collective silence before. I had lived for many years in a community where over a thousand people meditated together every day in a large hall. And when people started gathering there in the morning to meditate, the pull was indeed felt. But I had never experienced a pull quite like this, a silence quite like this. It was deafening.

I checked my clock—still more than an hour until evening satsang was to begin. I did not want to go into the hall so early. I wanted to finish my yoga and meditation in the privacy of my room. But soon the silence became irresistible and I had no choice. The yoga postures were forgotten. I found myself being drawn out the door, as if pulled by the force of some giant suction into the satsang hall.

In the hall I found only about fifty or sixty people—"sitting." They all sat absolutely still, not twitching around the way people sometimes do in meditation. Maybe there was more to this "sitting" stuff than I had thought.

I found my usual hiding spot under the plant and sat down to wait for my fourth satsang.

When Gangaji came in she first read several beautiful letters that had been put on her couch. They were like poetry, even scripture. I was impressed with the depth of understanding, spiritual maturity, and honesty they expressed. I began to feel like everyone was enlightened but me. From the arrogance of the night before the pendulum had swung the other way, to utter worthlessness—still caught in the pairs of opposites.

I tossed and turned most of the second night, once again without sleep, while my roommate snored blissfully on. The small bunk that served as my bed was not very comfortable. I lay there considering how long I'd been away on this retreat. Home and husband seemed light years away, eons away. It was startling to remind myself that it had only been a day and a half! That seemed impossible. It couldn't be. Something must happen to time around Gangaji. It got warped or stretched, or maybe collapsed altogether.

Finally, I decided to go next door into the satsang hall and meditate for a while. As I entered on stocking feet I found the hall dimly lit for the night. Two other people were sitting quietly in the semi-darkness, one on the floor before the picture of Papaji, the other on a couch in the back. I sat down on one of the couches to the side and tried to meditate. My body felt wired, buzzing, as though I'd been drinking caffeine—which I rarely do. What was wrong with me? Again I considered the possibility that I might be sick.

At one point I felt Gangaji's presence so strongly that I opened my eyes, half expecting to see her standing there in front of me. But the room was empty except for the two other silent sitters who sat unmoving in the semi-darkness.

In the early morning, still without sleep, I went back to my room to take a long bath, hoping it would relax me. My roommate had gone to breakfast already. Again, I didn't feel like eating.

It was later than usual when I finally got to the satsang hall, and found my safe place under the plant had been taken. A surprisingly intense irritation arose. I felt personally trespassed upon. I liked that spot under the plant. How dare someone take it! The spaces remaining on the floor were cramped and crowded, and the prospect of squishing together with all these people I didn't know made me tense. I decided to take one of the chairs in the back, which were supposed to be reserved for people who had requested them before the retreat. It had already been announced twice not to use these chairs unless you had reserved one. But in my contentious mood I didn't care about rules. I wanted a chair. It was undignified anyway for people my age to hunch together on the floor like kindergartners.

As I sat in the back, waiting for Gangaji to arrive, tears welled up in my eyes again. I couldn't believe what a basket case I had become. Crying was not something I normally did easily or frequently. But there was a feeling of desperation, of being at my wits' end, of being hopelessly lost. Not wanting to cry in public, I tried to hold it back, which made me even more tense.

By the time Gangaji arrived I was feeling almost hostile. Not at her, or at anyone, but at myself—at the way I had bungled my spiritual quest. I sat there just trying to hold it together until I could get back to my room, feeling separate from everything, not really listening to the satsang—until someone asked a question about "being seen."

I was curious, because I remembered how I'd wanted to be seen by Gangaji that first night at the Boulder satsang. It was a strong, inexplicable desire. The questioner asked, "What is 'being seen'? It seems to be so important for everyone."

That's right. Why is it so important? It's the same as being found, isn't it? And being found must evaporate hiding, or it's not really being found. So there comes a time, through the evolution of particular protoplasm, through the stages of single cell to multi-cell identification, where there arises this strong desire to be found, which is the desire to be seen. And then the search begins for that which can find me, for that which can truly see me.

So, of course, in this search there are many quasi-seeings and findings. But if any of these findings or seeings have attached to them some other motive than just to see, there's great suffering that follows.

For instance, many people will say: "I see you, you are beautiful. I love you, I want you. Will you be mine?" And at first it feels very good to be seen: "Oh, I am seen." But after a while it's recognized, what was seen was a particular external feature, or some energetic pattern that was wanted to be captured so that the one seeing could continue his or her search for being seen.

You follow this cycle of samsara?*

I followed it very well. I had known people who had developed great powers of "seeing," great powers of magic, powers of reaching deeply into the minds of others. But I had watched these powers being used for selfish, manipulative, and egotistical purposes more than once. And there was something deeply frightening to me about spiritual power being used in this way. It was one of those things I was careful to stay away from.

Gangaji continued:

But there comes a time when you are seen just to be seen, where nothing is wanted. And in that instant, you see. You see what you have been yearning for, you see who you are, you see what is. You are found.

There is an energy that is so strong from just seeing, that it evaporates, dissolves, burns up, removes, any possibility of hiding.

She glanced around the room slowly.

So, I'm quite happy to see you. And I do see you. Whether you are happy to be seen, this is up to you.

From my place of hiding in the back of the room I squirmed uneasily. I had been avoiding her eyes the entire time. And yet, I *did* want to be seen, to be found. Why was I fighting her, hiding like a frightened child on the first day of kindergarten?

A man related a dream he'd had the night before about being attacked by a tiger and how he'd punched the tiger in the face and stopped him. Gangaji said this tiger was reminiscent of the spiritual tiger that devours—devours everything that is unreal. This tiger is one's own Self. She suggested that the man re-dream the dream,

26

. . . and when it comes with fangs bared, you throw open your breast. And you say "dive in. Take me. I am willing to die."

Because this punch that you are speaking of, everyone can relate to that. That's the animal instinct, to keep danger, extreme danger, away.

We're speaking, of course, of the whole conditioning from the protoplasm on up. This defense. But in this recognition, real realization, there is defenselessness. And in that you are devoured by yourself—as guru, as tiger, as mountain, as Life. Devoured. Finished. Helpless victim of.

Yes, we are so trained to be empowered, to defend. And of course that has its place in the evolution of life forms. But what we are speaking of here is the power to be defenseless. The power to surrender—to this greater force, that has seen you, and is coming to get you, and may appear to disappear for a moment in the force of your defense. But I can guarantee you, it's just circling. Perhaps next, from behind! [laughter]

It was during this discussion about the tiger that something surfaced. I saw what had not been seen before. Through all my years of spiritual practice I had never really been willing to surrender, to let go of the "person" who was practicing. I had spent my life, even my spiritual quest, carefully defending, protecting, perfecting this entity called "me." I was afraid of being devoured, afraid to give up the personal. Afraid of being seen by the tiger who would eat me. It struck me like a flash of lightning—this is what she means by "willing to die." This is the missing piece!

Experiences came rushing to memory—of sublime meditations, where a vast limitless expanse had opened up before me, and yet I had drawn back from it every time, just as I was drawing back from meeting Gangaji's eyes now. The path I had traveled for so many years had taken me to the door of *Brahman** numerous times, but I had not been able to go through the door. At this moment a deep-seated fear became apparent, a fear that had kept me perched on the doorstep of the Infinite for more than a quarter of a century. It was the fear of personal annihilation. It was an unwillingness to die.

Emotion welled up inside and I felt on the verge of tears once again.

A woman named Barbara asked a question about devotion, and Gangaji spent quite a long time with her. Barbara cried through most of it, and she was sitting right up in front. I was impressed and encouraged by how this woman could just open up like that in front of a hundred and sixty people, in front of Gangaji.

The whole time Gangaji was speaking to this woman I thought about asking a question regarding this fear of being devoured. But even thinking about raising my hand made my heart race uncontrollably. Perhaps writing her a letter would be easier—maybe after the retreat, so that it wouldn't be read in satsang.

When Barbara was finished with her question there was a lull in the room, a moment of intense silence. No one was raising their hand. The room went into slow-motion, like that first night of satsang in Boulder. It was as if a timeless moment had opened up, penetrating time. And there was a strange sense that it had opened for me.

From my spot in the back of the room I found myself lifting my hand. Gangaji saw it immediately and nodded to me. As the cordless microphone was being passed to me I cursed myself for even considering asking a question in such a state. Surely I would burst into tears in the middle of it.

The microphone was pushed into my hands. I took a deep breath and stood up. I don't know why I stood up. No one else was standing when they asked a question. But it just happened that way. Carefully enunciating the words, trying to hide the emotion in my voice, I put my question before Gangaji: "How do you get rid of the fear of being devoured, and being seen?" The words were barely out of my mouth when Gangaji motioned to me and said:

Come here. I'll show you.

This was not at all what I expected, and completely threw me. There must have been a startled look on my face, for everyone laughed at my bewilderment, including Gangaji. But somehow I didn't mind the laughter. A deep inexplicable relief had come over me. Much of the emotional turmoil had miraculously drained out of me—instantly.

I stood there hesitantly, unsure as to whether Gangaji actually meant for me to come up to the front—maybe she was just kidding—until she again motioned for me to come. Still clutching the cordless microphone, I began to wend my way through the people who were sitting close together, packed tightly on the carpet, separating me from the couch where Gangaji was sitting. Some people were still chuckling and laughing as I stumbled between the bodies. When I was about halfway to the front, Gangaji said:

You can leave your microphone.

I stopped and looked up at her, wondering what this meant—maybe that I would not be required to speak when I got to the front? Obediently, I handed the microphone to someone near me and continued making my way toward her. There was a strange sensation of relief again, of lightness, as if I'd left off more than the microphone. Actually, with every step toward her it was like dropping more of some burden I was carrying.

When I got to the front I stood nervously beside the platform, my heart pounding like thunder. She smiled at me and patted the couch beside her, rather strongly. I believe my mouth dropped open. I had no idea she was going to ask me to come that close. I'd never seen her do that before. A moment of resistance to going up there made me moan, "Oh, no."

She laughed:

Oh, yes! Oh, yes.

Seeing that there was probably no way I was going to get out of this, I took another deep breath to steady myself and stepped up onto the platform. As I started to sit down on one end of the couch, as far away from her as possible, she took hold of me in mid-motion.

Nope, all the way.

She pulled me right up against her. I felt like an idiot, like a frightened child. A hundred and sixty people were staring at me, chuckling, laughing. My body was shaking. My mouth had gone dry. Gently she slipped her arm underneath mine and took my sweaty hand in hers.

You see, raising your hand and asking: "How do you get rid of the fear?" This is already a prayer, isn't it?

A profound silence began settling over me. I couldn't speak.

And it may be unexpected what the answer is. [laughter] But if you really had not wanted to get rid of the fear, or you really had not wanted to face the fear, you would never have raised your hand. You would have continued to allow fear to dictate this life experience.

She was right. Fear, staying safe, keeping unwanted stuff and people away, had been the dominant strategy of my life—more than I would have wanted to admit in that moment.

Or you would have left this retreat and written me some letter, "How do I get rid of the fear?"

I was amazed by how well she read me, and admitted quietly, "I thought about that." Everyone laughed again.

Yes, I'm certain you thought about that. And you have probably done that many times—in one way or the other. But here, you raised your hand. You said: "I'm afraid to be seen. But more than I'm afraid to be seen, I am <u>willing</u> to be seen." So, let yourself be seen.

30

I wasn't sure I wanted to be seen so deeply, known so deeply. It felt naked. But it was too late. She was already seeing me, already knowing me. It was out of my control. And, strangely, there was some relief in that.

I was looking down, staring at my knees. She leaned over and peered at me.

Your eyes open? Looking out?

She lifted my chin, making me look out at the people. My hair was slightly covering my face. With three or four gentle swipes of her hand she brushed my hair back behind my ears, so I could not hide behind it—just like my mother used to do when I was a teenager. Again I felt the nakedness, as if I was being unmasked.

Yes, you just be still here and you'll see. It takes care of itself. You don't have to <u>do</u> anything to get rid of fear. Fear is perpetuated by "doing" something.

Several times, Gangaji leaned over to look at me, trying to see into my eyes, but I kept turning away. It was too intense and I felt too shy. This also made everyone laugh, which was even more embarrassing. Finally, it seemed, I had no choice. I had to meet her eyes. It was why I had come.

As I turned finally and met them directly, just inches away, some ancient, incomprehensible recognition dawned. The thought arose: I know this person. Deeply.

"*Yes,*" she said, to my unspoken question. And with her eyes she welcomed me and drew me in—to a deep, unseen embrace.

After what seemed like several minutes she looked away, toward the group again and said:

So, heart may beat, mouth may dry up, body may shake—so what? So what?

The sense that I was totally naked in front of her flashed through me again. It was as though she could see everything I

31

was. And yet there was once again some strange relief in that—perhaps the relief of not having to hide any longer. I shrugged my shoulders and thought, Yeah. So what? It's just the stupid body. Then I realized I was completely quiet inside. The shaking had stopped. I felt peace filling my being, a peace like I had rarely felt in my life.

As I turned to thank her, she caught my eyes again and I could not turn away for what seemed like an eternity. This time as I looked into her eyes something shifted. I saw *behind* her eyes—and a huge expanse opened up. It was awesome, and not describable in words. At the very instant that this took place, Gangaji said:

> *Yes. You see? There's this shift. You are <u>seen</u>, and then there's this shift, you are <u>seeing</u>. And then you let yourself be seen. And there is seeing all around. Who can say how this seeing will radiate out? We will see. We will see.*

I had no idea what she meant, no idea what I'd seen. I was only aware of this vastness, and that I was completely calm and quiet in front of all these people. That, in and of itself, was enough to awe and amaze me.

She remained quiet for a while, looking out at the group. Just as I was beginning to wonder if she was finished with me, she spoke again:

> *Yes, we feel we crave to hide. But there comes a point when this longing to be seen and to see is stronger than the fear. <u>This is a very good point</u>.*

She slapped my knee three times as she said "very good point," punctuating each word with a slap.

> *This is the jail break.*

An intense wave of gratitude arose inside me. I felt a deep freedom and peace. Yes, like I'd been sprung from jail. How could I ever possibly thank her?

Then she asked me to look out at the people again. This time I was not so afraid to meet their eyes. In each person's face I saw something divine and full of light. "They're all beautiful," I said.

> *Yes. This is Beauty you are seeing. Beauty is seeing Beauty. It's irresistible. You are seeing your own heart. Don't withhold your Self from your Self any longer. It's unnecessary.*

It became clear, suddenly, that this was exactly what I had been doing all my life, withholding myself from my Self. I thanked her, withdrew my hand from hers, and bowed my head in a *namasté.** She put her palms together also, and bowed to me. Then I got down from the couch. But I did not return to my place in the back of the room. I sat down on the floor near her, actually in the only space available—in the aisle-way where she would walk out.

Immediately she picked up a letter, perused it briefly, then looked up and said:

> *Where's Hal?*

A middle-aged man near the front lifted his hand. She leveled her gaze on him, rather fiercely.

> *Hal!*

She tossed the letter up into the air and it fell behind her onto the back of the couch. Everyone laughed.

> *It's irrelevant, isn't it? After this morning? Irrelevant, yes. A kind of prayer, too. But now an irrelevant prayer. You are here. Just let yourself be here. Forget all concepts of enlightenment or unenlightenment. The concept of enlightenment has brought you here. Now lay it aside and recognize what is concept-less.*

You be still. Let the tiger come to you. You can't go hunting it. It's a very big, wise tiger. It waits for YOU. It likes to capture—by surprise. *

As she spoke of the tiger, I knew, on some deeply intuitive level, that she was speaking of the vastness I had seen in her eyes, the immensity I had been running from all my life. This man had been hunting it; I had been resisting it. Neither tactic worked. Just be still.

Throughout the remainder of that satsang this metaphor of the tiger haunted me in a strange and deep way. There was a sense that I had been captured by that tiger, captured by surprise. And yet on a conscious level I wasn't even sure what that meant.

That afternoon, after lunch, I felt the impulse to go for a walk, which I had not done before. As I set out from the lodge along a rocky path, I felt a sweet, all-embracing love surrounding me. It was as though I were a small child in my mother's arms. Was it Gangaji's love? I could not tell, for it was somewhat abstract, not exactly personal.

After a while I paused in a snowy meadow. The mountains loomed huge and unmoving above me. Then something dawned. I noticed that my awareness *encompassed* those mountains. The mountains were IN me!—and the trees, and the stones, and all the earth. It was the most startling, amazing feeling, and yet familiar, as though I had experienced this before, known this before. But there was no mental memory of it, just this familiar-ness.

A ground squirrel stuck his head up out of a hole in the ground and gazed at me for a long time. Shining in his eyes I saw, again, this familiar-ness, as though I were looking at my own self. And it was huge!

What had happened? What was this hugeness? This unity? I'd never quite seen the world like this before. But how could I have missed it? It seemed, in that moment, so obviously the Truth. An ancient expression from the Upanishads* came spontaneously to my awareness, "I am That, thou art That, and all this is nothing but That."

Awe-struck, I realized that's what I was experiencing. I *am* the mountains, the trees, the world. There is no separation anywhere. I was astounded, floored. And I knew then, beyond any doubt, that the teacher I had prayed for, had cried out to the universe for, was Gangaji.

4

ROMANCE OF THE SOUL

*T*hat afternoon, as I sat on the floor of my room meditating, a vision opened up to my inner awareness. In the vision, I was sitting crosslegged on a broad couch, absorbed in deep meditation. The couch was beautiful—covered in velvet, inlaid with gold, and richly embroidered with a symmetrical design like a mandala. I was sitting next to Gangaji, who was also absorbed inwardly. As we sat there together, a strange closeness became apparent, as if she was my mother or my sister or some deeply ancient friend.

Then something was revealed. I can't say how it was revealed, I just suddenly *knew* it—that the remainder of my life would be devoted to this Truth which Gangaji speaks and lives. Not that I decided that "I" would serve this "teaching," which I had now determined to be a good thing, etc. It wasn't like that. I didn't even know what she was teaching. In fact, she had said the day before, "I'm not teaching you anything." But there was just this "knowing," revealed, that my life was somehow *for* this. And there was a deep joy with that, even though mentally I wasn't quite sure what I thought of it yet or what it actually meant.

That evening in satsang I sat closer to the front. No longer did I feel a need to hide in the back. I had been seen. I had been found. And no longer did I feel like an outsider, but felt welcomed into this satsang family. Curiously, everyone seemed familiar now—like the ground squirrel.

After the silence at the beginning, Gangaji put her palms together and said, *Welcome to satsang.* Then she looked over in my direction. As my eyes met hers, I found my own hands spontaneously coming together in a *namasté*, and without my apparent volition my head went down in a bow to her. But it was more than just a spontaneous respectful gesture. Something profound took place in that bow. I felt something open in the top of my head, and some weight or some resistance departed. It was as if she took it from me in that bow. It was as if, in that moment, the separation between us was momentarily wiped out. The feeling afterwards was of being freer, lighter—and blessed.

During the satsang I felt tremendous joy just being there in Gangaji's presence, watching her strip away the misconceptions of those she interacted with. At one point she looked over at someone a couple of seats in front of me who was writing in a tablet.

> *I see you are taking notes. I saw you taking notes earlier. What will you do with these notes?*

The person remained silent. Actually, the whole room got very, very still. Gangaji continued:

> *Save yourself some time. I used to be a very good note-taker. I went to lots of classes and I got very proficient in taking notes. But you see, when you take notes, attention is split. And also, you are tricked by the notion of "getting it" later. You may read your notes later and be inspired, but the opportunity is to get it now. And when you get it now, you will see it's not in any word, not in any phrase. It's not in any injunction to do something, or not do something.*
>
> *So you try not taking notes for a day, and if you're not happy with that, start taking notes again.*
>
> *This is a kind of nakedness—no possibility of remembering where your disguises are. People think, "I have to remember it." Give up this illusion. To remember yourself you have to commit yourself to memory. You have already tried to commit yourself to memory. Satsang is about breaking <u>through</u> memory, breaking <u>out</u> of memory.*
>
> *Yes, naked. No possibility of remembering. No possibility of conceptualizing.*

Papaji says often, "The true teaching leaves no tracks. Nothing that can be followed." That's what those little scribblings are—tracks—that will restimulate some conceptualization that you hope will reveal Truth.

But Truth is here right now—as you.

It was beautifully ruthless, exquisitely clear. Every word rang true, deep in my soul. Every word was so familiar, as if I had said it myself, known it myself. It was ruthless speaking, but a ruthlessness of the utmost kindness—dispelling the illusions of mind, and guiding, pointing constantly back to That which one is.

The person being addressed quietly put aside her notes, and I did not see her bring them back during the remainder of the retreat.

That night I lay on my top bunk, expecting that after two nights without sleep surely this night would bring rest. But I was wider awake than ever. My body felt electrified, on fire. The huge picture of Papaji in the satsang hall hung exactly on the other side of the wall from my bunk. Strangely, I was aware of him and sensed him pulling on me, calling me. Was he the cause of this sleeplessness?

After lying there for about an hour, I gave up and decided to go next door into the satsang hall to meditate. Once again I found the hall in semi-darkness. I slipped quietly in on stocking feet, careful not to disturb the three other people who sat motionless, unable to sleep also—or so I guessed.

A quiet thrill wafted through me. I was beginning to enjoy these all-night vigils in the satsang hall. I sat down on the floor, in front of the giant picture of Ramana that hung on the wall to the left of Gangaji's couch. So far on the retreat, I had been doing my mantra meditation, as had been my daily practice for many years. But that night something different happened. As my eyes closed, the question arose: "What if I just 'sit,' without taking the mantra this time?" Immediately, some judgments arose about meditation. Why had I practiced it for so long? Had it been a waste of time?

Should I not meditate anymore? Inside my head, I heard Gangaji's voice: *Let go of that.*

I wondered how I could hear her voice like that in my head. Again she said: *Let go of THAT.* A fear arose as I felt myself struggling to let go of resistance. *Let go of THAT.*

As this internal dialogue continued, my mind began to relax more and more. Awareness expanded, deepened, again and again. Every time a thought would arise, Gangaji's voice would come: *Let go of that.* Until finally there was nothing. No *thing.* Only awareness of awareness.

It was the most delicious, sweet, silence. Totally without agenda of any kind. And mysteriously, once again, I felt wrapped in some subtle loving embrace.

I stayed there all night—letting go, letting go, letting go. From time to time, one or two people would come in, then depart after a while. But mostly I was alone—with Ramana, with Gangaji. It was Peace itself. I felt Ramana's presence in my inner awareness. It mingled with Gangaji's presence. I couldn't tell the difference. It was huge, awesome, untouchable by words. I couldn't get a grasp on it. There were no tracks, no images. No mind. Nebulous, unlocatable, undefinable are the only words that arise, but none of them come very close either.

One minute the presence seemed masculine, then it was feminine. Sometimes it seemed like the whole universe. Sometimes like Shiva himself. I recognized the presence of Shiva because once I had done a special fast to him when I was in India some years before, and during the fast he had blessed me with a vision of his presence. Something about what I was experiencing now reminded me of that awesome presence which I associated with Shiva.*

I was astounded. Who is this teacher?

In the early morning, I went back to my room to bathe. By the time I'd finished, my roommate had gone to breakfast. I sat alone on the folded mat I used for meditation and yoga, not meditating, not doing yoga, just sitting, staring at the mountains outside my window, bursting with gratitude and love for this teacher who had reached so deeply into my soul, leaving no traces or footprints. For as I tried to remember what Gangaji looked like, I could not bring up any image whatsoever!

Later, I waited quietly in the satsang hall for Gangaji to arrive. When she came into the hall my heart leaped—in love, and also in surprise. "My God, it's a woman," something inside of me responded. All night she had been with me inwardly. The unity of her awareness had filled my walk in the mountains the day before. Yet that presence, that awareness I was experiencing on an inner level, was so huge, so intense—often masculine in its aspect—that something in me could not believe all *that* could be contained or explained by this slight and beautiful woman's form.

There was some sense that I was experiencing more than one dimension at a time—that what seemed to be taking place (this situation of all of us being here at the retreat in the mountains) was an illusion, and what was really taking place was on some deeper level of Reality, unknown to the senses. I was seeing Gangaji in forms that were so vast and subtle, so celestial and divine, that even my senses couldn't quite believe it when she appeared in front of me in her form as female human being, with blond hair and that slight, charming, Southern accent.

In satsang that morning, someone asked about a great fear they were having regarding surrender. Gangaji responded:

> *It is very good that this fear is exposed. You think it's fear of annihilation; you think it's fear of suffering, of damnation. It is fear of freedom.*

The man said, "I would have said fear of annihilation."

> *Yes, because in your mind you have some idea of what annihilation means, some concept of annihilation. And with that is some concept then of freedom. Because these are opposing poles of the mind, aren't they?*
>
> *But I'm saying to you, you sit in satsang and this deep fear, maybe unknown before, arises. This is fear of freedom, divine fear of freedom. Let it bite you!*

The man said, "That's what I'm asking for, just to be seen and to be heard." Gangaji said:

Let it come. What you are speaking of is seeing this great fear as it arises. This is tremendous. Not about just feeling better sometime, or having a nice day. This is much deeper than wanting to correct some physical or mental or emotional or circumstantial aspect. This is from the root of Being.

I could relate to this man's question very well. It seemed he was speaking of the same fear I had asked Gangaji about the day before. But she was dealing with it differently.

You know these wonderful Tibetan tankas where they show all aspects of Being? The one I like quite a lot is called "Mahakala." Do you know Mahakala? Skulls as a necklace, ferocious, dark, great Kali coming to absorb you. A great deal of time is spent evoking Mahakala, Great Mother, terrifying Mother, obliterating Mother.
Very good that Mahakala has knocked at your door. Yes! It would be absurd to open that door casually. [laughter]

How well I knew this door. And it was not at all casual! It was the door I had feared all my life. When I was eight years old I had an experience which I understand now to be that of being thrown back onto my true Self. This happened from a little meditation I had invented. I would sit in my room and stare at two black knobs on my white closet doors. As I sat staring at these two black knobs, standing out against the white, they would start to pulsate. Then, suddenly, awareness would shift, and I would see the "reality" of my Self, recognizing, "Ah, yes. This is who I am. This is me. I am here, *now.*" And the world would fall away, and for some moments seem like a dream.

But by the time I was ten this experience of meditation had given rise to an awareness of a "hugeness" that began to frighten me. I imagined it was going to kill me, swallow me up. I began to stay awake at night, as long as I could, afraid to go to sleep lest this huge formless "nothing" devour me. So I drew back from it, and stopped practicing the meditation.

The same fear again surfaced at the age of twenty-two, when I consciously began my spiritual search and learned a deep meditation practice which reintroduced this hugeness to my awareness. Again I had drawn back whenever the experience appeared with too much intensity.

Now, reminded by this man's question, I thought about the question I had asked Gangaji the day before—"How do you get rid of the fear of being devoured, and being seen?" It seemed she had answered the "being seen" part of the question by bringing me up to the front, by seeing me, and then by helping me to see the beauty in the faces of all those present. Now I wondered about the other part of the question, the devouring part. Had she forgotten?

Sometimes it seemed she was this devourer. And this still terrified me on some almost unconscious level. I was not surprised that she relished the terrible image of Kali. There was something about her, in fact, that called up this image—ruthless, devouring Mother, ruthlessly committed to Truth, ruthlessly committed to exposing the lie.

The man who had told the dream about the tiger the day before, which had prompted me to ask my question, now raised his hand again.

"A very short report," he said. "Yesterday afternoon I took a little nap, and there was a retake of the tiger dream. You're a very powerful lady. You just called up this dream."

Gangaji shrugged playfully:

I have good connections.

The room erupted in laughter. After it subsided, the man continued, "Anyway, I just smiled at the tiger, and lunged. It was a delicious meal."

Yes, it's a delicious meal. That's right! Good, good. Allow yourself to be eaten and you realize you are _eating_. Excellent.

In the dream, the man had identified himself with the tiger and eaten himself. I realized that still scared me; I couldn't quite let go that much. I thought about asking Gangaji again about my fear of being devoured, but it seemed inappropriate and disrespectful to ask her the same question twice.

Visions continued all that day and into the evening. I'd had visions before in my life, but they were usually years apart. Never had so many come all at once like this in so short a time frame. Again it was revealed that my life was destined to serve this Truth, that Ramana had called me for this, and that my life would be very close to Gangaji's.

My mind tried to come up with all kinds of fabulous pictures and scenarios of what this might look like. Then, the same mind attempted to doubt the very truth of what had been revealed. "This is your imagination; this can't be real; how can you, idiot that you are, imagine a life close to hers?" Once again, caught in the pairs of opposites—arrogance/worthlessness—two sides of the same coin.

All the while my love for Gangaji kept swelling uncontrollably. At first it alarmed me with its intensity and power. It was not like any love I had ever experienced. It was an explosion deep in my soul, having a profound effect on all levels of my being—emotional, physical, mental, and beyond. I had never been in love like this—not with my husband, not with any boyfriend, not with any teacher. It annihilated every idea of love I'd ever known. And yet, somehow, I *recognized* this love. I had longed for it, written songs to it, and in a strange way had waited for it—remaining throughout my life, unnaturally cool toward the kinds of love offered by the world.

Another thing I'd noticed during this time was a voice inside my head. For much of my life I'd had a guiding voice of wisdom inside which I called my "higher self." This self had even given me its name, "Gayatri." But Gayatri was usually a very faint voice that I could listen to when I wanted and ignore when it was convenient. Now this inner voice had become quite loud, authoritative, impossible to ignore—and it had mysteriously developed a slight Southern accent! It seemed, in fact, that Gayatri had merged with Gangaji. Then I remembered one part of the prayer to the universe, which I'd made just prior to meeting Gangaji, had been for this inner voice, Gayatri, to become clearer in her guidance. I had even asked for her to manifest physically before me so that I could see her and talk to her. It occurred to me now that this was exactly what had happened, but in a way totally unlike what I had imagined.

Gangaji began the evening satsang by sharing a couple of "love letters" she had received. One went like this:

> Beloved, Beloved, Beloved, most Beloved One:
>
> The River rages, yet it's still in silence in its essence. It explodes into the bottomless, ever-deepening ocean, the ocean of peace. It expands endlessly, becoming Nothing, becoming All. How ironic this paradox called Reality. How exquisite. What appears as loss is the opening door to receive All. What is All is Nothing. Acceptance, allowance and non-resistance lead to freedom, to eternal Self-recognition. The mind must be still, for it could never possibly contrive or understand this unknowable mystery. The sweetest nectar flows from the flower of stillness and surrender. This Self lays prostrate before the unimaginable Truth.*

My heart was touched, awed by this beautiful expression of Truth and Love. I had remained silent about the love that was embracing me more and more deeply, and about the visions. The love made me feel shy, and the visions I didn't yet trust enough to express openly. But this letter had expressed so much for me. I was deeply grateful.

Again that night, there was no sleep, and again the satsang hall became my nocturnal sanctuary. Gangaji's presence was with me, guiding my inner experience in the most subtle and profound ways. My body still burned with an ever-intensifying fire. And I began to suspect that it was this fire that kept me from sleep. But what was it? Where did it come from? Why was it happening?

By dawn I felt an overpowering impulse to say *something*, anything, to this teacher of my prayers. Before going to satsang that morning I sat at the little table in my room, looking out onto the snow-covered mountains, and wrote her a letter that, as best I can remember, went like this:

May 4, 1995

Dear Gangaji:

I have known you for a week and it seems like lifetimes. I would like to tell you my story. Don't worry, it's short. I have been on a path of meditation and yoga for 26 years. And I am not free. I don't blame this path, for it has brought me to the door of Brahman many times. But I could not go through the door, so afraid was I of annihilation.

For a while, I thought I could gain enlightenment without going through this door. And the mind is very clever to rationalize and justify about why I shouldn't, or didn't need to go through it.

Recently I prayed for a teacher who could take me through this door. Last week, a friend brought me to satsang in Boulder. When I heard you speak, everything went still. Your words were like a cool balm of truth and like a raging fire. Instantly, I loved you and was scared to death of you—for in your eyes I saw the great devourer.

At first I wasn't sure if I could dare hope that my prayer had been answered so quickly and so perfectly—for I had specifically asked for a Westerner.

Even though there was a long waiting list for this retreat, somehow I got in. I went through a lot of fear and doubt at first, but hopefully, much of that has passed now.

As I saw the way you made me face myself, the way you make everyone face themselves, I realized you are the teacher of my prayers, the one who could guide me to face the great devourer without fear.

I feel tremendous gratitude for this grace which has finally brought me to your feet—and I'm *real* tired of being a seeker.

Gratefully,
Amber Terrell

I went into the satsang hall earlier than usual so I could put the letter up on Gangaji's couch without having to do it in front of the whole group. As I went up to slip my letter underneath the stack that was already collecting there, a man who was sitting right in front of the couch actually got up and offered me his spot.

I turned it down. I did want to sit closer that day, but wasn't quite ready to be that close. Even though I was aware of a sense that I was missing an opportunity being offered to me, there was no way I could accept it right then. For one by-product of this intense love I felt for Gangaji was that it made all the excruciating shyness of my childhood come creeping out of the closet. I thought I'd gotten over all that by "growing up." But I realize now that I had not gotten rid of it. I had simply become adept at avoiding situations which caused the shyness to arise. In the grip of this intense love, all my strategies of avoidance lay exposed, all my disguises uprooted. It was a kind of nakedness, and not at all comfortable for this very skillful hider.

I took a spot on the floor, about six rows back. It was as close as I could handle. As the satsang began I found myself desperately hoping that there would be lots of questions which would prevent Gangaji from reading her "mail." For I began to feel increasingly more shy about the letter. I had asked her to be my teacher. Was it even appropriate? I'd heard her say that she wasn't a teacher and that she had no teachings. Maybe she'd be offended by the letter. Or, what if she read my letter and tore it up?—as I'd already seen her do with a couple of others. Thoughts like these kept me dancing with anxiety the entire satsang.

Miraculously, thankfully, there were lots of questions, and the stack of letters never got read.

After lunch that day, I went over to a small card table set up in the dining room where we could write notes to the staff. My intention was to ask someone about my strange sleeplessness—for I'd now experienced four sleepless nights. It was amazing to me that I was still able to walk around.

The list on the bulletin board indicated that "Maitri" was the person who received questions of this nature. I knew who she was, because she had introduced herself at the beginning of the retreat and had made announcements several times before the satsangs. I liked her very much. She was radiant and natural, always managing to accomplish her announcements or other business in a very graceful and loving manner that did not disturb the silence at all.

At the table, I found that all the note paper had been used up. I looked around the dining room. It was mostly empty. Lunch was over and most people had gone—except for Maitri, who was having a late lunch and what looked like a quiet meeting of some kind with a man whom I later learned was her husband. I hesitated to interrupt her and break my silence, but I really wanted to ask her about the sleep situation. It was beginning to concern me.

I tapped her on the shoulder. She turned and smiled at me.

I whispered, "There's no note paper and I really need to ask you something."

She thought for a minute, then picked up a clean white napkin. "Here, write it on this."

So I wrote on the napkin something like the following:

Dear Maitri:

I've never been on one of these retreats before. I only met Gangaji a few days ago. I have not been able to sleep in four nights, and am becoming concerned. Any suggestions?

Amber Terrell, Rm #____

I put the napkin-note in Maitri's box on the staff table, then went outside for another walk. It was unusual for me to walk so much. I was not generally fond of walking. I preferred to ride my horse and let her do the walking. My physical body was not something I'd ever put much attention on. But I felt a definite "call" to go walking, perhaps originating from the new voice inside. In any case, I surrendered to it, feeling that the cool air might be good for the burning I was experiencing, and also maybe the walking would help tire me out so that I would be more likely to sleep at night.

Again, as I set out from the lodge, I felt the same loving embrace around me, and a happiness deep within. Both the happiness and the love, I now recognized, had a quality about them that was definitely flavored with Gangaji's presence.

My roommate was also starting out on a walk, so we walked together up the road, past some small cabins where many of the retreat participants were staying. She pointed to one of them. "Gangaji's cabin," she whispered. As I glanced over at the cabin she'd indicated, I saw Gangaji sitting out on her deck in a chair, reading, her feet propped up on the railing. Again, I felt the strange dichotomy of the vast inner presence I was experiencing contrasted with what the senses were seeing—this very normal, natural person, casually relaxing on her deck. I shook my head, as if to detach myself from some unreality. It made absolutely no sense to the mind.

I wondered if she'd read my letter. As I thought of the letter, the excruciating shyness came over me again. I had put my heart and soul on the line in that letter, laid them at her feet. Suddenly I felt like a small child, awkward, unsure, and mortally vulnerable. I thought, "Maybe I shouldn't have written her the letter; maybe it was stupid to ask her to be my teacher like that and tell her of my secret prayers."

Returning to my room that afternoon, I sat in meditation before dinner. As the awareness went very deep and the breath became very soft, I felt the bliss of samadhi* arising. According to my habit, I found myself "reaching" for it. I wanted it. I wanted to keep it somehow, for I knew how fleeting it could be. It had always been fleeting.

Then I heard Gangaji's voice like a clear bell in my head: *Don't reach for it. Let <u>It</u> get you.*

I'd never thought of that. Let IT get ME. Something seemed to open in my brain and I became aware of a sudden relaxation of effort, then of a deep letting go. And to my amazement, the bliss did overtake me. Just like that. I felt so stupid—all those years, trying to "get" the bliss. Now it suddenly became clear that with this impulse to get, I had been pushing it away!

An intense tremor of kundalini* energy in the spine brought me out of that deep state. As usual, my awareness was then drawn to the strong sensation. I'd had these sensations for many years. They always drew my attention away from consciousness and back to the body. I had always been under the impression that I had to deal with the sensation before I could get back to the depths of silence.

Again I heard Gangaji's voice: *The body has nothing to do with who you are. You don't need to pay attention to it. It'll take care of itself.*

These words rang true. I knew this was correct. I became aware, then, that I had been clinging to the sensations because they were interesting, fascinating in a way, and also because I in some sense validated my spiritual progress with these kundalini sensations—"I must be evolving, because I have these sensations."

Now I listened to Gangaji and forgot the sensations. In that moment I let go of the body, and found once again a deep state of awareness revealed. And the sensations did take care of themselves. How many years I'd wasted my meditation time giving them far too much attention!

Gangaji had reached into the inner depths of my meditation and corrected two long-standing mistakes in my practice. The gratitude and love swelled in my heart for this undeniable, omnipresent teacher of my prayers.

That evening, as I sat waiting for satsang, someone tapped me on the shoulder. I opened my eyes and the person who'd tapped me pointed to Maitri, who was standing near the door, motioning for me to come. I got up and followed her out into the hallway, outside the satsang room.

Alone in the hallway, Maitri asked, "Are you Amber?"

I nodded.

"Gangaji received your note about the sleep," she said quietly.

This disturbed me momentarily, for I hadn't expected that note to go to Gangaji. I had scribbled it on a napkin!

"I'll tell you what Gangaji said about the sleep in a minute," said Maitri, "but first I want to tell you something else."

I was feeling very hyper and wired from lack of sleep and also from not eating much. I hadn't mentioned about the eating in my note. It was not to the point yet where I was concerned; I had fasted enough in my life to know that the body doesn't need as much food as most people suppose.

Maitri must have sensed my hyperness because she rubbed my arm soothingly as she spoke. "When I walked into Gangaji's room this afternoon to give her your note about the sleep, she looked up at me and asked, 'Who's Amber?' I said, 'Oh, I was just bringing you a note from Amber.' So I told her you were the one who came up on the couch the other day."

For a moment I wondered how Maitri knew my name. It was a silent retreat. I hadn't spoken to, or introduced myself to anyone, except the lady who'd registered me. Then I remembered the napkin-note. Because there had been no note paper this morning, Maitri had been able to connect my face with the unconventional note signed "Amber." I became aware of a subtle orchestration of events which was somehow bigger than any human ability to comprehend or control. It had the same mysterious signature as the subtle orchestration of events that had landed me on this retreat, even though I was number 102 on the waiting list.

Maitri continued, "Gangaji had your letter in front of her on the table. Several times while we were speaking, she commented on how beautiful it was and how she was so glad you'd written to her."

An indescribable relief washed through me. Gangaji had liked the letter! I took this to mean that I was accepted as her student. And this confirmed something else I'd experienced a couple of hours earlier which had been so unusual, so monumental, that I hadn't dared interpret it or even think about it.

Just before dinner, I was doing some yoga postures on the floor of my room. Suddenly I felt an intense wave of love from Gangaji—or it may have been *for* her, or both; it was hard to tell the difference. Then I felt my whole soul go into—what I can only describe as "surrender." My life was at her feet. Just like that—without making a decision about it or even knowing it had happened. "My God!" I remember thinking, "she's my guru!" I felt a deep, deep connection with her, a connection like I'd never felt with another human being. And I *knew* what this was, because the Indian teacher I'd been with for many years had sometimes talked about the relationship with his Master. There is no relationship on earth that compares in intensity, in intimacy, in depth, in ruthlessness, and in love. Whenever he spoke about this relationship, I longed for it more than anything on earth, but knew that what he was speaking about was not exactly what I was experiencing with him. Now I recognized that all he'd spoken of was exactly what I was experiencing with Gangaji—and more, that could never be spoken. And what was so amazing was that this surrender had taken me completely by surprise. I hadn't *decided* to surrender, or decided she was my guru. It had just taken place. In the twinkling of an eye. Like a thief in the night.

For one instant I remembered my previous teacher with some nostalgia. Immediately I heard Gangaji's voice: *"No one is happier than he at this union."* And instantly I realized, yes, of course. No one could appreciate more profoundly the preciousness and auspiciousness of this divine partnership than someone whose life had also been blessed with such an alliance.

"With regard to the sleep," Maitri was saying, "Gangaji said to tell you that she is 'up with you at night.' "

My heart exploded even more with this confirmation, which destroyed all doubt. Her presence and her voice which I felt and heard so strongly all night long, all the time actually, were not just my imagination.

Maitri continued, "She also said not to be concerned about the sleeplessness. It is 'work that needs to be done. It needs to continue for some time, but it will not last forever.' "

That sounded ominous. I wondered what exactly "not forever" meant. A few more days? A week? A year? I sensed intuitively, with a shudder of dread, that it might be longer rather than shorter. Momentarily, I wondered if my physiology would survive. Already I could not hold my hand out in front of me with any steadiness.

Maitri added, "Gangaji also said to tell you that if the body needs sleep, it will take sleep. So, just relax."

I was standing there in a kind of stunned, awed state. "I . . . I've been with enlightened masters before, but this has never happened before."

She smiled. "Maybe it's the deep connection," she said, bringing her palms together to illustrate "connection." She shared with me that when she was first with Gangaji she would find herself unable to sleep whenever Gangaji would come into town. Then she suggested I drink some herb tea before going to bed, and asked if I was drinking any coffee or anything like that.

I said, "No. Caffeine and I do not mix."

She laughed, "Yes, you don't look like the caffeine type."

I thanked her, then went back into the satsang hall. That evening we were not actually having a satsang. A documentary film about Gangaji had recently been completed and we were all to have a preview of it instead of a regular satsang.

As I sat there waiting for Gangaji to arrive, contemplating the momentousness of what had been taking place, I found myself relieved that there would not be a formal satsang that night. I didn't know if I could handle the intensity of satsang just then. I was trembling inside—an ecstatic trembling, reminiscent of the poems of Rumi or St. John of the Cross who wrote about the awesome power of Divine Love the soul experiences when it is reunited with its Beloved, poems about the Self as spiritual bride on the wedding night.

How could I have even imagined a teacher so perfect? One who is "up with me at night." One who lovingly watches my meditations, correcting any mistakes, guiding me in every moment. In some mysterious way Gangaji had found me, from the prayer I had sent out to the universe. She was the one asked for, the one longed for, the one waited for—for eons. I was awed, floored, stopped—and hopelessly in love.

When Gangaji came into the room, my heart leaped. She looked radiant, beautiful, gigantic. It was as though the subtle visions of her and the experience of her through the senses were finally merging.

We closed our eyes for a twenty minute silence. It was pure divine ecstasy to just sit with her in silence like that. After the silence, Gangaji introduced Harp, the man who had produced the film we were going to see. Harp told some stories about traveling with Gangaji in India, where much of the footage was shot, and about how he'd had doubts during its production that maybe he couldn't do it or maybe he wasn't the right one to produce it. He had sent Gangaji a fax at one point and told

Gangaji

her as much, and she had faxed him back, "Well, maybe you're not the right one." He admitted that this was not exactly the response he'd expected or hoped for, and shared how it had snapped him out of his doubt so that he was able to complete the film.

Surprisingly, I felt a twinge of jealously arise, because he was sitting up on the couch next to Gangaji, and part of the time she had her arm around him. Immediately I felt stupid for feeling such a childish emotion. Yet there it was, arising in me.

The lights dimmed, and we watched *River of Freedom*. The film was beautifully done and the music melted in perfectly with the exquisite scenery. There were clips from Gangaji's first interactions with Papaji, and shots from early satsangs Gangaji had given in India at many sacred places. Papaji had asked her to give satsang at Bodhgaya, where the Buddha had sat under the Bodhi tree, and at other holy places along the Ganges River. Early satsangs in the United States were also shown, as well as photos of Gangaji as a child, as a teenager, and as a young mother with a six-year-old daughter. There was an interview with her husband, Eli Jaxon-Bear. And I learned that she had received the name "Gangaji" from her teacher with the instruction, "It's time for the Ganga* to flow in the West."

Right after the film, Gangaji left the hall. As I watched her walk out through the side door, a deep wave of love swelled in my heart and a longing to be near her—forever. She was everything I had ever loved, ever hoped to love, ever feared to love. She was Love itself.

I went back to my room and changed into comfortable jogging clothes. I wasn't even going to try to sleep that night, wasn't even going to get into bed. I knew it would be impossible, for the fire inside was raging. But I no longer felt a resistance to it, no longer feared that I was sick. I welcomed it as my teacher's Love.

Returning to the satsang hall as soon as it had emptied out for the night, I sat down on the floor before Ramana and let the stillness do its work.

5

Naked, Exposed,
and Willing to Die

The next morning I sat silently in the satsang hall for more than two hours, waiting for Gangaji to come. The love in my heart had swelled to almost unbearable proportions, such that I was actually concerned that my heart might physically explode when she came into the room. But it didn't. Something totally unexpected happened.

Sitting with eyes closed, I heard the hallway door open, heard Gangaji's bare feet padding firmly across the carpet toward the couch. Unbelievably, these quiet footsteps reverberated through my soul like the footsteps of *death!*

My heart began to pound, but not with love. With fear. A terrifying sense that something was "after me," that something was going to "get" me was present. I was shocked and confused by it. What is wrong with me? What is this terror? But there was no controlling it.

Gangaji sat down on the couch and closed her eyes as usual. I closed mine too, but could not settle down. My whole body, my whole being, throbbed with the most intense terror I had ever experienced. There was no doubt in my mind—*this teacher is going to kill me!*

When Gangaji opened her eyes, she picked up a letter to read. A tremor of extreme fear shot through me that it might be my letter. God! I could not handle that too, not on top of all this fear. But it wasn't mine. It was someone's who was sitting just behind me—which turned out to be almost as disastrous. As Gangaji's eyes fell upon the person behind me, and her gaze brushed over the top of my head, I shut my eyes in panic. I felt totally naked, exposed to the core, absolutely vulnerable. And I knew she could see it. So besides the fear, an agonizing embarrassment also arose.

I kept my eyes closed and my head down on my knees as she spoke to the girl behind me. *Why* did it have to be a letter from someone sitting right behind me? I felt stupid, pathetic, but could not stop the feelings. My mind and emotions were completely out of my control.

Soon I became aware that Gangaji had stopped talking to the girl and was now silent. My eyes were still shut, but I could *feel* her attention on me. It burned like a thousand suns—like all the burning I'd experienced so far magnified a million times. Perspiration began to moisten my forehead and shirt. Couldn't she turn her eyes somewhere else? Couldn't she take another question?

She did neither. She didn't move or speak—for what seemed like eons. Behind my closed eyes she appeared as the all-devouring Kali, skulls and all—blood dripping from her mouth, snakes streaming from her hair. It was absolutely terrifying. Everything I identified with as "myself" felt mortally threatened by her. I felt ripped wide open, filleted, torn apart. During that time, the exposure and the fear became so intense I almost lost consciousness—I actually came very close to passing out right there in satsang. I was that terrified.

Finally Gangaji said:

That's right. It knocks you out, you come back, you check again; still here. Still here.
You close your eyes and you check. You open your eyes and you check.

I didn't even consider whether she was saying this to me or to the girl behind me. I knew I had to open my eyes. I knew I was supposed to look into her eyes right then. It was the hardest thing I ever did. I practically had to pry my eyes open. But the command to do this was coming from some deep, mysterious level of my soul. Finally I managed to open my eyes a crack and wince up at her. She sat there absolutely unmoving, eyes half hooded, her expression severe. And yet through all that, I felt her love. Not a sweet, sentimental, motherly love. A huge, intense, ruthless love—like no love I had ever experienced before. A love that could swallow the whole known universe.

Finally, mercifully, she looked away and picked up another letter, asking where the author was sitting. Thankfully, this person was sitting on the other side of the room. Gradually, my anxiety relaxed a little, but still I felt confused and shaken by what I had just experienced. Where had all that fear come from? What had happened to the love and surrender that had overtaken me the day before?

A young woman named Tanya raised her hand and told Gangaji she wanted to marry herself to the truth with no possibility of divorce—to commit her life in surrender at Gangaji's feet. I was envious. How I yearned to be able to say something like that to her right then. But I could not.

Gangaji responded:

> *What you are speaking of is actually accepting. Truth has offered itself to you in marriage, and you are saying "I accept. I leave my known world behind. I leave the father I knew behind, the mother I knew behind, the life I knew behind." This is a marriage. "I surrender to the marriage of Truth."*
>
> *Then death cannot part you from that. Sickness cannot part you from that. Health cannot part you from that. Glory cannot part you from that. Disgrace cannot part you from that.*

There was a sinking feeling in my heart that I'd failed to accept the marriage, and that I'd disappointed Gangaji because I was shutting down, drawing back in fear, instead of opening to this gift I'd been offered.

> *You know, when you accept some marriage such as this, you can expect all your old lovers to come crawling out of the woodwork . . . [laughter] . . . with great promises, and kind of dance around you. Demonic lovers and godly lovers.*

When you have said: "I am married to no thing,*" all the "things" panic, and come to reclaim you as theirs. But if you are truly married to no thing, you* are *no thing. And they won't be able to find you.*

It seemed my old lovers—fear, resistance, keeping myself hidden, protecting myself from exposure and vulnerability—*had* found me. It did not occur to me until much later that it wasn't "me" that was panicking, but the "things," the old lovers, the personality I had identified with for so long as myself. In Gangaji they had recognized their slayer, their murderer. And they were terrified. At that point, however, I still thought I *was* that personality, that mind, and so was not able to see this clearly.

I made a conscious effort to relax as Gangaji spoke about spiritual effort.

You know, people love to give enormous credit to their effort. And that's okay. "It was my effort that got me here." "It was my effort in working on myself that I could hear you." But better than that, give the effort to all those who went before you. Give the credit to them. Give the credit to Christ, to Buddha, to Ramana, to all the unknown and known saints. Give the credit to their effort. They have done it for you. That's the great privilege of these times. Enough have gone before you that you simply can be carried by what is revealed.

Her words were beautiful, radiant with the most vital wisdom—not with the dead, intellectual wisdom born of interpreting some ancient scripture or sutra, but with the fresh, immediate, alive wisdom of her own awakening. And I did feel this sense of "being carried," that none of this was from anything I had done. Yet I sat there in extreme discomfort, hoping she would not look in my direction. Wanting to escape, bolt, get away. And wanting to *not* want that. Wishing it was not happening this way. Wanting to be able to say, as Tanya had said, "I surrender to you in love."

Then, perfectly, Gangaji spoke of discomfort in connection with effortlessness:

> *I'm not speaking of no discomfort. There will be experiences of discomfort. But to experience that is effortless. To deny that, to repress that, takes some effort, with the object in mind "I shouldn't be uncomfortable. I will effort to find comfort again."*
>
> *As long as there is this sensory apparatus, there is the experience of the polarity of mind. There's no problem with that, as long as you recognize and realize what this arises from—effortless, permanent, eternal Self. Life. Not personal, and not impersonal. Both personal and impersonal.*

I didn't understand what she meant by that—not personal, not impersonal. Also I was definitely not experiencing the fear effortlessly. I hated it, wanted it to be gone. Only as I look back on this do I understand why it was so painful and excruciating. She was telling me, "There's no problem with fear arising. It arises IN who you are, arises in satsang to be freed." But I was fighting it. I wanted the love to be there, not this fear. So I sat there "frying" in my own resistance to what was taking place, desperately wanting the satsang to be over.

Finally Gangaji put her palms together and said:

> *Okay, that's enough for this morning.*

I've never heard her end a satsang like that before, or since. But for me, at the moment, it was exactly appropriate. I could not have handled another three minutes. A great sigh of relief seemed to issue from my whole body as Gangaji left the hall.

I went quickly back to my room, in extreme agony, and cried my eyes out. I had told her she was the teacher of my prayers, that I wanted to be her student, that I loved her—and then this morning in satsang I'd drawn back from her with the most uncontrollable fear. I felt disgraced, confused, afraid—and imagined her anger and displeasure at my behavior.

After lunch I sat in the dining hall against the big rock hearth sipping a cup of hot tea, which was all the lunch I could manage, trying to analyze this fear. I thought surely Gangaji must believe the letter I'd written her was not sincere. But as soon as this thought sprouted, immediately, as clear as if she were sitting right next to me, I heard her voice: *I would have thought you were insincere if you hadn't been afraid.*

This made no sense to me at all, mentally, but it had that ring of truth to it her words always evoked. I tried to think about it, think it through, but my mind was not very clear and I soon gave it up.

That evening there was no satsang. The staff members of Satsang Foundation & Press were holding a meeting with us in order to introduce themselves, describe how the Foundation had been started in the basement of Maitri's house, and talk about volunteer opportunities. I sat through the meeting in a state of miserable depression, totally uninterested in anything that was being said.

After the meeting I went to my room and got ready for bed. I knew I could not go into the satsang hall to sit that night. I felt too upset, too vulnerable, too naked, too crazy. I needed to be alone in my room. Fortunately, my roommate was out late that night and did not return for some time. As I prepared to climb into my top bunk behind Papaji's picture, I heard Gangaji's voice: *You must be naked, exposed, and willing to die.*

Naked. Exposed. The words themselves made me shudder. But suddenly I became aware of the uncountable masks I had built for myself and had become adept at hiding behind— masks that even looked like spiritual effort and sincerity, but in reality were just clever ways of hiding. It was excruciating to have them ripped from me like this. In front of Gangaji that morning they had all lain exposed. Yes, I had been rendered totally naked. And I had panicked.

By writing her that letter of surrender I had declared to her, to the universe, to my Self, that I was ready to die to all these masks, to all that was false. And the declaration was being tested. All the old lovers of fear, resistance, and hiding were rushing in to defend their threatened territory. I could feel them almost tangibly in the room.

As I stood at the foot of the little ladder that led up to my bunk, a brief fight ensued between this surrender that was calling me and the "things" that were battling for their existence. But finally, it was the intense love for Gangaji and for this Truth being revealed to me that won out. I felt I would rather die than lose Gangaji as my teacher. And there was a hopeless feeling at that moment that I'd already failed an important first test. Again her voice came to me: *naked, exposed, and willing to die.*

Still standing by the ladder, I sucked in a deep, shaky breath. "Okay," I whispered, "then death."

I climbed up the ladder into my bunk that night willing to die, willing to shed every mask, willing to relinquish every strategy. I lay there in the darkness for some time, burning with the hottest fire yet, aware of a willingness to give up everything and yet not knowing how to let go of all my habits of protection.

Then, what I can only describe as a miracle, as the most unimaginable Grace, took place. I saw Gangaji's physical form hovering over me. Before I had time to be surprised or afraid, she reached out her hand and raked it down the length of my body. As she did this, her hand became larger, almost like a bear claw, gouging deep into my soul, as if scooping something out. It was painful, excruciating, but not in a strictly physical way. It was akin to the pain of ripping off a bandaid that has been on too long, long after the wound has healed.

Afterward, I felt strangely relieved, lighter, easier, as if some huge sludge of resistance had been removed in that raking. She appeared in this way several times that night. Each time, more resistance was raked out of me. I felt tangibly the scraping, the gouging, sometimes like the ripping open of my flesh. But the pain of it was as if at a distance.

Gangaji's presence and form stayed near all night long. By the morning satsang I felt calmer. The fear had subsided. Still I could not meet Gangaji's eyes, and sat toward the back of the room. But the insane fear of her had left me.

The first person that spoke said, "I'm being torn apart, and I want to be free."

Gangaji said:

What's being torn apart?

Through tears, the person answered, "Thoughts..."

Find out what's being torn apart.

"I know it's thoughts."

Oh, good! Then these are tears of joy.

"Yes."

Find out what can be torn apart. Find everything that can be torn apart, and let it be torn apart. Let them be torn apart. Even this experience of "this body is being torn apart." Yes, let it relax, let it go. This sense of holding the body, holding thoughts, holding the imaginary "I" together—let it be torn apart.*

These words seemed like they were designed for me, and struck deeply at my discomfort. This was the struggle, this was the discomfort—trying to hold the illusion of this "person" together. Let it go.

It was strange how every question seemed to be mine, every answer seemed to be for me. Again I was subtly aware of a huge presence orchestrating everything—for Its own awakening to Itself.

An announcement was made that the evening satsang would be a musical satsang. Gangaji would be present, but would not speak. It would be the last satsang of the retreat, for there was to be no morning meeting, just a breakfast before going home. I was disappointed by this announcement, even though usually I loved music. In these last precious hours of the retreat it was Gangaji I wanted to hear, not some people playing their songs. And so that prospect was agonizingly uninteresting.

That night as I sat listening to the musicians offering their beautiful songs and chants I felt some soothing effect on my besieged body, mind, and emotions. Music has always had a magically transforming effect on me. I had been an amateur songwriter since about the age of ten, when I began taking Christian hymns from church and re-writing them with different words that were more meaningful to me. Tonight, however, though I was aware of the soothing effect, I sat there feeling unusually numb to the beautiful melodies. I was not ready for the retreat to end. I was not finished. I was still shying away from Gangaji's eyes when she looked my way. I was still vacillating back and forth as to whether all the wonderful and terrible things I'd experienced on the retreat were real or imagined, and questioning what all this would mean to my life.

Toward the end of the evening the whole group, including Gangaji, sang "Amazing Grace." It is one of my favorites. As I began to let myself sing and open to the beauty of this song I realized how powerfully and amazingly Grace had poured into my life in this meeting with Gangaji. I glimpsed, in that moment during the singing, all that had taken place on the retreat, as excruciating as some of it had been, as unbelievable as some of it had been, was just that—*Grace*.

The next morning, I woke to the sun streaming in my window and felt relieved that I'd finally been able to sleep for a few hours. But soon after waking, a wave of depression and fear overtook me. The retreat was over. I was being tossed out into my life, a complete physical and emotional wreck. How could Gangaji do this to me? How could she leave me like this? I couldn't possibly face my husband, my friends, my work, in this dismal state.

As I lay there in bed, not wanting to greet the morning, not wanting to face packing and going home, the most insidious fear gripped my mind—that I'd never get back to "normal," that all the beautiful experiences and visions I'd had were illusions, that I was losing all sense of reality. It was as if all the fears I had ever entertained in my life suddenly came rushing to meet me—at once.

In the depth of all that, as I felt myself being sucked deeper and deeper into a vortex of uncontrollable fear, I thought, "This must be what insanity is like." Then I heard Gangaji's voice, strong and clear, with an authority that could not be ignored: *You are free. You are Light. This fear has nothing to do with you. It is only thought.*

I sat up in bed. Instantly my mind cleared. I felt bathed once more in the love and peace I had come to associate with Gangaji's presence. I was amazed and awed once again. Where had all the fear gone? Now it seemed like nothing. A phantom. I felt Gangaji's presence tangibly near. It was not as if her presence had pushed out the crazy thoughts. The thoughts were just seen as nothing, seen as never having been anything.

It occurred to me then that maybe Gangaji wasn't leaving me. Maybe she's right here. Maybe the retreat isn't going to end.

I went to breakfast feeling very strange. My body was still on fire, shaky, wired. The crazy fear-thoughts and depression kept fading in and out—fighting, it seemed, with that loving presence which had just saved me from insanity.

I hadn't eaten much in several days and now, finally, felt hungry. But as I sat at the breakfast table and tried to bring a spoonful of oatmeal to my mouth, my hand was shaking so badly I could barely get it in without the oatmeal falling off. Some people sitting across from me were staring at me, watching my futile efforts to eat. Feeling embarrassed and self-conscious, I finally gave up on the oatmeal. I went to the buffet table and picked out an apple from the fruit basket, then sat down in a different spot, alone, to figure out how to eat it without looking stupid.

A young woman came up to me and told me how much she'd liked my presence on the retreat, how much she'd loved it when I'd gone up on the couch—which now seemed like a long, long time ago. Since silence was no longer being observed on this last morning, we talked and introduced ourselves. Caroline was from Switzerland and had been with Gangaji for over a year, having met her in India and then followed her around the world—from India to New Mexico, to California, to Hawaii and then to Colorado. She told me some of her experiences with Gangaji, the intense love she felt, and how she felt Gangaji inside of her, speaking inwardly to her constantly.

I was relieved beyond anything I can describe. Someone else was experiencing this. "You mean, I'm not crazy?" I said.

"Oh, yeah, we're all crazy," she laughed easily.

I began peeling my apple as Caroline went on.

"Sometimes Gangaji ignores me," she said, "but it's good, you know, because I have this ego I can't let go of, and she's working on that."

I asked Caroline what it was like being away from Gangaji, and told her I was freaking out about the retreat ending.

She said, "Sometimes it's good to be away from her, because then you see she's always right here." She put her hand on her heart. "The teacher is within you. Gangaji is your own Self."

As we spoke, I felt more and more at ease. Even the shaking had subsided somewhat. We talked for some time as Caroline related more of her experiences with Gangaji. I was drinking it in. It was healing nectar to my soul. The longer we spoke, the more the love came to the foreground of my awareness and the more the fear grew dim.

I asked Caroline how old she was. "Twenty-six," she told me. I said, "How beautiful that someone so young has found a teacher like Gangaji, at the age of twenty-six!" I told her that was how long I'd been seeking.

Caroline gave me a very important satsang that morning. And I had the sense once again that the meeting with her had, in some mysterious way, been "arranged" by this incredible Presence that had been orchestrating everything since that first satsang in Boulder less than two weeks ago. And I began to see too that satsang was not just "formal" satsang in Gangaji's physical presence, but could happen anywhere, any time. For I felt vividly that morning, beyond any doubt, that Gangaji was speaking to me, as Self, through Caroline.

I had found a ride back to Boulder with a lady named Kara, so I called my husband to tell him that he didn't have to drive up the mountain to get me. He seemed a million miles away. Talking to him didn't seem real—as though we were in a play, assuming roles of husband and wife. I couldn't imagine what it would be like to be back in Boulder. It felt like I'd been on another planet, and that at least a year had passed since I'd been gone.

As I was driven back down the mountain by Kara, we talked about the retreat, about Gangaji, about truth. Actually, I mostly talked while Kara mostly laughed. Finally I asked her why she was laughing so much at everything I said. Through more laughter, she replied, "Because it's so beautiful, everything you're saying. You're speaking satsang."

6

DROWNING IN
THE RIVER GANGA

*M*y husband greeted me warmly as I came through the door. I still felt a little strange. The interaction with him, as well as just being in the space of our home again, had a dream-like quality about it, as though I'd never really seen any of it before. I was still experiencing alternating moods between intense love for Gangaji, and a deep depression that I'd never be normal again, that I should never have gone to the retreat in the first place. It made absolutely no sense. And the fact that it made no sense alerted me to the possibility that the fluctuations were not real. Yet they were being experienced, vividly experienced.

I did not want Toby to suspect what I myself at moments suspected—that I was not stable, mentally or emotionally. So, while I was experiencing one of the alternations where I was flooded with love and gratitude, I quickly sat him down on the couch and told him as much as I could put into words about what had taken place at Estes Park.

He was awed, amazed, and happy for me. A part of him knew the profound significance of what had occurred, for we had both been on a spiritual path for a long time and had served the same Indian teacher for many years. But another part of him had not yet grasped the depth and extent of the changes I was experiencing.

After I finished my tale, Toby began telling me about his plans for the summer. He wanted to book our flights to Cape Cod for mid-June to go visit his family. I stared at him blankly. Cape Cod and the trip he was proposing seemed even more unreal than everything else. I had no desire whatsoever to go to the Cape. I couldn't imagine having to interact with his family in my present condition. And besides, I had just met the teacher of my prayers. She would be going to Santa Fe in a few days and then returning to Boulder in mid-June, offering public sat-sang four times a week for most of the summer—and I had no intention of being anywhere but at her feet.

Toby was shocked, disappointed, angry. I had always gone with him on these summer visits to his family, and they would be expecting me. But I knew in my heart there was nothing that could drag me away from Boulder this summer. I had waited for this teacher for uncountable time, and was not about to miss this opportunity. Though I felt his disappoint-ment and distress, there was nothing I could do about it. I could not go.

This refusal to travel to the Cape with him was the begin-ning of a test in our relationship which intensified over the summer. He could see that I was "gone," that I was not there for him. He would say sometimes, "I want my wife back." But I could not bring her back. I couldn't even remember who she'd been! There were so many cataclysmic upheavals going on inside of me that, for some time, I could not handle anyone else's perspectives or needs.

I went up to my room that night, a loft above the living room, and lay down on the futon. A picture of Ramana Maharshi as a boy sage of sixteen or seventeen sat on my bed-side table. Achala had given it to me just before the retreat. As I looked into the eyes of that awakened youth, an intense fear of being devoured arose again. Suddenly, everything that boy's life represented was terrifying—Advaita Vedanta, unqualified non-dualism, the absorption of all that is known into the unknown. What was I doing, getting back into this Indian stuff again?

I lay there feeling the fear burning inside me like a volcano. Then, a half hour later, I felt intense love for Gangaji and grat-itude for the tremendous Grace I could see had flooded my life. A picture of Gangaji, which I'd purchased at the retreat, also sat on my bedside table. As I looked into her eyes an explosion of love erupted in my heart. It was so intense it alarmed me. I actually felt as if my heart was physically exploding out of my chest. I realize now it was probably the spiritual heart, but the sensations were so tangible, so concrete, that it felt very physical at the time. The love was on the order of magnitude I might have felt upon recognizing an ancient, deeply cherished lover, returning finally to collect me after eons of separation. And I must admit that this very straight, conservative mind had no way to relate to this experience in any logical, comfortable way. But there was nothing I could do about it. It was simply taking place—all by itself, out of my control.

I would have to look away from the pictures, of both Ramana and Gangaji. Then the fear would arise again. Then the love. Back and forth. I couldn't stop the fluctuations. I lay there all night, burning, feeling fear, feeling love. It was exhausting, confusing.

This went on for two more days. Not sleeping, not eating. Fear, love, terror, depression, my husband feeling more and more alienated. Looking back on this time, I believe the deepest fear was that I might never recapture the profound euphoria I had felt on the retreat in that first explosion of Self-recognition, and especially the ecstatic joy and love I'd experienced when the surrender first took place.

Finally, in desperation, I called Satsang Foundation & Press and asked to speak to Maitri. It was all I could think of to do. She was not available and I was put in touch with her voice mail. I left a tearful message on her machine that I was still unable to sleep, unable to eat, and didn't know how much longer I could exist like this.

After I hung up the phone my eyes fell mysteriously, miraculously, upon some of Gangaji's words. A newsletter put out by the Foundation, called "Satsang With Gangaji," lay open on the floor of my loft. It was part of the literature Achala had given me that first night at the Boulder satsang. The text was from an interview with Gangaji.

The interviewer asked, "You don't go into some fear that you have somehow lost your Self when your bliss may dissipate for a while and you move into a more ordinary space?"

Yes, I thought. That was it. The fear of moving back into "the ordinary" after the sacred space of the retreat, after the blissful revelations that had taken place there.

Gangaji replied:

> *No. When I was first with Papaji and first leaving him, that fear would definitely arise, "Oh no, I have lost it!" But the great beauty of this teaching, this self-inquiry, is to question, "Who has lost it?" In that, the mind is thrown back immediately to its source; there is no one there who could have gained or lost anything. There is only consciousness present.*

Reading these words, something clicked, and my awareness shifted profoundly. I felt Gangaji's presence right there in my room. I read on.

> *The sense, "I have lost it," then serves as a vehicle for the revelation that you cannot lose who you are. You can lose states that appear, you can lose forms and ideas that arise— and all of that will be lost. I say, lose it all right now and see what cannot be lost!**

Just reading these words threw my awareness back, deep into Self-recognition. Suddenly I felt once again the peace and clarity and vastness I had felt sitting beside Gangaji that day on the couch.

Then the phone rang; it was Achala. She asked how I was doing, and I told her the truth—wonderful and horrible. We talked for a while and she spoke about being with Papaji and the deep awakening she'd experienced there, about how this presence was one's own Self and not in another person. After we hung up, I felt a lot better.

Remembering the message I'd left on Maitri's machine, I felt embarrassed that I'd bothered her with my problems and decided to call her back. Again I reached her voice mail. I left another message saying, "I'm okay, sorry I bothered you, please disregard my previous message, I'm fine."

That afternoon I lay down on the futon in my loft to take a nap. Sleep did not come, but finally my awareness settled into a deep state, half awake, half asleep. Then a vision opened up.

Gangaji appeared, hovering over me once again in tangible, visible form, even more real than the time before on the retreat. Her form came closer to me, as if she was going to merge right into me. Startled, I drew back, shook myself from the vision and quickly sat up. "What was that?" I thought. "What's happening?" My heart was pounding.

I decided it must have been a dream, and lay back down. After a short while, I again drifted into a half-wakeful state. Gangaji appeared again. This time, before I knew what was happening, her form and presence merged right into me! There is no way to describe this adequately in words. I felt her love, her awareness, her stillness to be the same as myself. I was aware of something indescribably huge that wanted to swallow me. But there was no fear. All fear had vanished. Subtly I could hear Gangaji asking me to let go into that hugeness. And in an instant of the most unfathomable trust and Grace, I let go. I let go of "me."

The huge expanse of what I can only describe as the whole universe, what the Vedas describe as Brahman, opened up inside of me, all around me, encompassing everything, swallowing everything. An ecstatic explosion of awareness followed. In this merging with her consciousness I could see clearly this infinite vastness I had feared, whose doorstep I had lingered on for so long and which I had imagined would annihilate me, to be *my own Self*, to be her Self, no difference—all loving, all embracing, all beautiful. Gangaji's being and my being had become one. I had drowned in the River Ganga.

In this seeing I actually remember feeling a little ridiculous. How could there have been so much fear of this which in reality is my own Self? I heard the answer clearly in her voice: *False identification with mind as who one is.* And I knew then that it was my own Infinite Self I was seeing in Gangaji, my own Self I was loving. That's why she had reminded me of myself so uncannily in that first satsang.

She had not forgotten the other part of my question, "How do you get rid of the fear of being devoured?" But she had not answered me in words. She had *shown* me—by allowing me to drown in her; by allowing me to merge with her own consciousness long enough for me to see, that this which I had feared would devour me was and is my own true essence.

I was awed by the poetry and striking metaphor of what had occurred—she's the River, the holy River Ganga, and I had drowned in her. I sat up on the edge of my bed, reached for my guitar, and this song flowed out quite effortlessly.

> There's a Holy River in the heart of India
> And the sages say her waters
> Quench the fire of samsara
> And they say she flows with Grace
> In a never ending stream
> And they say that those who bathe in her
> Awaken from a dream.
>
> Oh, River Ganga
> Flowing to the sea
> Let this soul drown in you
> And be forever free.
> Oh, River Ganga
> Flowing to the sea
> Let this soul drown in you
> And be forever free.
>
> Once this Holy River flowed across the sea
> Knowing that the Western world
> Was longing to be free
> Though it remains mysterious
> How this came to be
> I have seen the Ganges flowing here
> From sea to shining sea.
>
> Oh River Ganga
> Take us to the sea
> Let us all drown in you
> And be forever free
> Oh River Ganga
> Take us to the sea
> Let us all drown in you
> And be forever free.

When Toby came home that evening I tried to tell him what had taken place. I told him how terrified I'd been of losing what had been realized on the retreat, and how Gangaji had shown me that there is no separation, that she is always with me, and that the realization continues to deepen. I didn't know whether I had expressed it very well, so I played him the song which I'd named "River Ganga." He was deeply moved and said it was the most beautiful song I'd ever written.

That night I lay in bed, still merged in the Ganga. My body felt strange, numb. When I'd try to move my arm or leg, nothing would happen. It took a while to realize what this was—my body was definitely asleep, while my awareness remained wide awake. It was something I'd experienced a few times before in my life, but never quite this vividly.

I felt Gangaji's presence and love so intensely. At some point in the middle of the night, I felt another presence. Then I saw Ramana, standing nearby, watching. I heard Gangaji's voice; she told me to sit up. It took a while to get my body to obey the command. But finally I managed to sit upright and draw my legs up into a half-lotus position.*

It seemed that Ramana was approving of me in some way. Then, in front of me, I became aware of another Indian man whom I did not recognize. He was performing some kind of ceremony, which seemed to be an initiation. Later I realized this man must have been Papaji.

Gangaji was right there with me, a part of me, as if inside of me. There were times during this "initiation" when I felt fear arise, perhaps because everything seemed so strange and huge and other-worldly. At such times I would call out to Gangaji and she would assure me that she was *right here*. At one point I asked her if I had been devoured by Brahman yet. She laughed, *Devoured? You're being digested!*

Then I laughed too, at this wonderful humor I was beginning to recognize as hers. Gangaji then spoke with Ramana about me. She told him that she was able to connect with me very deeply, because of some resonance between our two forms. I couldn't make out all of what they were saying, but at one point it seemed Ramana was confirming that, yes, I was accepted. I would be able to serve this lineage.

I was awed. I could hardly believe what was happening. Once I remember the thought arising, "This has got to be some kind of gigantic ego-trip or something."

Gangaji's voice rang out strongly, *Can you find any ego here?*

I looked for an "ego" and could find none. In fact I couldn't find anything that I used to call "me." Everything was so expanded and huge, drowned in the River Ganga. And the Ganga seemed bigger than the whole universe, what the universe arises *in*.

After the initiation was completed, Gangaji told me that she was going to start training me. I asked: "When?" She said: *Starting tomorrow.*

Then the vision faded out and I sat for a while in stunned and grateful silence. Finally I lay down and slept long and deeply for the first time in nearly ten days.

The next day was May 9th. I remember the date because I awoke that morning a very different person. The huge, blissful presence which I associated with Gangaji was felt in every cell of my body. My awareness was endless, not located just in my physical form. Everything I did seemed to be taking place in some great wholeness that was me, and that was Gangaji, that was everything. And for the first time in my life I felt beyond any doubt—I am no longer a seeker.

Later that morning, I went to the market to do some household errands. Every face seemed beautiful. Every action seemed effortless, blissful, perfect.

In the afternoon I called Satsang Foundation & Press to find out if Gangaji had gone to Santa Fe yet, and found out she was leaving the following morning. I was disappointed, because I wanted to record the song I'd written for her and give it to her before she left town, but knew I couldn't get it together that quickly. I did not have adequate recording equipment and would have to find something to borrow. The lady at the Foundation I spoke with said she herself was leaving for Santa Fe the day after Gangaji, and if I could get something to her before that she would take it to Santa Fe for me and deliver it to Gangaji.

That night, I went over to Achala's and borrowed her tape machine. In the morning I recorded the song for Gangaji and, before taking it down to the Foundation, enclosed a brief letter reporting that the intense fear had gone, and that my heart had filled up with love—especially for her. I realized later that the way I had written this was inaccurate. The love had not filled my heart because the fear had departed. In the dissolving of separation the fear had ceased to exist, and the Love that had always been present now shone forth, naturally.

This intense love, however, still caused quite a lot of shyness to arise, and I did not know how to explain to Gangaji about the visions and the merging. I did not know whether I should try to explain it, or what it actually meant. So I left out that part and just let the song speak for me.

Bhagavan Sri Ramana Maharshi

7

WHO AM I?

*S*oon after I'd sent the tape and letter off to Santa Fe, my friend Moksha called from Florida. She had heard that I'd come into contact with the lineage of Ramana Maharshi, and had recently come across a video about Ramana's life and teaching called "The Sage of Arunachala" which she was sending to me. She thought I would enjoy it because she knew how much I loved animals, and Ramana, like Saint Francis of Assisi, had a mysterious rapport with them. He had even been able to bring his pet cow to the state of total liberation during the last moments of her life. This interested me a great deal because I'd often wondered about the possibility of an animal reaching spiritual liberation. All my life I'd had close relationships with animals and had felt sometimes that animals were a lot more in touch with universal presence than humans.

The video arrived in a few days and without wasting a moment I pushed it into the VCR. The narrator began with the story of Ramana as a young boy. He was not the best of students, having little interest in books and study. He loved swimming in the river, visiting temples, and reading about saints. At the age of sixteen he became aware of a powerful fear of death. From the description given it sounded very much like what I had experienced at age ten—a huge nothingness threatening to devour me. But unlike myself, who had resisted it and tried to avoid it, Ramana had just lain down and met it, experienced it, headed straight into it, without calling for help, without running to a doctor. And in that direct meeting he discovered what cannot be touched by death, what cannot be devoured because it is itself the ultimate devourer—one's own infinite consciousness.

Instantly I loved this being and felt I knew him, felt this lineage was my true spiritual family, the true teaching I had longed for all my life. His teaching, if it can be said to be a teaching, can be distilled into the question "Who am I?" I had asked myself this question much of my life, from as early as I can remember. It began as a child when I noticed that around different people I would feel and act differently—parents, siblings, friends, teachers. I wondered how my personality could have all these facets, and felt there must be something unchanging at the basis of all this that constituted the real "me." And so the question would naturally and constantly arise, "Who am I?" I had even once written a little song to this question which went something like this:

> Who am I
> When I'm really me?
> Who am I
> Deep inside of me?
> Who am I
> When I don't try
> At all?

The video went on to explain that this question turns the seeker's awareness back onto itself, revealing the questioner, the seeker, the true Self. Much later I would hear Gangaji say that although the question "Who am I?" may have long been a static philosophical axiom contained within the body of Indian lore, this question had now become, through the gift of Ramana's life, surcharged with a powerful transmission of Grace and Silence which allows the seeker to "be still" so that the answer, the Truth of one's Being, can be revealed.

I had experienced this transmission directly. When I first came into Gangaji's presence that first night in the Boulder satsang everything had gone still in my mind—the moment she walked into the room. And it is clear to me now that when I looked into her eyes at the retreat the vastness I had seen behind her eyes was my own true Self reflecting back at me. That's why, directly afterwards, I was able to perceive the mountains as my Self, and the trees and the animals and all the universe. It was as though the question had been asked enough, and was just waiting for this transmission of stillness and Grace for the answer to be revealed.

The video went on to describe Ramana's life after his awakening. Still only a boy of sixteen, he now found his schoolwork to be even more tedious than before, and so decided to embark on a secret pilgrimage to a holy mountain called Arunachala. Though it was not mentioned in the video, I found out later that Ramana was born with the sound "Arunachala" repeating in his head. It was not until Ramana was about twelve that he found out through a relative that this sound was actually a place one could go to, that there existed a holy mountain in South India by that name.

Stealing a little money from his brother to pay for the trip, Ramana quietly departed from the world he had grown up in, leaving a note for his family stating that he was going "in search of his father," that it was on an honorable mission he embarked, and asking them not to waste any money or time looking for him.

Arunachala was situated near Tiruvannamalai, north of the town he was living in at the time with his uncle. A three-day journey finally brought young Ramana to the temple at the base of the holy mountain, which is said to be an incarnation of Shiva. I wondered if this was who he meant by "his father," and remembered how the presence of Shiva was definitely lively in those first days with Gangaji at Estes Park.

Ramana took up residence in the main temple at Arunachala, sitting unmoving for weeks and months at a time, absorbed in the bliss of Divine Union. People would sometimes offer him food, but he was not interested in eating. Even when someone would place food right in his mouth, upon returning the next day they would often discover the food still there in his mouth, unchewed, unswallowed—so absorbed was the young sage in the Infinite.

Schoolboys visiting the temple and seeing a boy about their own age sitting so immovably like a renunciate, would often taunt Ramana by throwing stones at him or try to disturb him in other ways. But he remained unmoving. Sometimes vermin gnawed at his legs (scars from which remained all his life), but still he did not move.

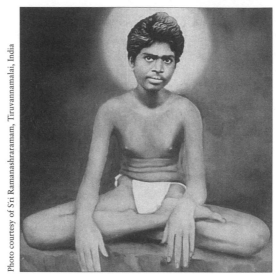

Photo courtesy of Sri Ramanashraramam, Tiruvannamalai, India

Ramana, at about 17 years of age.

News of the boy-sage soon traveled across India and seekers of truth began to gather around him for his *darshan* (holy sight). But for several years he did not seem interested in having students or in being a teacher. He was not concerned with outer phenomena of any kind. He rarely spoke, rarely moved. Even so, aspirants continued to come from afar, even from the West, to sit in silence at his feet. In the video, many stories were related of great awakenings that took place just from sitting with Ramana in silence. His teaching was transmitted not in words, but passed silently from heart to heart.

The video had a powerful effect on me. One particular shot of Ramana gave a start and a thrill to my soul, because in it he looked very much as he had appeared to me in the vision of a few nights before. I was also especially struck by the fact that he had had no outer teacher. His guru was the mountain, Arunachala. He loved it, had walked in the course of his life every inch of it, and had composed beautiful devotional hymns to it. Later I learned from Gangaji that she had asked Papaji once, "What does 'Ramana' mean?" And Papaji had replied: "Ramana is that which dwells in the heart of all Being."

After watching the video twice, I climbed the stairs to my loft and sat for several hours, aware only of a deep silence and Grace.

That evening, I picked up a little booklet that Achala had given me entitled *Who Am I? The Teachings of Bhagavan Sri Ramana Maharshi*. The introduction stated that in spite of its size, it is still praised as the clearest, most concise exposition of the essence of Ramana's teachings. The book was in dialogue form, beginning with the opening question, "Who am I?" Ramana answers:

> The gross body which is composed of the five humors, I am not; the five cognitive sense-organs . . . I am not; the five vital airs . . . [breath, etc] . . . I am not; even the mind which thinks, I am not; the nescience [deep sleep] too, which is endowed only with the residual impressions of objects, and in which there are no objects and no functioning, I am not.

The questioner continued, "If I am none of these, then who am I?" Ramana answers:

> After negating all of the above-mentioned as "not this", "not this", that Awareness which alone remains—that I am.

The questioner asks, "When will the realization of the Self be gained?" Ramana answers:

> When the world which is what-is-seen has been removed, there will be the realization of the Self which is the seer. *

I closed the book. My mind felt tired and unable to grasp any of it. As I lay down and tried to sleep, Ramana filled my awareness with his stillness and hugeness.

I was only four years old when Ramana left his body in a strange country far away from mine, after having lived a life mostly of silence—and yet here was his life and silence touching my life so deeply, so tangibly, so perfectly through this incredible teacher whose master had named her as the Holy River Ganga.

8

WHAT DO YOU REALLY WANT?

*U*p until this point, I had no intention of traveling to Santa Fe. It just hadn't occurred to me that this was an option. For one thing, I didn't know how far it was, having lived in this part of the country for only nine months. For another, I knew that in just four weeks Gangaji would be returning to Boulder for the remainder of the summer, and public satsangs would be offered four times a week at the same Unitarian Church where I had first seen her. But a few days after sending the "River Ganga" song to Santa Fe, and after viewing the Ramana tape, the pull to see Gangaji became irresistible. I had to go. It was as if I was being "called."

At first Toby refused to consider it. He was doing some Latin translation work for his Ph.D. that took a lot of focus and a trip right then was the farthest thing from his mind. "Gangaji will be here all summer," he said. "What's the big rush about trekking all the way to Santa Fe now?"

Yes, it didn't make sense. But neither had a lot of other things since meeting Gangaji. The pull to Santa Fe was definitely not coming from a logical, practical mind. Yet I felt a strange sense of urgency about seeing her, as if only this moment mattered. Summer might never come. The world might come to an end next week. What if Gangaji changed her plans and decided not to come back to Boulder at all? Anything could happen. This call could not wait. I could not miss this opportunity to be in her presence.

Miraculously, as the weekend approached Toby changed his mind. Something deep inside him, unconnected to his rational self, also felt a pull to see Gangaji again. So on Friday night we packed up the mini-van for a weekend trip to Santa Fe.

It was a seven-hour drive through the beautiful high desert of southern Colorado and northern New Mexico. Toby studied, while I drove and listened to audio tapes of satsang with Gangaji, some of which I had purchased and some that had been loaned to me.

The satsang coordinators in Santa Fe had made available names of people associated with satsang who provided rooms in their homes for those coming from out of town to see Gangaji. So we had arranged to stay with an artist/healer from the satsang group who lived on a quiet street near the edge of town.

The satsangs were being held at a small theatre on the campus of the New Mexico School for the Deaf. We arrived in the late afternoon more than an hour before satsang was to begin, having been told by our hostess that space filled up quickly in these public meetings. As predicted, a fifty-foot line of people had already formed at the doors, which would not open until about half an hour before satsang.

As we waited in the hot sun, Toby grew uncomfortable in the heat and went in search of a shady spot where he could study. But the heat did not faze me. There was a very deep sense that this was exactly where I was supposed to be, and nothing in the outer circumstances mattered.

A man named Govind was circulating among the waiting crowd making a list of those who wanted to see Gangaji in a smaller group after the large satsang was over. Toby encouraged me to sign up for this, but for some reason I couldn't. A maddening shyness was still gripping me.

Finally inside the theatre, we got a seat about halfway back from the stage, which was set up with couch, flowers, and pictures of Ramana and Papaji. About four hundred people began filling up the small auditorium. We sat in silence for a while, waiting. When Gangaji came in, my heart felt a thrill and a deep peace. She was even more radiant and beautiful than I'd remembered. How could anyone be that beautiful? Though I'd heard her say it and I had experienced the truth of it, I kept forgetting that what I was seeing was the beauty of Infinite Reality, the beauty of my own Self reflected in her.

After about twenty minutes sitting in silence, Gangaji opened her eyes and, putting her palms together, said:

Welcome to Satsang.

She looked around the room for a moment, bathing everyone in a radiant smile, then began:

I have a question for you, and it is a very important question. It can reveal maturity or immaturity. When immaturity is revealed, then maturity is possible.

The question is: What do you really want? What is it you finally want?

If you answer, "Well, I want a good lover, a nice house, a good job"—then this is a reflection of immaturity. Because in that, there is some belief that a good lover, or a good house, or a good job will give you peace, fulfillment, and lasting happiness. Of course, in all of those, there is temporary, passing happiness and pleasure.

If you can see that what it is you have thought you wanted has not given you what it is you <u>really</u> wanted, then this is very good. This is maturity revealing itself.

I am not speaking of maturity in terms of age, or education, or spiritual practice. I am speaking of a ruthless intelligence and telling the truth. The truth that, no matter how much you have enjoyed and loved your house, and your lover, and your job, still, those things have not given you that which is lasting and eternal.

This recognition is a kind of rude awakening called disillusionment, and it is very important. Until disillusionment occurs, there is a kind of trance-like state where you wander through life—this life now, your life as a teenager, your life as a child, your life as an older person, your next life—and you grasp for the things that you want, and reject the things that you don't want, in the hopes that you will receive what it is you really want.

In this disillusionment, this rude awakening, this ruthless truth-telling, you have the opportunity to actually discover and declare within yourself what you really want.

All I could think of that I wanted in that moment was her. I didn't even know what that meant. I just knew I wanted what I saw there in front of me, in her, as her, through her, from her. The presence she radiated I wanted more than anything I had ever wanted.

> *If by chance what you really want is eternal truth, then you are very lucky. Then I say to you—stop looking for it anywhere. Have the courage to stop looking in any "thing" for eternal truth. Whether this thing be some worldly thing, or some philosophical thing, or some spiritual thing. Just stop looking. In that instant of stopping, you will then know where to look for That.*
>
> *It takes less than an instant.*

Toby glanced over at me; he looked worried. It was only his second satsang and I wondered how he was doing with it. But we would have to talk later. Every word Gangaji spoke was like nectar, like a perfect sutra,* and I didn't want to miss a single one.

> *If you are unlucky, and you discover that what it is you really want is security, and comfort, and knowledge, and personal power, then you will continue your search. You will continue to accumulate knowledge, personal power, and an appearance of security.*
>
> *That is okay. Satsang has appeared in your consciousness, so at least these words have been heard. However deeply you hear these words, they have been heard. They carry within them that which cannot be heard, but can be realized—in the instant you stop <u>looking</u> for the truth, happiness, and eternity. When you stop looking, you discover where to look.*
>
> *I am not suggesting that I can give you truth, or eternity, or whatever it is you want. I am simply confirming that what you want is who you already are.*
>
> *Stop all your conceptualizations of who you are. Stop looking to be something, and stop looking to not be something. In*

that instant, who you are is revealed, and this is what you have been searching for throughout time. You have been searching for your own Self, and you have looked everywhere except where you are!

I am not asking you to accept this as truth. I am asking you to see for yourself—to see your Self, for your Self, by your Self, through your Self.

I am that same Self. That's how I know who I'm talking to.

There was a quiet ripple of laughter. These words had a powerful effect on me—*I am that same Self.* I didn't really think about them; they just went in very deep.

So I am asking you, my own Self, to see for yourself and then to get busy spreading the news to your Self everywhere. To be used by the Truth of your Self, spreading to all aspects of your Self, all faces of your Self, throughout all time—past, present, and future.

So that is my welcome to satsang. *

Something about this sounded familiar—"Spreading to all aspects of yourself, throughout all time." Many years ago the Indian teacher I'd been with for so long had once written me in a letter: "You will take all the wisdom of life to light every corner of time." I wondered back then, and still wondered now, how is it possible to take wisdom to the past and future. It sounded like science fiction fantasy. Again, the mind collapsed in resignation. Like so much of what Gangaji spoke, I could not figure this out with my mind.*

After satsang we drove back to the house where we were staying. Toby was very quiet. Anxious for him to receive this truth, I asked him how he'd liked the satsang.

He said, "I'm in shock."

"Why? What happened?"

"I realized something," he said.

I was ecstatic.

"No, don't get excited," he warned. "It's not good. I've been thinking about what she said today, 'What do you really want?' and when I ask myself that very question, the answer that comes back is 'respect.' What I *thought* I wanted above all was enlightenment, but that and all the other things I've wanted—money, success, a Ph.D.—I realize now are just ways I think I'll get respect."

I was thrilled. "This is beautiful that you've realized that."

"But what shall I do now? Enlightenment isn't really my main desire. I want it, of course, but I need respect first. This is devastating. It's not maturity."

"This is great, though, that this has been revealed. Gangaji said today that immaturity must get revealed, otherwise there's this trance and you go on pretending. This is the opportunity for maturity." But he did not yet see the beauty of it. I encouraged him to ask Gangaji about it the next day in satsang.

The next day there were lots of questions in satsang and though Toby raised his hand a couple of times, he wasn't called on. I figured it must not have been the right time for the question.

We had originally planned on driving back to Boulder after that Sunday satsang, but decided instead to stay another night so that we could attend the morning satsang the next day. In the morning we got to the College nearly two hours before satsang, which is about how early one had to arrive in order to secure a place near the front of the line. I had the desire to sit up closer that day. But even though we were about fifth in line, there was such a rush when the doors opened, that somehow we still ended up five or six rows back.

As we sat waiting for satsang to begin I was thinking that during the entire weekend Gangaji hadn't seemed to notice me or recognize me at all, even though her eyes would often sweep the entire hall many times during a satsang. The visions and profound experiences I'd had in the past two weeks had tempted me to think that I was in some way special to Gangaji. I heard her voice in my head speaking to me all the time. And she had said in the vision with Ramana that she would start training me. But she definitely gave no outward indication that she even remembered me. I began to doubt that the visions were true and wondered if it was all my imagination, a big ego-trip after all, wondered if it would be better to just drop the memory of those visions all together.

At one point near the end of the satsang a man sitting behind me began to speak to Gangaji. "I just wanted to express deepest gratitude for your presence," he said.

She flashed him a radiant smile.

Oh, thank you.

He went on, "And in your presence I just feel incredible silence and bliss."

Very good.

He added, "And the really good news is that I never seem to be out of your presence."

That's right! Now what can that mean? How is that possible? Clearly he's not talking of this form. We haven't spent any time in physical presence other than in this satsang experience. So we know he's not talking about form.

The man continued, "I asked you to push me and I felt completely immersed in the River Ganga."

She chuckled.

Yes, it takes everything, and leaves you naked. And in this nakedness—with no name, no form, no history, no relationships, no past work, no future work—then you recognize, "I am that presence. It never leaves me."
One presence. Infinite manifestations of one presence.

During this discourse I began to feel that maybe I wasn't so special after all. It seemed this man too had drowned in the River Ganga. This was further confirmed when he continued saying, "I hear your voice wherever I go."

Gangaji laughed.

It's your voice. That's how you can hear it wherever you go. It is the same voice, using particular tonalities, maybe, that you associate with some aspect of yourself that came to yourself at a particular time and said "Now!" [laughter]

Yes. Ask to be pushed. Ask to be pulled. Ask to be delivered. Ask to be found. Ask to be saved. And realize—I am That.

Then you realize you push yourself—deeper and deeper into realization—whether you call yourself Gangaji, Papaji, Ramana, Dan, Sue, Bob, Hare Krishna—whatever, doesn't matter. Ask for Truth, and you will answer yourself with Truth. Ask for more objects and you will also answer yourself—with more objects.

You are infinitely giving and merciful. Then you know to ask for nothing—and nothing, no "thing" is revealed. This is what is meant by "stop," by "being pushed"—pushed into silence, drowned in silence.

Once again she had answered my question perfectly. The voice inside my head that sounded like hers was my own Self, which somehow, mysteriously, had taken on the attributes and qualities of Gangaji-ness.

I felt a subtle sense that I'd been chastised for my arrogance and this brought up a burning sensation again. It began to dawn on me that everyone Gangaji spoke to was equally special, equally her own Self, equally invited to drown in the River Ganga. She loved every one of them—unconditionally, intimately, totally. It was not personal and it was not impersonal. And it was both personal and impersonal.

The man's talk of drowning in the Ganga reminded me of the song I'd written for Gangaji. All weekend I had wondered if Gangaji had received the tape I'd sent and if she'd liked the song. Now I resigned myself to the possibility that I might never know.

She fielded a few more questions, then put her palms together and said, *Om Shanti.* The Satsang was over. She stood up, gathered up her "mail," smiled warmly at several people sitting in the front row, then exited the auditorium through a side door to the right of the stage. As I watched her walking out, a strong pang of longing arose in my heart, as if I was being separated from something precious, from someone deeply loved. An intense, intimate attachment for her had formed deep in my soul and yet there had been no acknowledgement from her side, openly at least, that she even remembered who I was. Again I was reminded that this was a most unusual relationship, not graspable by the mind.

After Gangaji left, Govind announced that those who would be attending the small satsang should get up first and come behind the stage. The rest of us were requested to sit quietly for a few minutes more. I suddenly felt a great frustration with myself. I longed to go to the small meeting, but the longing and the shyness were fighting with each other. And the shyness was still winning.

We hung around in the foyer, looking at the books, tapes, and videos for sale on the tables. I bought a video of a satsang in Santa Fe from the year before entitled, "The End of Ego." Meanwhile, Toby had bumped into a friend, someone who had lived in a large spiritual community which we'd been a part of for eight years and which we'd left about four years before.

"Come here," Toby grabbed my arm. "I want you to meet someone. This is John. Do you remember him?"

The man seemed vaguely familiar, but I'd never had a very good memory for people. John smiled and said to me, "I remember *you*. I recognized you at Estes Park, but we were in silence so I didn't say anything to you. It was so beautiful when you went up on the couch. It really melted everyone's heart. You were so scared at first. Then it was obvious that you just got quieter and quieter."

Toby and John talked a little about how we had each found out about Gangaji, and also who else we might know from that old group who had been attracted to satsang. My attention faded out for a while and I wasn't listening to them. Out of the corner of my eye I saw Maitri standing near the sales table. She glanced over at me and smiled. "You're here from Boulder?"

I nodded. "Just for the weekend," I said. As I turned back to the conversation with my husband and John, I heard Toby telling him about the beautiful "River Ganga" song I'd written for Gangaji.

John said, "Oh, River Ganga? Gangaji recently played a song on tape like that—in a small satsang for volunteers last Wednesday night."

I turned to John with excitement. "She played it in satsang!"

"Yes. A song about the River Ganga."

"Did it go like this...?" I sang him a couple of bars.

"Yes. That's it. That's what she played for us."

My heart exploded with joy.

And so, purely by chance it seemed, I found out in this surreptitious way that Gangaji had liked the song. It was similar to the coincidental way I'd found out that she'd liked my letter at Estes Park. Indeed, there was something maddeningly secretive about this relationship—the expression even occurred to me "seductive" in a mysterious and divine way. In the months that followed I would come to understand what a skillful seductress the Self really is when, having grown impatient with the postponements of mind and the indulgences of personality, unable to be put off any longer, it comes at last like a beautiful devouring tiger to claim its own.

9

THE MYTH OF ENLIGHTENMENT

 *D*uring that week we were invited to a couple of social events in Boulder—a departmental party at the University, and a dinner with some friends. Feeling reclusive and inward, I tried to get out of them both, but Toby insisted I attend. Since I was not going with him to the Cape, the least I could do was accompany him to these events. The party was mostly gruesome. The flow of alcohol was plentiful and about an hour into the evening everyone had a glaze over their eyes and over their brains that put an end to any kind of depth in the conversation.

Alcohol was something I had given up at an early age. Once, when I was about eighteen or nineteen, I had imbibed too much liquor at a party one night, and while attempting to drive home had scraped my car against a roadside marker. The car was a '56 Chevy which I had just purchased a few days before. The next morning, as I surveyed the scrape on the right fender, I felt very stupid for having damaged the car so soon after acquiring it. I did not fix the scrape, but left it there to remind me never to be so stupid again. And that was the end of my brief experimentation with alcohol.

The dinner with friends on Thursday night was interesting. Silvine and Stewart were recent friends we'd met since moving to Boulder. Also present were Tom and Nancy, an enjoyable couple whom we'd met only once before. Silvine was particularly interested in hearing about Gangaji and about my experiences at Estes Park. Up until then I hadn't tried to explain these experiences to anyone. Even Toby hadn't really heard the whole story.

Somehow, at dinner that night, the whole thing just came tumbling out. At a certain point I realized everyone was staring at me in awe. Silvine, especially, seemed to be "stopped."

Her mind just went still. This was quite evident to everyone because Silvine is known for having a very active mind. She has a Ph.D. in Literature and, as a university teacher, lives an intensely "mental" life. But she had seen something in my eyes, felt something in my presence, which from her description must have been similar to what I'd experienced with Gangaji. Perhaps the vision of Ramana telling Gangaji that I could serve this lineage might not have been imaginary after all. Maybe Gangaji *was* training me—quietly, secretly, intimately—in a way that made it very difficult for the mind to cling to.

All week long Toby had been adamant that we were certainly not going to Santa Fe again that weekend. But by Friday my longing to see Gangaji had become unbearably strong once again. I had to go. Since our one car belonged to both of us, I could not just take it without Toby's consent.

As Friday afternoon approached, Toby miraculously changed his mind. No, actually I can't say that he changed his "mind," for that was definitely still resisting (all the way to Santa Fe, as a matter of fact) but something inside of him, deeper than mind, knew that we had to go and he was beginning to listen to that and to surrender to that more and more.

Saturday morning we arrived at the School for the Deaf fairly early. Govind was circulating with his list of those who wanted to go to the small satsang afterward. I was still experiencing an excruciating "hanging back" and was too shy to sign up for it. But Toby had decided that he would go, because he wanted to ask Gangaji about the respect issue that had come up for him the weekend before. He thought it might be easier to get called on in a small group.

When the doors opened, the rush of people wanting front row seats again took us by surprise. In spite of the fact that we had been nearly at the front of the line outside we ended up in about row six again.

That day in satsang there were lots of questions about enlightenment, such as: What does it really mean? How do you know you are "getting it?" What is the difference between realization and simply a profound spiritual "experience," etc.

Gangaji spoke beautifully on this topic, similar to the way she had spoken at Estes Park the night my "yogi staff" was broken. But that day I wasn't listening to her words so much as to the breath between her words which seemed to draw me deeper into silence, beyond the words.

After the satsang Toby went to the small meeting and I waited for him out in the foyer, talking with our new friend John. When Toby finally came out he was with a couple, Dan and Jennifer. They had traveled to Santa Fe from the Midwest where they lived in the same spiritual community which Toby and I and John had all once lived in too. As Toby introduced them to us I recognized their names, for we had some mutual friends, although I had never met them before personally. Dan was the one who had spoken the weekend before about being immersed in the River Ganga and hearing Gangaji's voice inside his head. Jennifer had asked many of the questions that day about enlightenment. Toby wanted me to tell her about my experiences at Estes Park. So Jennifer and I sat down on the sofa together in the foyer and talked. She asked how the path of self-inquiry compared to the mantra meditation that we had all been engaged in for so many years. I said that meditation was beautiful and has its place, but finally one must ask the question, "*Who* is the meditator?" She asked me lots of other good questions and I enjoyed talking with her; it felt like satsang

After Dan and Jennifer left we decided to go to lunch and invited John to come with us. As we sat together at an Indian restaurant John had recommended, he told us about how he'd had a very good job back East, but had given it up when a close friend, Sandy, had been killed in a car accident. I knew Sandy well. We had kept our horses at the same stable for many years and had often ridden together. John related that when Sandy died so suddenly and unexpectedly, in the middle of her life, he had realized that one cannot postpone the spiritual call, imagining there will be a time to "do it later." There may not *be* a later. Who knows how short or long this lifetime will be? So he had quit his successful job and embarked on a spiritual pilgrimage, which, after visiting and traveling with several saints and teachers, had finally culminated in a strong call to be with

Gangaji. He had been in Boulder for satsang that Spring, attended the Estes Park Retreat, and had then come to Santa Fe where he was now a volunteer helping with the set-up crew and with ushering during the satsangs.

He expressed that he felt a call to serve satsang, but had no idea how it was supposed to look. Without actually mentioning the visions I'd had, I told him that I too had definitely heard the call and also had no idea how I would end up serving.

John chuckled. "That's easy. You'll write music that expresses satsang, and sing it."

I shook my head adamantly. "I may write a song once in a while, but this personality was definitely not cut out to be a performer."

He just smiled and looked at me like he didn't believe a word of what I was saying. This irritated me slightly, but I dismissed it, thinking, "He just doesn't know me very well yet."

As we sat there speaking I felt a huge all-embracing presence vibrating in everything—us, the restaurant, Santa Fe, the earth, and on and on. Everything moved in That, was That, came from That, and was perfectly orchestrated by That. Though I was aware of this hugeness most of the time now, there was still a fading back and forth between identifying with That as myself, and identifying with my mind and personality as myself.

The next morning I was up early. I sat on the patio among the cactus plants in the early dawn and let go of everything into the expanse of infinity. The bliss of samadhi arose and filled every cell of my body—no, every cell in my body was *in* That. It took my breath away—literally; the breath was sucked right out of me. This sudden loss of breath had happened several times since Estes Park. Sometimes I would get alarmed by it and find myself gasping for air, although I knew, intellectually, that in samadhi the body doesn't need breath; it is in a suspended state. I guessed that the gasping was because I was sometimes only half in that state of suspension and half in identification with body.

After sitting for a while, I decided to write a letter to Gangaji. I don't remember all that I said in that letter, but it went something like this:

> Dearest Gangaji:
>
> This 'hugeness' which I experience every day now used to terrify me. I used to draw back from it in fear, afraid that it would annihilate me. How ridiculous that seems to me now! You allowed me to connect with you so deeply that all sense of separation (the cause of fear) was annihilated long enough for me to see that this great devourer I so feared was none other than my own Self.
>
> How can I thank you for this? I only hope that I can somehow be used to serve this Truth. In deepest gratitude,
>
> *Amber Terrell*

Toby was not interested in going to the auditorium early that morning, since no matter how early we got there we still didn't get close seats. But when we arrived, John informed us that he was the usher that morning down in front and he had saved us seats in the second row center.

When Gangaji came in, my heart leaped in love. I was awed and overwhelmed by the close proximity of her presence. It was the closest I'd been to her, physically, since Estes Park. Again the shyness and nervousness arose along with the love. It was as if this love reached so deeply into my soul that it made *everything* arise, everything I'd ever longed for and everything I'd ever tried to suppress. But it would be several more weeks before I came to realize that this "arising" was nothing to get upset or anxious about. It was only necessary to just *let* it arise, without resisting it, without following it, and let the identification be burned up in the Truth of Being.

That weekend Maitri and Govind, as well as John and Toby, had all encouraged me to sing the "River Ganga" song in satsang. I had brought my guitar with me to Santa Fe this time on the off chance that I might miraculously snap out of my shyness, for I really did have a desire to sing the song for Gangaji in person. Shortly after arriving in Santa Fe the day before, however, it became clear to me that I was not ready to sing in front of four hundred people and Gangaji.

That morning Gangaji opened the satsang with the most powerful exposition on enlightenment I have ever heard. Toby felt sure it was inspired by the questions of the day before.

Welcome to Satsang. Welcome.

Her smile radiated out with the most boundless, unfathomable, unconditional love. She glanced around the auditorium in silence for a few moments, then began:

I want to speak just a few words about this concept of enlightenment, because you know . . .

She took a deep breath, looking out over the faces before her—

. . . this is a big deal, isn't it? [laughter] And it's ironic that something that is so precious and so fulfilling and so eternal gets very subtly turned into some "thing," some object of the mind. And in that, the preciousness is ruined. And the opportunity to realize what enlightenment points to is overlooked once again.

So, it's an important concept as it first arises, this realization or this insight that "my God, I have been living in ignorance. What I want is enlightenment. What I want to leave is ignorance." This is so important, such an evolutionary point in a life-stream. And then time is spent being more deeply aware of the ignorance and being more fueled to reach for enlightenment. This also is very important.

There is the resolve and the courage to turn one's back on the forces that support ignorance, and to turn toward the force that supports enlightenment. All, very important.

Then there comes a time when for an instant, by some miraculous mysterious Grace, you are struck dumb of all words, all concepts, all searching, all striving, all identification—either with some entity who is ignorant and unenlightened, or with some entity who is free and enlightened. And in that moment, that instant out of time, there is the realization that who you are, really, has never been touched by any concept. And this in fact is what "enlightenment" points to, this very instant of realization.

My meeting with her was that realization, that instant out of time. Gratitude welled up and flooded my heart. Just then, Toby glanced over at me. She was addressing questions we had often talked about in the past couple of years, between ourselves and with our seeker friends: "What is enlightenment? Why, after all these years of practice, has nobody we know gained anything remotely resembling enlightenment or freedom?"

With her next words Gangaji answered everything.

The habits of mind, of course, are very strong and they are likely to reappear. "Oh, I got it, I'm enlightened." This already is a habit of mind. This already presupposes some entity separate from consciousness, separate from that which is realized, revealed in that instant of the mind ceasing. And in that "Oh, I got it, I'm enlightened," there must follow, "I lost it. I'm unenlightened."

She smiled and looked out across the sea of faces.

Right? You must have been through this many times. Of course, they are the same coin—thought. "I am some<u>thing</u>." "I am ignorant; I am enlightened." Thought.

And then in following that thought as reality, there once again reappears the experience of unnecessary suffering. Either in "Oh, I got it, I'm enlightened. Now what can I do with it? What can I make? How can I . . . etc, etc." Or, "I lost it, I am ignorant, I am unenlightened." This is unnecessary suffering. All based on a lie.

How painfully lucid was her description of my own previous experiences. How many times in years past had some deep explosion of awareness and bliss been followed by just this kind of thought, "Ah, now I've got it. This is it. Now I can have everything I want, do anything I want." And in following these thoughts, immediately the re-identification with mind would occur and the sublime awareness vanish. Then the perception of needing to "get back" to it, to find it again would arise. Until now I had never understood why I couldn't "keep it."

> *Who you are has no need of, no desire for, no fear of either ignorance <u>or</u> enlightenment. You are free of these concepts. Ignorance points to not realizing that. And enlightenment points to realizing that. But the moment you cling to any concept of ignorance or any concept of enlightenment as reality, you are already in the experience of ignorance again.*
> *You see how subtle the workings of the mind are? How <u>subtle</u>?*

Not only had the emanation of Gangaji's silence and presence drawn me deeply into Self-recognition, but with the brilliance and clarity of her speaking she was alerting me to the subtle tricks of the mind, the subtle ways in which one can turn from the Truth even after it has been revealed. She was exposing this tendency of the mind to claim realization for itself. The moment the thought arises, "*I realized That,*" there is separation again, the "I" and the "That." <u>In true realization there is no one left to claim it.</u> There is no one left to "keep it." There is no sense of having attained something or of having achieved something. True realization just is, and always has been.

> *The great <u>gift that Ramana</u> offers you as his own Self is to be still. <u>To not look to the mind as the reference point of who you are</u>, mind being "thought"—mental thought, physical thought, emotional thought, circumstantial thought. To be still. What can be said about what is revealed in stillness? Nothing has been said that can touch it. Much has been said that points to it. Words such as enlightenment, realization, Self, Truth, God, Grace—all of these words point to that. The moment they are conceived as some "thing" they point <u>away</u> from that. And then you begin this ridiculous practice of comparing yourself with someone else.*

Gangaji's tone and voice up to that point had been fairly serious. But now she laughed, as if this "comparing" was the most absurd kind of joke.

Toby glanced over at me sheepishly, for he had been doing some comparing recently with regard to me and what I was experiencing with Gangaji.

All in the hopes of reaching something, or leaving something. And these all based on the idea that you are some "thing".

She glared at us with playful intensity.

YOU ARE NO "THING" AT ALL! Everything that appears, appears in you, because of the vastness of the mystery of you. When you identify yourself as some "thing"—something mental, something physical, something emotional, something circumstantial—and you believe this identification to be real, you overlook the reality of the vastness of being who you are.

It is so utterly simple. This is what has held it as the deepest secret.

Again, I was awed by the profound, concentrated Truth her words conveyed and by the transmission of stillness I felt. I had never heard anyone speak so clearly, so brilliantly, so freshly about this trap of mental identification.

So all of your strivings, all of your practicings, all of your comparing, all of your taking notes on, is realized to be worthless. In this moment of realization of the worthlessness of that, there is ultimate freedom. If there is the slightest clinging to that as worthwhile, as worth something, there is once again being caught in identification.

The opportunity for the mindstream that you have identified as yourself, the opportunity is, in the midst of that, to realize you are that animating force that gives the mindstream its apparent power. This can be realized immediately—in simply being still. You will never realize it by searching for it in thought. You may have intellectual understanding, and I would say you all have this intellectual understanding, but you aren't satisfied with that, because you will never be satisfied until you embrace yourself, the truth of who you are. Luckily you will never be satisfied. You will not settle for second best. Luckily.

This is the greatest gift—this gift from Ramana, through Papaji. This opportunity to stop, midstream, to stop, and recognize who you are. All discussion before that and after that is worthless, is some mind game. Maybe beautiful, maybe horrible—but worthless.

An intense stillness fell over the room. For a few moments, everyone remained absolutely silent. No one, it seemed, could even breathe. Her eyes swept over the quiet faces a moment more, then she added:

You can't make stillness. You <u>are</u> stillness. Be who you are. Be still—absolutely, completely still—and see That which is prior to any thought, any concept, any image of who or what or when or how or why. *

Her voice and eyes and body language revealed an intense passion for everyone in that room to hear this, deeply. And yet, paradoxically, there was clearly in her manner a perfect dispassion, an unsentimental detachment, an exquisite freedom; whether we got it or not was completely our own business.

She began to take questions and read some of the letters that had been placed on the couch. Every word she spoke was charged with the most vibrant pure silence. It was infinite Self speaking to Itself. After a while she put her palms together, bowed her head to us and said, *Om Shanti.* And that was the end of the satsang.

As she walked out that day I felt the pang in my heart once again and the intense longing. I did not often form deep attachments to people. I had been careful not to form deep attachments, seeing at a fairly young age how personal attachment causes misery. My life had carefully navigated a course of fierce independence, even with close friends, family, and hus-band. And yet here was this intense love and attachment to Gangaji. I had no control over it. Again the reminder, there is something mysterious here, something about this relationship that is not what it seems, not personal and not impersonal, both personal and impersonal. It could not be captured in mind.

10

THE ROSES

*T*he next Saturday we made the trip to Santa Fe for the third weekend in a row. This time the satsangs were being held at a junior high-school on the other side of town, which we found without difficulty. We saw John right away, and he and Toby immediately started campaigning to get me to sing the "River Ganga" song that weekend. I told them to leave me alone about it. I just wasn't ready to do it.

One evening after one of the satsangs, Toby had a beautiful experience of stillness. We were sitting on the bed in our room, Toby leaning against the headboard and me sitting on the end of the bed with my guitar. Suddenly, and quietly, as Toby relates it, there was a shift in his awareness. He *became* pure consciousness. It differed from previous experiences of transcendence he'd had in that he just suddenly found himself as That—very clearly and simply. Not that *he* was having an experience of *That*. After some time I asked him a question about something and as he collected his thoughts to answer it, he found himself coming back into mind. As he related this experience to me, he asked, "Why can't I keep it? Where does it go?"

I said, "It can't go anywhere. It is who you are."

But this gave him no consolation. He lamented the loss of this experience for several weeks, until finally, after Gangaji returned to Boulder, he was able to ask her about it directly.

That night I wrote another letter to Gangaji. I wanted to express to her how profoundly the connection with her had affected me. The experience of her presence, continually, deep in my soul, had served to connect me with the huge timelessness of my own Being. This is the first letter I can quote word for word, because she eventually read this one in satsang and so I was able to transcribe it from the tape:

Dear Gangaji: June 3, 1995

When we first met a little over a month ago, a connection took place between us which was not "in time." And
a relationship developed, also not in time, which began to
enliven this huge timeless presence in my awareness—because
the relationship existed there.

The mind got all upset about this and started saying
things like: "this isn't real, this can't be happening, this is
your imagination," or it would try to grasp it, place it in
time, or make some "thing" out of it. Finally it shut up,
because recently this timeless presence has become so vivid
that it has begun to overshadow the space/time reality,
causing it to recede sometimes into the distance and to
appear like a dream. There is so much fulfillment present
when this happens, that all desires have been fulfilled. The
mind still says things like "hey, wait a minute, fulfillment
can't be this simple," or "what about all your plans?" But
these voices, while not completely gone, grow dim and
have lost their power. For in this awareness (which is like
a river of Grace), the *Leela** of space/time seems in some
sense perfect and there is less inclination to "plan" or to
"touch" it in any way. It just unfolds, and as long as I stay
quiet in this Grace there isn't much to "do" but enjoy the
unfoldment.

And all because of this "meeting" out of time. If this
is a metaphor for a marriage, then it was an arranged marriage, because I didn't "do" anything for this. I didn't
"decide" to surrender or anything. It just "took place"—
and then it continued taking place, as if the surrender itself
is infinite. Is this what you mean by saying the "finding"
the Self-discovery is endless?

There is so much fulfillment in this realization—the
Self revealing Itself by Itself to Itself. Right? In this timelessness I know we are one, because I experienced this
merging very concretely. But in this space/time Leela, there
is this delightful separation where I am at your feet and in
total awe. Thank you for being my door into the Infinite.

Gratefully,
Amber Terrell

P.S. I know I've sent you three reports in three weeks, and I
hope this isn't too many. But so much is revealed every day,
every moment, and it helps to verify it if I write it to you.

I put this letter up on her couch the last day of our stay in Santa Fe, carefully burying it in the stack of letters already piling up. That weekend there had been so many letters that she could not read them all in satsang on any one day. She would take them home with her and sometimes bring one or two back the next satsang to read to the group. It seemed a sure thing that she would not get to my letter that day and would then read it later. This was a relief because at that point I still felt that I would probably die of embarrassment if she read one of my letters in satsang.

Thankfully, she did not find my letter that day, and when she finally did read it the next weekend, there was no one there to be embarrassed.

The next week Toby left for his trip to Cape Cod. Although that weekend would be Gangaji's last weekend in Santa Fe, I had decided not to drive down by myself, even though some new friends, Steven and Tanya, had invited me to stay with them if I decided to come. Gangaji would be in Boulder soon anyway, and I felt the seven-hour drive all by myself would be too exhausting. But as the weekend drew near, I could no more stay away from her than I could stop breathing.

I don't remember how it actually happened, but somehow the people at Satsang Foundation & Press had connected with me before this trip and had asked me to take a few things down to Santa Fe, as none of the Boulder staff were going down that weekend. The items consisted of video equipment for a man named Rob, and luggage for another man named Lee.

On Friday morning I stopped by the Foundation on my way out of town to pick up my cargo. While I was there, someone told me that Maitri wanted to see me. I was shown downstairs to her office. She greeted me warmly and asked me when was I ever going to play my song for Gangaji. I replied, "I'm not a performer."

She looked at me in the same dubious way that John had looked at me the week before, not believing a word of it. "Gangaji really, *really* liked that song," she assured me. Then she asked me if I'd take a package to Gangaji, and handed me a large manilla envelope. "Gangaji's mail," she told me. I felt deeply honored and thrilled to bring Gangaji's mail. But as I took the package I asked, "How shall I give this to her? I mean, who should I give it to?"

Maitri said, "Give it to Gangaji! You could give it to her in a small satsang."

"I've never gone to the small satsangs," I said. "I'm too shy."

Maitri laughed in disbelief. "Oh, so beautiful," she said. I wasn't sure why she thought this was beautiful. Shyness was my curse, just the way this personality had been born. Then she added. "Well, you could give it to Govind then, if you want. But if I were you, I'd give it to Gangaji myself."

I arrived in Santa Fe just before dark, but had trouble finding Steven and Tanya's house. I must have taken a wrong turn somewhere and got terribly lost for a while. It was close to ten by the time I found them, and I was tired, frustrated, and near tears, partly because of the frustration of getting lost and partly because of the "holding back" I was still experiencing with Gangaji. It was driving me crazy and yet there seemed to be nothing I could do about it.

As Tanya came out to welcome me and help unload my things from the car she saw my guitar, which I had brought just in case I felt like playing—alone by myself. "Oh, are you going to sing?" she asked. I was about to respond, "No, I don't perform," but before I could say this she added, "That's perfect, because it's Gangaji's birthday on Sunday."

"Her birthday!" I gasped. And right then I knew—I was going to sing.

That night, as I lay in bed unable to sleep, I felt for the first time the unmistakable presence of Papaji. It wasn't exactly a vision, but it was definitely him—his Presence and Grace filling the room, filling my being, filling everything. Then I remembered that I had written him a letter about three weeks before, to thank him for sending the River Ganga to flow in the West. It takes about three weeks for mail to get to India and get delivered, so I figured he might have just received the letter. Silently I thanked him, once again, for my teacher and for the Grace that

H. W. L. Poonjaji (Papaji)

transmitted through her, and asked for his blessing in being able to open more to her and to be able to sing for her on Sunday.

The next morning I went over very early to the junior high school where satsang would be held to drop off the things I'd brought from the Foundation and also to find Govind to give him Gangaji's envelope. There was no one in line yet, and only the volunteers who were helping with the set-up were scurrying around, busy with their jobs. One of the first persons I ran into was our friend John. I told him I'd brought some sound equipment for someone named Rob, some luggage for someone named Lee and a package for Gangaji.

He told me to come inside and said he would take me to Rob. I followed John into the school, past the door monitors who were posted there to keep everyone out except the volunteer staff. He led me into a big gymnasium where volunteers were busily setting up the hall for satsang. I saw my roommate from Estes Park doing the flower arrangements next to Gangaji's couch, and my friend Caroline from Switzerland helping on the set-up crew.

When I was introduced to Rob, I recognized him as the cameraman who had videoed all the satsangs at Estes Park. He was an athletic-looking, blond Australian—evident from his accent—and I figured he must have about the best job on earth.

After I delivered Rob's equipment a lady named Margo, whom I recognized as one of the organizers there, came up to me and asked if I was Amber, who wrote the "River Ganga" song. When I said yes, she told me they were planning a low-key celebration the next day for Gangaji's birthday and asked if I would sing the song then. There was no hesitation; immediately I found myself saying, "Yes, I'd be happy to."

Later on I saw John again and told him I was finally going to sing. He just smiled knowingly. (I found out later he had been the one to suggest it to Margo.) I asked John where I could find Lee, in order to give him his belongings. John told me Lee wouldn't be there until Gangaji arrived, because he was the one driving her to and from satsang. "We'll have to get that stuff to him later," he said.

"What about Govind?" I asked, anxious to get my other very important piece of cargo into the proper hands.

"I haven't seen him around," said John. "Someone said he was sick and might not be here at all today. Why don't you give Gangaji the mail yourself? You can stand outside when she drives up and give it to her then. I'm going to be standing out there myself today, because I'm the usher on the side door."

"No, you give it to her," I said, and tried to hand him the package.

He frowned at me and refused to take it. "Why don't you think about it? I'll check with you later."

So I sat down in the line, which was now starting to form, holding the package on my lap and asking myself, "Okay, what are you afraid of? This is the teacher of your prayers. You love her. She loves you as her own Self. What's the problem?" I didn't know how to answer that. I just felt extreme contraction when I thought about standing outside the gym and giving her the package. I suspected it had something to do with a certain level of embarrassment I still felt for this crazy, intense love and attachment to her which made no sense whatsoever and clashed mightily with this image of myself as straight, conservative, dispassionate, and independent.

But as I sat there in the shade of the awning which covered the school entryway something let go deep inside. Again, as I'd felt that morning at Estes Park, when the room had gone quiet and I knew it was my moment to ask a question, I knew now it was my moment to give her this package.

When John emerged again from the gymnasium, about half an hour later, I told him I'd changed my mind. I was going to give Gangaji the package myself. He didn't seem at all surprised. "Good," he said, "I'll come and get you when it's time and show you where to stand."

Sometime later, after we had all gone inside and everyone was sitting quietly waiting for satsang and for Gangaji, John appeared silently in the front aisle near where I was sitting and motioned for me to follow him. I followed him across the gym floor, out the side door, down a short hallway, and out onto a small terrace. Outside, I stood at the top of a short flight of steps, waiting quietly, with butterflies in my stomach. John stood by the door, relaxed and steady, like a royal sentinel.

After a while a very lovely woman came out of the gym and stood beside me. She introduced herself as Gayatri, Govind's wife. Instantly I liked her. She was beautiful and natural and her presence was very soft and loving. And besides all that, her name was the one my inner self had once given to me.*

"I hear you're going to sing tomorrow," said Gayatri. I nodded, still wondering how I was going to pull it off without falling apart. Gayatri added, "Gangaji doesn't really want any kind of a fuss made. But I told her we were going to do *something*, so she might as well choose. We decided on some songs, and then tea and cookies afterward."

I thanked Gayatri for sharing that with me. Then she invited me to go to the small satsang that day. I happily accepted, amazed that the fear about going had suddenly vanished. Gayatri glanced at her watch, then descended the steps to wait below by the drive. The time for satsang to begin was approaching and I had already learned that Gangaji was notoriously punctual. Then I saw Gayatri's hands draw up into a *namasté* as a white Toyota sedan pulled up in front of the steps and stopped, right on time.

I had no expectations that Gangaji would say anything to me or even recognize me. My mission was just to give her the package. But as she stepped from the car and turned to see me standing there she said, "Oh, Amber! I'm so glad you're here. I have your letter," she held it up, "which I'm going to read today."

I gulped. Read my letter!

A couple of men got out of the car after her, and John told me later they were Lee (the driver) and Eli (Gangaji's husband), but at the time I didn't really see either one of them. My eyes were totally fixed on Gangaji as she walked up the steps toward me. That strange sense of slow motion and timelessness began happening again. When she got close enough I reached out to give her the package. "From Maitri," I said quietly.

"Oh good," she smiled and light-heartedly took the package. It barely touched her hands. She passed it immediately to one of the men who walked behind her. "Let's just put this in the car for now," she said to the one taking the package.

As Gangaji walked by me she flashed me a radiant smile, then put her hand on the side of my cheek and patted it lightly. "I'm so happy to see you here," she said. Then she disappeared into the dressing room which had been set up for her in a small anteroom near the gym entryway. As John led me back down the hallway to the gym he said teasingly, "Can I touch you?"

I was in an ecstatic daze. "I . . . I didn't know if she'd even remember my name," I stammered in a whisper.

Back in the gym I hurried to my seat so I'd be sitting still when Gangaji came in. I had barely gotten seated when Gangaji ascended the platform up in front, sat down cross-legged on the couch, and closed her eyes.

We sat in silence for about twenty minutes. I felt strange, like I wasn't there, or like I was everywhere—actually there didn't seem to be any difference.

After the silence Gangaji greeted everyone:

> *Welcome to satsang. Welcome.*
> *I have a couple of letters I want to read that really point, in these particular ways, to what is universal—and can't even be pointed to, really.*

She began to read:

Dear Gangaji:

Because I don't know whether or not I will raise my hand to give a report, I would like to write my report. I am very grateful for your being here in Santa Fe and for our time, all of our time, together. I'm learning so much, but it is not head-learning. Involvement is part of that learning. When I first came to the satsangs I would drop by only if convenient and stay on the periphery. What an analogy for my life.

As my commitment to being here has grown, so has my commitment to being—this sweet and wondrous vastness that I am. Also, it really is about continual surrender, isn't it?

She looked up and said:

Yes. That's right. There is often the tendency to say, "Oh, I surrendered to that. Oh yeah, I did that, ten years ago, last year . . ." [laughter] "Oh yeah. I saw the truth and I surrendered."

But this, the Truth, is <u>continual</u> surrender. This is the challenge of this experience of incarnation. This is the joy, the victory. Victory in surrender.

She continued reading:

I realize that even reference points of being must be surrendered. Then there is the excitement and wonder.

She held up the letter and said:

Excellent!

Then she picked up another letter. It was mine. As she started to read I waited for the feeling of embarrassment to arise, or self-consciousness, or fear, or something. But there was nothing. Just vastness and peace. When she came to my P.S. at the end, where I asked if I was sending too many reports, she looked up at me and said, in the most loving and tender way:

No. Not too many. Not too many. Just right.

Then she read another letter with similar content, about surrender and intense love and attachment for her. The author had realized that this too must be surrendered,
    I sat there feeling I could have written all three of these letters, or I could have written none of them. I felt no differently when she read "mine" than when she read the others. There was no sense of ownership, no sense of "me-ness," just a vastness that included everything. I realized that something profound had happened when she'd patted my cheek just before satsang. The

only way I can describe it is that the identification with mind and personality had dropped. Just like that. Gone.

At the end of satsang that day, after Gangaji had left the hall, it was announced that the small meeting had been cancelled—by Gangaji. I felt some disappointment, and yet there was also a humorous recognition of the irony of this divine play. When finally I had surrendered to going to the small satsang, she'd cancelled it.

After satsang I waited for John to finish his duties, because he had offered to take me over to the place where Lee was staying so I could deliver his luggage. This turned out to be Govind and Gayatri's house.

As we pulled up, a man with a British accent named David came out of the house and helped John unload Lee's things from the back of the van. As the two of them carried the luggage into the house I closed up the back hatch, then noticed a man with silvery hair standing quietly beside the van, watching me. I didn't know at first that it was Lee. Though he had been the driver for Gangaji that day and must have walked right by me when I stood outside the gym, I had not seen him. I hadn't seen anything but Gangaji.

Now I looked up at him, standing there with such a quiet presence. He asked if I was Amber, who'd brought his things. When I nodded, he thanked me and then stood for a moment, completely expressionless, looking deeply into my eyes. In that moment I saw his "being"—a beautiful loving soul, but one that was a little troubled at the moment. Then something else unusual happened. I heard some of his thoughts, as clearly as if he'd spoken them to me, although his lips had not moved. It was a strange experience and I had no idea what it meant. I looked away from him then, because his eyes were too intense.

John and David returned from the house and we stood in Govind's driveway talking about satsang and Gangaji. I noticed soon afterward that Lee had disappeared, as silently as he had first appeared. I thought, "What a strange person." And yet I liked him and recognized him and sensed that he was a friend, perhaps from long ago.

John was talking with David about a get-together at someone's house that some of the volunteers were having. He asked
if I would come along and sing the "River Ganga" song for
them. He suggested I could teach them the refrain and then
they could help me with the singing of it the next day in satsang. Usually parties aren't my thing, but I was feeling so
unbounded that it didn't matter what I did or didn't do.
Everything was blissful and unmoving and felt like Gangaji. I
also liked the idea of having some help singing the next day, so
I went along to the party.

When we arrived, the man who'd had the dream about the
tiger at Estes Park greeted us at the door. He and his wife were
visiting from southern Colorado. During the course of the
evening I had an opportunity to tell him how important that
dream had been for me, and how Gangaji's response had
prompted me to ask a very important question—the most important question of my life. After some socializing, I played "River
Ganga" and taught everyone the refrain. They all promised to
help me with the singing of it the next day in satsang.

The next afternoon, just after Gangaji opened the satsang,
Gayatri was the first to raise her hand. Gangaji said suspi-
ciously:

Yes, Gayatri?

Instead of asking a question Gayatri arose from her seat and
approached the couch, bearing a beautiful lei of roses in her
hands. Respectfully, she put the roses around Gangaji's neck.
Gangaji chuckled:

Uh oh. Here we go.

Gangaji bore the attention patiently, gracefully, though it
was clear she didn't want any kind of a "deal" made out of her
birthday. After the garland had been positioned comfortably
around her neck, she thanked Gayatri and everyone and took
a moment to admire the roses.

Beautiful Santa Fe Roses.

And then, as always, she used the occasion to express the most beautiful words of Truth.

If this is your first time here, you may wonder what all the fuss is about. [laughter] It has to do with seeing and being seen, and the love that naturally reveals itself in true seeing, and in truly being seen.

Someone once asked me if I minded all these people who were devoted to me. And I had to answer in truth, "But they are not devoted to me. They are devoted to what they see in me, and what sees through me-ness—sees through their particular me-ness. Sees the seeing." And this is my own Self. And finally I can say in truth, I am quite happy to love my own Self, to serve my own Self, to meet my own Self—everywhere I appear to go, everywhere I appear.

I am happy to find my Self here in Santa Fe. To see my Self here. To greet my Self, and to invite my Self deeper into realization of that one Self—that one Self that is beyond both unity and multiplicity, and includes both unity and multiplicity. I am devoted to That myself.

So if, again, this is your first time here, just so there's no misunderstanding, when I say my "Self," I'm not speaking of thoughts, I'm not speaking of emotions, I'm not speaking of physical sensations, I'm not speaking of circumstances. I'm speaking of what all of those arise in, and exist because of, and return to.

And this is what I see in you. This is what I love in you. Whatever name you go by, this is the truth of you. Whatever the particular life history you remember, this is the truth of who you are. And I see that happily, joyously, devotedly.

And I will take no excuses from you that you can't see that. [laughter] You are that, so of course you can see that. And when you see clearly, you will see Love. Not love like you think of love. But Love as it is. Ruthless, universal, playful, serious Love.

At that point you have the opportunity to be devoted to That—which sees. And to live That, and to give That. In other words, you have the opportunity to be Love itself. That which you have searched for, cried for, bargained for, sold for—this is who you are. This is who I bow to.

She then bowed her head to all of us, and you could hear the whole gymnasium breathe in awe.

My friend and hostess, Tanya, was sitting next to me, for she and John had agreed to sit on either side of me that day and hold the microphones when I sang. Tanya raised her hand to speak and Gangaji called on her.

Tanya began, "Hello Gangaji"

Hi.

"I hope I can speak to you without crying this time."

Oh, please cry. Crying is beautiful when speaking—like laughing.

"I just couldn't have you leave Santa Fe without . . ." her voice began to break with emotion, ". . . without expressing this eternal gratitude. Since we were at the Estes Park retreat with you and I made this commitment to marry the Truth, it has been a profound unfolding. All the untruths that I have believed in have come very strongly, with a loud voice, to reveal themselves. And I feel that, for the first time I feel so hopeful, like you've pointed me in the direction of true sanity, and . . . you know I've been in therapy and done all this self-help stuff and on and on, and thought that I'd met my anger and my shame, but really I'd only touched them and was still keeping them at bay. And something you said permeated so deeply in me. You said, 'to neither deny nor discharge.' "

Gangaji was ecstatic.

Finally, I have been heard! [laughter] Millions of times I have said this! I have never heard it come back! Excellent!

116

"It went into such a deep place."

Yes, it must have.

"And I realized, even in therapy and things, I was still trying to get it *out* of me. Like, I've got to get this anger out. One day I'll beat enough pillows and then finally stop hating my mother . . .' "

Yes, "And THEN I'll be all right." Yes! Yes!

"And instead . . . I wrote you a letter this week, just reporting on this new commitment I'm making to really meet this shame and anger. And yesterday I had an experience, like a million times in my life, some little thing happened and the anger and shame came up and it was triggered by that. And in my mind, instead of going 'okay,' to the person who I was with, 'you're responsible for this; now fix this,' or 'fix me,' or whatever, I just said, 'all these feelings are coming up and I know you're not responsible,' and I just went by myself to be with them. And the most amazing thing—it's just, it's your promise! It's your PROMISE! They dissolve into nothing. And after that there's this new clarity and love and seeing with these eyes. And I'm just free."

Yes! Yes! Hallelujah! Hallelujah! This is it. This is the promise. This is the guarantee.

"And this great gift of you here mirroring—no, you being my own Self—I'm seeing my own Self everywhere, and this limitlessness . . ."

That's right!

"Thank you for your eternal blessing, this eternal Grace. What great luck, to be in this life, and to have this—satsang with you. All my gratitude to you."

Yes. What great luck! To recognize this. Yes. This is the gratitude to my master. This is what I said to him. And he spoke to me of the gratitude to Ramana. And Ramana is That which abides in the heart of all being. That which is in your heart, your heart of hearts, the core of your being.

Pure, pristine Truth, revealing itself in the core of anger, in the core of shame, in the core of bliss, in the core of pride—when experienced <u>directly</u>. Covered, when denied, when ignored, when explained, when justified.

Yes, yes. This gratitude. As there is no end to this enfoldment in Self, there is no end to this gratitude. This gratitude is samadhi. It is a waking, regular-state samadhi. And all the suffering of all the past, when it meets this gratitude, is prostrate—and reveals itself to be also gratitude.

What luck. What a lucky lifetime. Everything leading to this, supporting this. <u>Everything</u> supporting this. Not everything but what bad happened to you once. That too supporting this. This is the ruthlessness of Truth. The absolute unsentimentality of Truth.

Endless. That's the promise. Endless. And, you see also, beginningless—always has been. And in that, this identification with "I am that which is born," therefore "I am that which is subject to death" is cut. Naturally. Not because you go take some psychic machete and carve it down. Cut because it's only a <u>thought</u>. And a thought is nothing. It's illusion. Of course, this thought can cause enormous experience of suffering. But when this experience of suffering is met, suffering itself is also revealed to be nothing. Nothing!

This is the nature of direct investigation, of "Self-inquiry." This is Self-inquiry—meeting yourself everywhere, in all form, in all states, in all degrees. And this mystery of unfoldment into that which is eternally unfolded—this is the dance of life. This is the promise, the potential, of this experience of incarnation. And that's what we celebrate. What a mystery. What a marriage. This experience of incarnation married to that which is never born. True marriage. True Love. True Self.

What a report! That's satsang. When you speak like this, you are declaring the Truth. You are not content to declare,

and declare, and declare the lie, and the hope for the truth,
or the belief in the truth. You simply stop speaking the lie.

Then the Truth is spoken. You don't even have to speak
it. You just be quiet. The Truth will use your vocal cords, will
use your experiences, will use your intellect, will use your
form, will use your hand, will use your pen, will use your
life—to speak Itself.

After a few more questions and reports, the entertainment organizers signaled Gangaji that they were ready to begin. She said happily:

Oh, is Amber going to sing now?

Apparently they had told her that I was going to sing and she seemed very happy about it. So, I sang first. There were close to five hundred people present. And I can tell you truthfully that I have never been so relaxed while singing in my life. All the fear I was so used to giving in to suddenly had no power. I saw it as merely a habit of mind—like an old tape that kept playing because someone had forgotten to shut it off, or like a chicken with its head cut off still running around the barnyard in circles. I realized its "real-ness" had been fading ever since the moment I had first looked into Gangaji's eyes.

As I reached the last verse of the song I noticed that no one was singing with me. All those people I'd taught the song to were supposed to be helping me, at least on the refrain, but the hall was silent except for my voice and guitar. I asked one of them about it later and she told me that they had all been so moved by the song that they were in tears and couldn't sing. When I finished the song I looked up at Gangaji. Her eyes were still closed. When finally she opened them, she looked down at me with a smile.

Very good, very good, very good.

I put my palms together in a *namasté* and bowed my head to her. In that bow, once again, I realized there was no separation from her—there was not someone bowing and someone to bow to. It was just Self. It was all One. Actually the whole room was all One, all my Self. That's why I couldn't be nervous or afraid. How can one be afraid within one's own Self?

A couple of other people sang and Gangaji appreciated each one lavishly. Then she put her palms together and said, *Om Shanti,* inviting everyone to stay for tea and cookies afterward. And that ended the satsang sessions in Santa Fe for 1995.

With eyes closed I sat silently in my seat, my guitar in my lap, while Gangaji and the satsang volunteers left the gym. My eyes were still closed when I suddenly smelled the strong, wonderful scent of roses close by. I opened my eyes to find Kathy, one of the staff volunteers, placing a lei of roses around my neck.

"Gangaji wanted you to have these," Kathy whispered. My mouth dropped open in astonishment and awe and my heart broke open in love. They were the roses that had been around Gangaji's neck during the satsang.

11

THE SWORD

As I drove back to Boulder that evening the roses lay on top of a large flat box which took up most of the back part of my van. Inside the box were the big pictures of Ramana and Papaji which had hung in the satsang hall all month long in Santa Fe. I had been asked to transport the pictures back to Boulder since I had a mini-van, and the box containing the pictures would not fit in a regular-sized car. Periodically I glanced at the roses, drying in the hot wind as I drove. I would treasure them forever.

The weekend had been perfect. Everything that had taken place—with Gangaji, with the new friends I'd met, with satsang—everything had been absolutely perfect. I saw how there had been no mind identification, no personality, no preconceived ideas of myself getting in the way. Just the silence and vastness of Being, expressing effortlessly in all my actions and speech and circumstances. I found myself reflecting, *Life* could be this way—all the time.

I also became aware of a subtle apprehension that I might not be able to keep it, that being in Gangaji's physical presence was very important in order for this mindless-ness to be sustained.

As I drove north on Interstate 25 I felt a thrill in my heart knowing that Gangaji was coming back to Boulder now and would stay all summer. There would be satsang four times a week. Then something inside me said, "Wait a minute! That's not enough! Four days a week isn't enough." My desire to be near her could not be satisfied by sitting in satsang only four days a week. I wanted to be near her every possible moment. A resolve began to form in my mind to try to get a job cleaning her house or doing her gardening or something like that. I had already told the people at the Foundation that I was willing to do anything.

I glanced at my roses. They filled the car with their heavenly scent. About halfway back to Boulder something unusual about those roses began to dawn on me. Suddenly it seemed they were not exactly what the personal self wanted to make of them. There was a sense that what appeared to be happening in the gift of the roses was not really what was happening. On one level, the roses signified that Gangaji had drawn me closer, and that I had opened to her more deeply. I felt embraced by her again, by Self again, as I had felt at Estes Park. Yet the tendency of the mind was to attempt to capture all this in memory and project some kind of personal meaning onto it. Clearly there was something about it that could not be captured that way, something unlocatable, unimaginable, ungraspable. A haunting "knowing" inside, a foreboding actually, alerted me that there was something else going on here, something I had not yet seen. The roses signified something more than a hug and a kiss from the teacher. They signified something huge and vast, something that was designed to annihilate "me" even more completely.

When I got home our two cats were happy to see me. Achala had checked in on them a couple of times in my absence, but they had been mostly alone. A message from Toby on the answering machine asked me to call him in Massachusetts. When we connected, he informed me that he had decided to stay another week at the Cape. His mother was moving up to their beach house for the summer and needed him to help with the move. I told him that was okay with me. I needed a lot of time alone these days.

Much of my time was spent sitting—not meditating, just sitting in silence. Actually, even when I tried to meditate, the mantra would only come for a moment and then disappear into the silent vastness. At first this bothered me and I wondered why I couldn't meditate anymore the way I used to. After all, I had been devotedly spending from three to four hours a day with this meditation for over a quarter of a century. It was somewhat shocking to see it suddenly fall away like this. But there was nothing I could do. The mantra simply would not arise—or if it did, it would stay only momentarily.

Later, I learned that this same experience had occurred to Papaji shortly after he first met his own master, Sri Ramana Maharshi. Papaji had been doing Krishna *japa* (repetition of the names of Lord Krishna) for 25 years—about the same number of years I had been meditating. He would do *japa* every morning from 2:30 to 9:30, at which time his wife would call him to get ready for work. Soon after meeting Ramana, however, he noticed that his *japa* would not arise. When he would sit for meditation, only silence would be there.

Papaji was living in Madras at the time and asked several nearby teachers about this strange occurrence, but did not receive any satisfactory answers. All of them wanted Papaji to sit in their satsangs and follow their practices and teachings as a cure for this sudden inability to meditate. But Papaji suspected this was not the true answer. Finally he traveled to Tiruvannamalai to see Ramana and at the first opportunity asked his Master about this inability to meditate. Ramana remained silent for a time and then finally asked Papaji, "How did you come here to the ashram?" Papaji replied, "By train." Ramana asked, "Where is the train now?" Papaji said, "At the station, of course."

Ramana then asked Papaji how he got from the station to the ashram. Papaji told him, "I hired a bullock cart." Again Ramana asked, "Where is the bullock cart now?" Papaji was getting annoyed at this point and replied impatiently, "I sent it back to town."

Ramana then suggested that when one has arrived at one's destination, one no longer needs the vehicle. Papaji finally understood—*japa* was the vehicle which is naturally left behind once one reaches the destination. Seeing Papaji's recognition, Ramana added these confirming words: "You have arrived."*

After my return from Santa Fe the mind stayed completely "gone" for a few more days. Activity was effortless, blissful, moving in motionless silence and love. I helped out at Satsang Foundation & Press, and focused on a couple of personal tasks which needed attention. The inner voice I had become so familiar with, which now sounded like Gangaji, had given me two strong instructions after the Estes Park Retreat, neither of which I had any desire to do. But they could no longer be ignored. This voice had a compelling authority about it. One instruction was to have some dental work done that I had been postponing; the other was to sell my horse.

I had raised Starlight from a newborn foal, and had been attached to her from before her birth. As her body had grown and matured for eleven months inside the womb of my mare, I had felt her soul coming to us from the stars. But the voice of Self was stronger than this attachment: *It is too dangerous for you to ride her now. This form is not yours to take chances with.*

There was some resistance to this instruction, resistance to the authority of it. But finally I reminded myself, "This is my own voice speaking," and surrendered.

Though Starlight and I had a very beautiful and trusting relationship, it was true that she was young and a little wild. Even though I put off this instruction to sell her and argued with it at times, I had only ridden her twice since Estes Park—at moments when I was in the grip of some rebellious mood.

Now I made a concerted effort to find her a new home, which at first seemed like a monumental task. It couldn't be just anyone that I would entrust with my baby. And the price we were asking was not for the

Amber, Toby, and baby Starlight

"budget" horse-shopper. Starlight had championship blood-lines and we wanted her to go to someone who would appreci-ate her lineage and who would be interested in breeding her to a fine stallion someday.

At first I hired the trainer who had been working with Starlight to search for the right new owner. I figured the trainer would have more contacts in the Colorado horse-industry than I did. But after several weeks the trainer had not come up with anything, nor did I get the impression that she was really try-ing. I realized I would have to do it myself. As soon as I put my attention on it, quickly, miraculously, the perfect new owner appeared. Alice and her husband owned a resort ranch in a small mountain community above Boulder which included a riding stable and restaurant. They owned thirty horses which were rented out for weekend rides. But Alice was looking for a horse of her own, a personal horse that she could feel a con-nection with. She and Starlight hit it off wonderfully and the price we were asking was not a problem. In addition, I would have unrestricted visiting privileges with Starlight anytime I wanted. The arrangement could not have been more perfect.

Next I made arrangements for the dental work to be done. I hated dental work, and there was in fact nothing medically wrong with my teeth. But one of my front teeth had been very crooked since I was a teenager, and as a result I had suppressed my smile much of my life. Over the years I had contemplated getting it fixed a number of times, but because of my anxiety about dental work in general had always decided it wasn't really that important.

My inner voice now assured me that it *was* important and time to open up my smile. This did not make any sense, actu-ally. Who cares if I smile or not? But the voice was strong. It was Gangaji's voice, it was my voice, and there was no getting out of it. So I arranged to begin the work, which actually took about seven or eight visits over the course of the entire summer to complete. I was surprised to find that there was none of the usual anxiety in the dentist's chair. For that, too, is only in mind. Although the strong experience of "no mind" only last-ed a few days after returning to Boulder, once the mind has really been stopped, it never quite has the same power again. Later I would hear someone ask Gangaji if the "I" ever arose in her any more. She replied:

> *Once the Master has severed the identification with this 'I' arising, maybe the 'I' never arises again, and maybe it does, but if it does, it can never be believed totally again.* *

Just before Gangaji returned to Boulder I got a call from a lady named Shivaya Ma. I remembered her from the Estes Park retreat, because she had made an announcement one day and it looked like she was about as uncomfortable making that announcement as I would have been. She seemed like a very shy and reserved sort of person and I immediately liked her and felt a kinship with her.

Shivaya Ma informed me that she was calling because she needed help getting her house ready for Gangaji and she had been told by the Foundation that I had volunteered for this kind of service. She explained that another house had been rented for Gangaji in Boulder, but it would not be ready for a few more weeks and Gangaji was arriving in two days. So, Shivaya Ma's house was going to be used in the interim, since Gangaji had stayed there before and was comfortable there.

As we spoke, I got the impression that Shivaya Ma had some concern about whether her house could actually be made ready in time. She had just returned from a trip back East for her daughter's wedding and had not even unpacked. I said I'd be happy to help, and so she asked me to be there at 9:00 the next morning.

When I reported for duty the next day, I learned that the project was not only cleaning the house and moving Gangaji's things in, but moving Shivaya Ma's and her family's things out or into storage areas. I set to work happily, unconcerned with the amount of work ahead or even with any thought that it was work at all—just this timeless, moment to moment joy of serving my teacher.

Shivaya Ma first gave me one of the bathrooms to do. I cleaned that bathroom like I had never cleaned a bathroom before. It crossed my mind once or twice how unusual it was for me to volunteer for such a project. As my husband would be quick to affirm, this particular personality was not at all fond of housework. But the personality was in surrender.

There were two other people who came to help that day, Ray and Shanti. Like Shivaya Ma, devotion to Truth and to Gangaji clearly radiated from these people and I enjoyed meeting them and working with them. We worked diligently all morning, cleaning and scrubbing and rearranging, then broke for lunch at noon. Shivaya Ma made us all sandwiches and we sat out on the patio and ate and talked.

They had all been at Estes Park and remembered me, commenting on the deep opening that had obviously taken place when I'd come up to the front that day. We talked about Gangaji and how she radiated the Truth so purely. Shanti noticed my intense attachment to Gangaji and said to me, "This is your own Self you see in her. This is Truth appearing as Gangaji." Ray added, "It is Truth that you love, not a person."

I understood that they were gently informing me that Gangaji does not encourage attachment to herself as a person. I said, "Yes, I understand that. But you see, although I've been with enlightened beings before in my life and read the beautiful expressions of Truth in the *Upanishads* and in the *Bhagavad Gita*, it was not until the Truth came to me, shining through this particular personality in the form of Gangaji, that I really "got it," that I really heard it. So I *am* attached, totally and completely attached. And there's nothing I can do about it."

They all sat silently for a moment after this speech, which was delivered with some intensity, and glanced at one another suppressing smiles. Shivaya Ma looked at me with loving understanding and admitted, "We're all attached too."

About four o'clock the cleaning part was done, and Ray and Shanti had to go. But the "moving in" part and the "moving out" part was nowhere near finished. There was no way I could leave Shivaya Ma to do the rest alone. She tried to convince me she'd be fine, but I told her my husband was out of town and assured her I had nothing else I would rather do than help her. Besides, Gangaji was arriving the next day!

We worked steadily through the evening, taking periodic breaks to talk or have a snack. Being with Shivaya Ma was like being with Gangaji, and I felt the Presence strongly. Every time we would feel a little tired, we'd just sit for a moment together and Shivaya Ma would tell me some beautiful story of her time with Gangaji in India, or in Boulder when they first met. Instantly our fatigue would vanish into bliss. It was after nine o'clock when we actually began transferring Gangaji's things into the closet of the room which would be hers. As Shivaya Ma and I passed each other in the hallway, she carrying a load of her own clothes out and me carrying a load of Gangaji's clothes in, she inquired as to how I was holding up. I grinned happily, "This is pure satsang." Shivaya Ma seemed relieved. She knew she had met someone as crazy-in-love as she was.

We worked until about ten-thirty that night and got everything ready. And we have been the dearest of friends ever since.

On Thursday evening, June 22nd, public satsang in Boulder began. I arrived early and got a seat close to the front. I had brought a letter with me I'd written to Gangaji that day, in which I'd reported my experience with the singing in Santa Fe and how effortless it had been and also the experience of "no mind" that had taken place during and after that weekend. But at the last moment I yielded to some intuitive foreboding and decided not to give it to her. Somehow I sensed Gangaji's mood that night even before she arrived. What I was picking up was fiery, ruthless intensity. And I was right.

She opened the Boulder summer satsang session like this:

Welcome to Satsang.

Her eyes swept the room for a moment. The intensity of that gaze was enough to burn up all of Colorado.

Someone was speaking to me the other day about how long this Gangaji Satsang has been happening in Boulder, and I said it was a long time. And she said, no, it was actually only three years.

Here Gangaji chuckled, finding it amusing that this person thought three years was not very long. Obviously Gangaji thought it was long enough!

> *But there have been maybe five sets of satsang in Boulder. And the value of formal Satsang occurring in a place over a period of time is really immeasurable.*

I could tell right away that she was speaking differently to this group than she had spoken in Santa Fe. In Santa Fe it was like she was speaking to "the public." There were usually new people present who had never been in satsang before, and Gangaji usually greeted these new people in a cordial, friendly, introductory manner. Here she spoke as if to her family, to people she had spoken with for a long time, and with whom the introductions, the formalities, the "coddling" was finished.

> *So the usual pattern of phenomena is for this formal satsang to appear in one's consciousness, and either there's some doubt or resistance or there's some immediate recognition. And then maybe the doubt or resistance falls into recognition and then there is deeper recognition, deeper recognition.*
> *And then, <u>usually</u>, [laughing softly] when the honeymoon . . .*

The room erupted into laughter. Apparently, everyone had experienced the honeymoon by now. But I thought, "She can't be talking to me. I just met her. My honeymoon can't be over yet." But it was over.

> *. . . when the phenomena, the adrenaline, the ecstasy, the awe at realizing what was always present within oneself is what one was always searching for—the absolute shock and awe can begin to be replaced by some slight casualness, or taking for granted, or some sense of "Oh, it was so easy at the first; now it is getting difficult."*
> *This is when the true marriage with Truth comes into play. And I will tell you, continually, that it <u>is</u> easy. It is easy if you are true to Truth. Not if you are true to particular*

phenomena, not if you are true to adrenaline, not if you are true to particular biochemical firings.

If you are true to that, then you will go the way that conditioned existence has been going throughout time. I promise you this. But you don't have to even take my promise as truth. You tell the truth about your experiences throughout time, and you will see that this is so.

It's a hard truth. Because there is some kind of infantile idealization of the way things should be—just <u>sparkling</u>, and firing—yes, it's an adolescent mistake.

I swallowed hard. I didn't even feel like an adolescent. I felt more like a six-year-old. I wanted to sit in her lap, be her favorite singer, sleep on her porch, cherish this "being in love" feeling. Suddenly, ruthlessly, I saw all that as "phenomena."

But this hard truth, if it is met in this resolve to be absolutely true, is <u>nothing</u>. Is easy. No effort. The effort, the struggle, the falling comes from trying to cling to some kind of phenomena—or trying to "get it" again, or someplace else. Whether this is phenomena called personal power or phenomena called sexual excitement or phenomena called enlightenment, spiritual power—it is all a trap of the mind.

There is nothing wrong with phenomena. Some phenomena are quite delightful, and some are quite horrifying. But all phenomena are simply phenomena. And if you cling to any of it, or if you reach or grasp for any of it, you will go the usual way that has been gone throughout time. You will be following the mind—subtly or grossly.

And so the value of satsang appearing in your consciousness again, over time, is to point this out. I can tell you that all the books, all the teachers have always said this is very rare, the awakened being is very rare.

This is true in the past, your past and the collective past. Whether it is true in the present and the future is up to you, now. And this takes a resolve that is <u>unknown</u>. It is so total that it is unknown. And when it is so total, then resolve itself is easy. Do you get this? Good. Good.

Again, I was tempted to think, "She couldn't be speaking to me. She knows I want truth. I've written to her about my experiences, my resolve. She liked my letters. She read one in satsang." But she *was* speaking to me.

> You know, I often have occasion to read the most exquisite letters of opening, of deep realization—ah, <u>some</u> of these letters, so deep—and they have inspired you and they have inspired me, and they have inspired whoever has seen them on the video. But finally, these letters mean nothing. <u>Nothing</u>. Because I can also tell you that some of the writers of the deepest letters, actually when push comes to shove go for some temptation, some phenomenal temptation.
>
> So the letters display truth. But your life, as you live it, now, this is the truth of what it is you really want. And if what it is you really want <u>is</u> Truth, then live it in surrender to that and not some phenomenal display.
>
> You may enjoy the phenomenal displays, or you may hate the phenomenal displays, but surrender to the truth that no phenomena has ever touched, and you are free, and your life itself is free, and your life is a beacon of freedom. Freedom having nothing to do with comfort or discomfort, likes or dislikes, excitement or dullness. True freedom.
>
> This is the opportunity for everyone in this room. Because the truth of who you are <u>is</u> this freedom. And these phenomenal displays are simply masks, clothes, passing clouds, chemical/electrical moments.

It was ruthless, unsentimental speaking. And I found both my resolve and my love for her deepening as she spoke.

> So the usual is to slip back into trance. The usual is when what has been cast aside then comes in another way, through another door, promising more glory, more beauty, more thrills. The usual is to say, "Oh, yes. I have waited for this forever. I'll get back to truth later." That's the usual.
>
> So from the first satsang I ever held in Boulder, I have said over and over this is not casual, this is not trivial. This

is in fact the most special, the most extraordinary, the most rare, the most unusual possibility for your life.

And in this possibility of embracing and surrendering to the most rare, most unusual, most special, most extraordinary potential, you have the support of every awakened being throughout time, and before time and after time, in all realms—and still it is totally UP TO YOU.

You are supported, you are cheered, you are shook, you are cajoled—and still, it is up to you.

So I will say again, it is not casual. The surrender, truly, to Truth, is the most ruthless act of a lifetime. It is the willingness to die to all pleasure, all pleasure. The willingness to die to that. Then see what is received. You can't die to that so that you get some more pleasure. You've tried that. And what you get is more suffering, with some pleasure.

Someone told me about a particular event of temptation and they said, "Oh, but it's so beautiful and it's such a...it's so deep and it's so vast." And I said, "Did you expect it to look like a Mack truck getting ready to run over you?" [laughter]

You must expect the deepest, vastest, most thrilling displays of phenomenal temptation. You must expect what in the latent, latent recesses of your mind you have hungered for—as if that would give you who you are.

How painfully precise was her reading of the deepest most secret desires of my heart. I had hardly been aware of it myself. The music. I had written music all my life and never thought there was any possibility of being able to perform it or share it because of my shyness. Now, with this experience of the dropping of the mind, I had tasted this freedom from the bondage of my nervousness and had seen that all the fear was just an illusion. So there was this possibility arising of sharing the music at last, of recognition of my talent as a songwriter at last, of success at last. What could be wrong with that?

She had said, clearly, what could be wrong: *as if that would give you who you are.* That is the trap. Anything looked to in this way, to give you who you are, becomes a distraction away from surrender to the Truth of your Being.

In that moment I let go of this secret desire. I didn't care if I ever sang or wrote again. I wanted the Truth of my Being.

Whether this is some display of personal power like flying or levitating, or some appearance of the hungered-for soulmate, or some winning of the lottery—do you understand?—or some recognition, or finally, some control. Latent tendencies, subconscious, all will present themselves, because they lie in wait.

This is not a trivial matter. What makes it difficult and hard is holding on to some idea of personal gratification. This in itself is hell. This is hell.

When you are willing—I don't mean willing to be a martyr so that you'll get in heaven; that's not what I'm speaking of; this cannot be a martyrhood—when you are willing to face whatever temptation, horrible or exquisite, fully and completely, you die to all fantasies of personal gratification or personal lack of gratification. And you discover gratification itself as WHO YOU ARE.

Her words seemed to be ripping something out of me. It was a disillusionment of the deepest kind. How deeply ingrained was this sense of the personal; so deeply ingrained that even with a glimpse of enlightenment there can be the tendency to grab it for the personal self, to possess it, to boast of it, outwardly or inwardly, and use it as some kind of personal attainment. Then once again there is the spin into hell, the hell of identification with the mind.

There was a kind of death happening inside of me. I could feel that quite tangibly. Layers of personal attachment were peeling off, as if I were shedding layers of skin, like a lizard.

Yes. This is the invitation that is spoken in satsang. This is the invitation of Ramana and Papaji. And you can be expected to be pushed and pulled, to be flipped, to be attacked from the side and the back. To be presented with

*flowers and sweets. To be clubbed. This is called Leela.
Leela plays very hard.*

It was all becoming clear now—the flowers, the sweet smiles, the pats on the cheek. It's all part of the game, all part of the Leela. It's not what it looks like. There will be tests— to verify what is really wanted. She was warning me that she will play hard with me. This is not trivial. This is not causal. To surrender to the Truth of one's Being is the most ruthless act of a lifetime.

> *If you are surrendered to Truth, this play will only push you deeper into That. If you are in fact surrendered to some phenomenal experience, you will be pulled out of experience of your own Being as gratification itself and into the search for more, or different, or better. Which is the name of hell. Okay?* *

She appeared to lighten up a little after that and took some questions. I even asked a question about the experience of the mind dropping and then coming back again. But the most ruthless part of that satsang was when she closed her eyes at the end. I'd never seen her do that before. Usually she just put her palms together and said, *Om Shanti*, to end a satsang. But that night she closed her eyes, and for quite a while at the end she just sat in silence with us.

I was sitting right in front of her, only a few rows back. And in that silence I felt her reach into my heart and rip it apart. I swear I could actually *feel* it being torn. It was the most excruciating, deep pain. I began to cry, and I couldn't stop. I cried all the way home and three-quarters of the night.

As I crawled into bed in the early dawn, exhausted, slain, shaken to the core, the wreath of roses lay drying on my bedside table. My heart had always thrilled just looking at them, for I imagined that they symbolized Gangaji's love for me. Now they began to look more like funeral roses, my funeral, signifying another deeper death of the ego self. I began to wonder, how many times must "this" be killed?

12

NOT MOVING TOWARD,
NOT MOVING AWAY

*W*hen I awoke in the morning my heart felt like a truck had run over it. My mind was filled with thoughts like, "What have I gotten into? I don't know if I can handle this. I'm a pretty delicate person. Maybe I need a teacher who will be more gentle and loving with me. Maybe this isn't going to work."

That morning I was supposed to go over to Shivaya Ma's to help with the weekly cleaning for Gangaji, but I felt resistance to going. I felt horrible. Slapped. Ripped apart. She was being more ruthless with me than I felt I was ready for. The thought arose, "Get away from this teacher; she's hurting you."

Then, somehow, I began to see that the resistance was only thought. And I could see exactly where the thoughts were coming from. The egoic impulse for survival and comfort is tremendous. The human organism is conditioned to move away from pain and toward pleasure. So, when it gets painful at the guru's feet, the conditioning is to get away, to retreat back into the mind, back to something comfortable, something known. That particular morning all the conditioning held in my very cells from eons past was shouting: RUN!

By some mysterious intervention of Grace—her Grace, the Grace of this lineage, the Grace of every awakened being—I did not run. I was tired of running. I had been running for millions of years.

I went to Shivaya Ma's and cleaned with Shanti and Ray. Shanti asked me if I was all right, probably noticing the red puffy eyes. I said, "I'm okay. It was just a very powerful satsang last night." She agreed. But I figured she was in a position to handle it better than I. She'd been with Gangaji for a couple of years, had even lived with her for a while, and was probably used to this "death by guru" experience.

In the few days that followed, as the pain from the "slaying" I'd received stopped smarting, the most amazing thing happened. I experienced a freedom and a relaxation of effort and an expansion of awareness beyond anything I'd experienced before. I had "stopped" once again, and this new depth of "stop" brought a deepening of the recognition of Self. I also felt unbelievably closer to this ruthless teacher who had obviously facilitated this deepening. I recognized what she'd done—caused latent tendencies of mind, old patterns of egoic thinking, to arise in the purity and intensity of satsang in order to be burned up in the Truth of my Being. And so the love and gratitude deepened also. I wrote Gangaji a note reporting this deepening and thanking her, which she read in satsang on June 25th.

That day I placed my note underneath the stack of letters on the couch, hoping she wouldn't read it during satsang. But she went right to the bottom of the pile and picked out my letter as if she were looking for it. When she saw the signature she looked up and said:

Where's Amber?

I raised my hand. She looked over at me with a playful scowl and appraised me for a moment, saying, *That's good,* then began reading my note.

Dear Gangaji:

On Thursday night I thought you were being too ruthless.

She looked up and burst out laughing, and so did the group. I felt a little embarrassed and exposed, but somehow I did not mind. Her attention was precious to me, however it appeared. Still chuckling, she said:

I got a lot of letters about Thursday night.

She continued reading:

> My heart felt like it was going to break apart. Now I see
> how this was necessary, and how it has brought a new
> depth of realization and surrender.
>
> Your Kali aspect used to terrify me, but I am coming
> to love that as well. Thank you for your ruthlessness—and
> for the roses too.
>
> With ever deepening love and trust,
>
> *Amber*

She put my letter down, smiling to herself, as if remembering something amusing.

> *Yes, you know, I've told this story often about first being
> with Papaji, and being his pet, being his darling. He'd say:
> "Come over earlier than the others," and "Let them go, you
> stay." So, you know, it's like . . .*

She made a motion like putting her thumbs into imaginary suspenders in blissful pride as everyone laughed.

> *Who can't love that? It's lovable. It's an embrace. It's a
> welcome. It's like saying, "Yes, you are the one! That's right."*
>
> *Then, I went away from him for some time—some
> months, two, three months. I came back to him, dah dah!*

She put her arms out, as if ready for another embrace; everyone laughed.

> *Yet he never even invited me over for tea. "What are you
> doing back so soon?" is what he said.*
>
> *"Well, I'm back for more, of course."*
>
> *So I felt the slap. What you call the Kali aspect. What a
> beautiful slap. What a beautiful aspect—*

She glanced over at me,

> *—just in case one thinks "being the one" is one particular
> way. That it looks like or feels like something in particular.*

137

The welcome is beautiful.

An interviewer recently asked me in Santa Fe, "When Papaji saw you, did he welcome you as 'the one?'" I said, "Yes. And everyone I have ever seen him see has been welcomed as that same one."

You will see all life, as you said, brings you "a new depth of realization and surrender." All of life. The welcome, the kiss, the rejection, the slap. Then you are free. Free for deeper, wider, bigger, higher, smaller, more subtle, more sublime, realization and surrender.

Very good, Amber.*

I could tell she was pleased with me that day. I had received a slice from the guru's sword and had not run. But I had no illusions that I would be able to rest on that for long. I could see she was going to push me hard and fast, wasting no time whatsoever with me. And for this, I was grateful, while at the same time still harboring an underlying fear that I wouldn't be able to handle it. By then I had heard some of the stories about Papaji's fierce ruthlessness with her, and did not at all perceive myself to be as strong as her, or as capable of handling the same treatment.

It was only a few days later when I felt the sting of her slap once again. Sitting outside the satsang hall one morning I met a new friend named Terry, who was Gangaji's cook. She was looking for some people to cook on her days off, and encouraged me to try out for it. At first I would not even consider it. I'd been cooking vegetarian for nearly twenty-seven years but my cooking was very simple and, according to my husband, a little on the bland side. When I mentioned my reservations to Terry she said, "That's great! Gangaji loves bland food." So we talked about it for a while and eventually I agreed to try out a few dishes on Terry.

We were both sitting very close to the front of the line that day. Terry said she was determined to sit in the front row. I told her I'd never sat in the front row before. There was a certain amount of aggressiveness needed to get a seat that close, which was not typical for my nature. Besides, sitting so close to Gangaji would probably make me feel too exposed. Terry said she didn't have a problem with it and when the doors opened, sure enough, she got right up front, on the rug just below Gangaji's feet—while I ended up a couple of rows back.

But I must have been destined to sit up front that day, because Terry and a guy named Steve and another fellow named Hal, who were occupying the "rug" that day, all repositioned themselves to make a spot for me, front and center. I hesitated to take it because it was so close, right at her feet, and I could already feel the shyness and feelings of exposure arising. But there was so much pressure on me to take the seat they'd made for me that I finally succumbed.

There were about five or six of us that day, sitting on the rug in a semicircle around Gangaji's feet. During the satsang, Gangaji made a point of giving a big smile to every person in the semicircle—except me. In fact she didn't even look at me. Her eyes skipped over me every time. Inside, a feeling of rejection started to arise. Then the familiar impulse to avoid rejection quickly arose to counter it—"Hey, I don't care. I don't need her to look at me." This was a personality pattern that had manifested all my life, in all my relationships. If it hurts, get away. You don't need it.

The first time I remember this pattern arising was with my mother when I was five years old. I accidentally broke a milk bottle on the front porch. She got very angry and yelled at me. It was the first time I remember her being real mad at me like that. Stifling tears, I turned and went into my room. Feelings of rejection were coming up which I was not willing to experience. The defence arose: "Hey, I don't need this. I'm outta here." I packed up my little toy suitcase with pajamas and teddy bear, and quietly left home.

I walked two miles across a field and through a wood to my grandmother's house, and there spent the night. I didn't realize until later that Mom had sent my older brother to follow me to see that I arrived safely, and also that my grandmother had secretly called my Mom and Dad to tell them I was okay and that it was fine for me to spend the night. The incident was forgotten the next day when Grandma took me home, but the pattern remained all my life—get away from uncomfortable feelings, disharmonious people, or distasteful circumstances.

As I sat in front of Gangaji that day, experiencing the rejection, the impulse to withdraw from her arose. I felt my heart actually shrinking back, pulling away; it was so automatic. I told myself, "I don't care. I don't need this." I told myself it was probably my imagination anyway that she was ignoring me. But after satsang Terry commented in her unabashedly direct way, "Hey, that was amazing. Gangaji looked at everyone in the front row except you!"

Terry's comment was perfect; like the last escape route closed. There was no way out of it, the feeling had to be met. Inside I was dying. Inside, I knew—in Gangaji I had finally met someone I could not run from. I had finally met someone who could stop me, stop this movement into the mind. She could stop me because she herself had stopped.

I went home and cried my eyes out. All night I let the emotion arise, let it all be felt, all that I'd run from, all that I'd avoided meeting throughout my life. I realized that I'd been somewhat proud of this ability to just leave whenever I wanted. As a teenager and young college student, I'd seen so many of my friends get into painful relationships and then stay there because of the illusion that they "needed" the relationship for happiness. I knew I didn't need anything, and I felt this knowing was freedom. My motto, from about age nineteen, was, "When you don't need anything, then you'll always have everything you need."

Now a new perspective on all this was dawning. This "freedom" I was so proud of had been created in my mind. It was not real. It needed constant strategizing to avoid what I didn't want, and to draw to me what I thought I did want. Gangaji was exposing this play of mind for what it really was—illusion.

I'd heard her speak a number of times in satsang about "meeting" whatever arises. I didn't understand this at first. It sounded Buddhist. And whenever she would mention it I'd think to myself, "Well, I don't have to do that," or "That's just coming from her Buddhist background."

Now I saw the truth of this "meeting." It is a "staying still." It is a ruthless "not moving." It is taking refuge in the Truth of one's Being, instead of taking refuge in phenomena, in the illusion of some phenomenal temporary comfort or some mind-created sense of "getting away."

I was beginning to see that *everything* arises in satsang, including everything one has never wanted to see. The opportunity is to not move. The opportunity is to surrender what arises in mind and let it be burnt up in the fire of Self-recognition.

A couple of days later, the opportunity to "not move" presented itself to me once more. I was sitting close to the front again that day in satsang. Gangaji looked especially beautiful and radiant. Suddenly, she turned and smiled at a young girl sitting a little to the side and in front of me. Gangaji said to the girl:

Have we met?

The girl shook her head. Gangaji gazed at her lovingly for a moment, then said,

I believe you're an angel. Did you know that?

The girl nodded shyly, but said nothing. I could feel the intense love coming from Gangaji toward this girl. And then, to my surprise and embarrassment, the most excruciating jealousy arose. It shocked me actually, for jealously is not an emotion I have often felt in my life. But there it was, undeniably filling my consciousness, right there in satsang, right there in front of Gangaji.

Thoughts arose like, "Hey, wait a minute, I want to be your angel. I want the love you are giving to this girl." I felt mortified that such childish thoughts and emotions could arise. I struggled with them, tried to suppress them, but it was no use. I was sitting too close to the front!

All during that evening, Gangaji kept looking over at this young girl, giving her the most loving and adoring glances. Each time she did this, the jealously would arise. At first I tried to beat it back. "Bad jealousy! Get out of here! Go away!" But finally something relaxed inside. By some Grace I saw that this jealousy must be welcomed, welcomed to satsang. As I relaxed with it, stopped fighting it, a true "seeing" began to emerge. I saw that this jealousy was only thought, only latent tendencies of mind arising in satsang. I saw the mind as the magician that creates the illusion of separation, the illusion of "mine" and "me" as separate from "another" and "them." I saw how Christ's instruction, "Love your neighbor as yourself," can never be lived as long as life is lived through the mind, through the eyes of separation. It can be modeled, it can be pretended, it can be attempted, but it cannot be *lived* until one sees that one's neighbor *is* oneself, until all separation is seen as illusion.

Gangaji kept looking over at this young girl, and the feelings in me kept arising. At one point I just laughed at myself and at this play that I was watching. Finally I saw that this love going to the young girl was going to me also. And not only going to me, but it was actually *my* love going to the young girl. It was Self loving Itself!

Something profound must have shifted in my awareness, because the rest of that evening *everyone* Gangaji spoke to appeared as my own Self speaking to Itself. And I noticed that when Gangaji walked out of the hall that night, for the first time I did not feel a great gaping longing inside as I usually did when she left. I knew, deeply undeniably *knew*, that what I longed for was not leaving, was not going anywhere. It is my own Self, right *here*, always.

Then I saw how perfect it was that this young girl had been present in satsang that night and sitting so near me. Mysteriously, I never saw her again. Perhaps she really was an angel, appearing that night to help reveal to me this truth of "no separation."

After that it seemed easier to meet everything that arose, both in formal satsang, as well as in interactions with Toby, friends, and strangers. And in this meeting, a new depth of "stopping" was revealed. I wrote a letter to Gangaji soon after that, reporting all this, and she read it in satsang on July 9th.

My heart thudded as she picked up my letter. There was still an excruciating, anxious fire that arose inside whenever one of my letters lay there in her hands—as though my head was on a chopping block, as though everything was exposed. This time, she looked up at me and smiled reassuringly before beginning to read:

> Dearest Gangaji,:
>
> It's been 10 weeks since meeting you, and there have been so many beautiful realizations and so much Grace. Yet I have felt there was something I wasn't "getting," something that kept drawing me back into separation. Finally, I believe, the cause of this has surfaced.
> When you speak of "meeting" everything fully, completely, I realize how foreign this is to my life, and how I have subtly resisted this idea whenever you have mentioned it in satsang. My habit has been to keep at a distance anything distasteful, disharmonious, or uncomfortable.

She laughed, looked up at me, and asked jokingly:

Well, how much success have you had?

I said, "A lot. I've had a lot of success." But I don't think she heard me because there was quite an upsurge of laughter throughout the hall at that point.

> *If you are successful in this, I say, "fine." I'm not opposed to it if you have found success there.*
> *But I would say more your habit has been to attempt to keep at a distance anything distasteful, disharmonious, or uncomfortable— attempting and attempting and attempting.*

It was true. Much as I liked to boast about what a great escape artist I was, when I examined it carefully I had to admit—it's an awful lot of work, keeping so much at bay. There was always the hope that if I could just keep enough of the impurities of other people and the world away, then I'd be free. But it was not an effortless project. There was a constant need to retreat, to protect, to run.

143

She continued reading:

> This is probably not unusual.

She looked up at me and smiled.

> *That's right.*

> But what is unusual is that I have been fairly successful at
> it, mainly because I don't especially need anything in this
> world—people, situations, or things—badly enough to
> stick around if things aren't pleasant. I possess a ruthless
> ability to just leave, escape, and have mistaken this ability
> for freedom.

She was very happy with this realization and looked up at
me again.

> *That's very good. It's a power you have, a siddhi you're
> speaking of. Powers are beautiful phenomena, but to mis-
> take them for freedom is a big mistake. Very lucky that this
> mistake is being corrected.*

> This escape pattern has even surfaced a couple of times as
> the impulse to run from you. But I see now what a false
> freedom this pattern of escape has fostered. For I know
> that what I see in you is true freedom, and that this free-
> dom and beauty and Truth that I see in you is the seeing of
> my own Self.

> *That's right! That's seeing. That's hearing.*

> I see now that in this running I inadvertently create
> "things" separate from myself and give reality to them,
> thus perpetuating the lie of separation. Now I find that,
> just as you promised, by meeting phenomena fully, com-
> pletely, willing to die, they are revealed as nothing . . .

> *That's called the "end" of phenomena. Not because of
> running from, not because of acting out, not because of
> ignoring, not because of denying, but because in a true*

meeting only what is remains. This is the secret meaning of the word "meeting."

> . . . they are revealed as nothing, revealed as Self, and the lie stopped. So I am resolved to stop. Stop retreating. (As many times as I've thought I've stopped, a new level of "stop" keeps being revealed.)

That's right! And THAT is endless. That can't be stopped—if you stop your mind.

This is all within the mind—retreating, running, powers, comfortable, inconvenient, uncomfortable. This is all within the mind. This is the world as it has been known through the mediation of past concepts, internalized or rebelled against, one way or the other. That's called "activity of the mind." That's called "a life lived indirectly," maybe with a "sense" of personal power, with a sense of freedom—until, in a very lucky meeting, you recognize, "what I thought was freedom was some 'thing,' was some 'capacity,' was some 'strength,' was something relative to something else."

In that moment you can stop, and you can hear, and you can see what is revealed in "meeting." Meeting does not have to do with going toward or going away. It has to do with remaining absolutely—not relatively—absolutely still. Relatively, you can be in motion or not, and be absolutely still. Relative motion or not occurs in absolute stillness, which since it is absolute is always still.

You don't have to go and get stillness, or find stillness, or make your mind be still. Simply recognize absolute stillness that is present at every moment, in every retreat, in every advance. And in the recognition of that, the mind is stopped, is prostrated, is finished—as it has been known.

She continued reading:

> This resolve is going to be a challenge, because there is such a long habit of not meeting things fully that it is very subtle, almost unconscious sometimes.

That's right. That's right. It's a challenge. If you don't want a challenge, leave now. Run from challenge. Try to avoid challenge. Attempt to get away from challenge.

Yes. Good luck. If you're successful, wonderful. Then you have found your proper teacher.

Inside, I reacted fiercely—No! the world has been my teacher long enough! I am ready for my true teacher. I have found my true teacher. I will stay here, at your feet and meet any challenge that arises.

But if you recognize "challenge," really CHALLENGE, then you can hear this "stop" as surrender, surrender to stillness, surrender to the Truth of who you are.

Then see what is challenging. Yes, then challenge will regroup. The challenges will come up from deeper in the subconscious. Then maybe you will even take on the challenges of your neighbor, or your country, or your species, or your planet. What a game now! You have left behind this melodrama of personal discomfort, and personal inconvenience, and personal power, to play fully, completely, without moving, this challenge that Leela presents. Leela means "play of God, play of the Self."

Yes, you will be challenged to move. You will be prodded to move. You will be threatened to move. You will be seduced to move. What a challenge! What delight! Then you can speak with certainty of "Why the senses?"..."Why this body?"..."Why this lifetime?"..."Why these circumstances?"..."Why this past?"..."Why this present?"

You follow this? Good! Good!

I didn't follow the last part. But she didn't notice my puzzled look. She was looking out at the rest of the group at that point. Then she looked down at my letter again. I noticed that she was cutting out certain sentences, editing it as she read it.

But in this past week as I surrendered more to this stopping, it seemed like *every* situation encountered, every person spoken with, became self-inquiry . . .

THAT is correct. That's the Truth.

. . . throwing awareness back onto itself. While this recognition is not always immediate yet, I am beginning....

Suddenly she stopped reading and jabbed her finger several times into the page.

No! That's not true. That's not true.

She gave me a hard look.

It is always immediate. You just take that sentence out and you see. Then that sentence has no power. You don't follow that sentence. "Oh, I'm not through, I haven't . . . I'm not fully . . ."

I read an interesting article the other day about the issue of enlightenment, and "fully" enlightened. The person being interviewed really said a very beautiful thing—that to say "fully" enlightened is really to lie because there has never yet been pointed to, or spoken about, or revealed, an end to this that is enlightened.

This fullness has no end. There is no container that can hold it, that can then be said to be full. You understand this? This is endless.

We have heard this word "fully" enlightened with some idea of something "finished." What is finished is the idea of something finished. [laughter] And in that finishing, the revelation of what is permanently, absolutely, more and more full is revealed. More and MORE.

You just have to stop identifying that you can collect a certain amount where then you can say, "Okay, I'm measuring at pass," or "I'm measuring at A-plus." You are That already, immediately and always. And that which you are is endless. There is nothing that can hold it. It is full beyond measurement. And it is more full and MORE full.

So give up this idea of some finite measurement, or some finite measurER, and be fully That, which you are, FULLY! You are FULLY That! More and more fully! FULLY!

These words were hitting me like bullets, with a force that pushed me back into my seat with each punctuation.

Until finally you just—stop trying to speak about it.

Again she resumed reading:

> I am beginning to see how it is possible for *all* phenomena, if met fully, truly, to actually serve Truth, rather than distract from it.

Hallelujah! That's correct understanding. Then there is no NEED to move—no need to move away from, no need to move toward—when this understanding is revealed.

How everything that occurs can be the teaching . . .

I wouldn't say CAN be the teaching, IS . . .

. . . the teaching of the Satguru.

IS the teaching. Everything that occurs is the teaching of the Satguru. How does your mind relate to that teaching? If your mind is floored, if your mind is prostrate before the Satguru, then everything serves That. The Satguru, the Truth guru, the guru who is alive within you always and who has always been present, has never left you—and has presented to you many images or forms of teacher, guru—but the true everlasting guru presents <u>everything</u> as a teaching, every instant, every emotion, every thought, every circumstance, every comfort, every discomfort, every measurement, every denial, every affirmation.

You recognize <u>that</u> and then it's not even a challenge. It is just blissful, eternal surrender—to this prostration of mind to Self. True Self. Not image of Self, not thought of Self. True Self. That which cannot be imaged or thought.

> I feel continually more grateful for the Grace that has led me to you, and that flows from you in a never-ending

stream. Thank you for meeting me fully, ruthlessly, again and again, deeper and deeper.

Ever more carefully listening,
Amber

Very well said. Very good. This is Truth, really recognizing an ally, a friend.

She related a story that Papaji tells about a violent samurai warrior meeting his master, feeling resistance enough to actually want to kill the master, then finally realizing this was his greatest friend and ally, and falling at the master's feet in surrender.

When she finished the story, she looked over at me again:

I am happy to hear you are stopped. That's all that's required. No credentials. Just the willingness to stop, and in that, investigate for yourself. Then you see—for yourself.*

In all the times I'd heard her speak of "stopping" I don't believe I ever really understood what she meant by it until then. I saw it so clearly in that satsang. It was the stopping of the mind. It was the stopping of the following of the mind, the retreating into the mind, the indulging of the mind. It was staying absolutely still in Self, in *who one is*, no matter what arises, no matter what temptations, horrific or divine, come to challenge you to move.

After that, I began to notice when I was moving and when I was not moving. And even though I saw that sometimes I still moved, just in the seeing of it there seemed to be a weakening of the mind's illusory power, and this facilitated the burning of the tendencies of mind that caused this movement. And in that, I finally began to see the truth of what I'd heard her say several times already: it is so *utterly* simple.

149

13

ATTACHMENT TO THE TEACHER

*T*hroughout that summer the silence, the love, the "not moving," the awareness of Self just kept unfolding. As early as Estes Park Gangaji had promised that this deepening was endless. But I couldn't quite believe it at first. The explosive awakening I had experienced when I first met her was so intense, so vast, so profound I could not imagine how the bottom could keep falling out. But it did—and continually, it does.

Looking back on that summer I believe this deepening was facilitated by the ever-increasing love and attachment I felt for Gangaji. Continually, I was annihilated in this love. In her presence I felt like a child, or at times a love-sick adolescent— even though in this life I am only four years younger than her. Sometimes I questioned this attachment, struggled with it, wondered if it was even healthy or appropriate. None of what was happening made any sense; none of it was controllable. There was nothing I had done to bring it about, and there was nothing I could do to stop it.

I realized at one point that all my unfulfilled wants had been transferred to her. All the love I'd ever longed for, all the recognition I'd ever sought, all the passion I'd ever suppressed, all the most secret desires of my heart were laid at her feet. She became, in effect, the object of every unburned desire. When this first became apparent to me I thought it was stupid, madness, to transfer all this onto her. But, besides the fact that I had no choice, since it had taken place spontaneously, I later saw that this was perfect. Gangaji had appeared in my consciousness as the fire of Truth, as my own pure Self. How perfect that all unburned desires got thrown into this fire.

My husband saw all this and felt left out. He saw the surrender that I, in my characteristic independence, had never really given to him now going to Gangaji. It made all his own insecurities and respect issues arise. And there were times when we talked about separating. I had no desire to separate, nor did I have a desire to stay together. By mid-summer I felt a deep sense of personal fulfillment that was not related to anything in my outer circumstances. I knew I belonged to this Truth now, that my life had somehow been given to that. It was not mine anymore and it was not Toby's. I let him know that if he was too uncomfortable, I was willing to release him in love. I wanted his happiness. The outer circumstances of my life did not seem very important.

In spite of his discomfort Toby "hung in there" all summer, attending every satsang. Gradually he began to see, gradually he began to release his personal attachment to how he wanted the relationship to look, and to perceive the beauty and mystery of all that was taking place. This was quite amazing, actually, and reveals the true depth of his commitment to Truth, for I must not have been the easiest person to live with during this time. My body was still going through tremendous upheavals. Often I would cry all night; much of the time I was unable to eat or sleep. When I wasn't in formal satsang with Gangaji I spent most of my time at Satsang Foundation & Press, or helping out in the satsang hall, or cooking or cleaning for Gangaji.

In the fall I wrote to her about this time:

> It has felt like my whole body, gross and subtle, has been being transformed, reborn even, in the fire of this work. It is quite intense and often exhausting, physically and emotionally, and sometimes I felt like running—but by your Grace I did not follow that. And sometimes I felt like complaining to you that I couldn't handle the intensity— but I didn't do that either because, truthfully, I am not interested in wasting any time.

Often I would be aware of a tremendous flood of love coming from Gangaji, and yet experience a frustration with myself because I could see that I was not fully open to it. Shyness was still arising around this, and I realized how deeply this pattern of hiding, of staying aloof and of keeping a safe distance, had been seated. It had produced a personality with a great deal of repression, inhibition, and resistance to intimacy of any kind.

All this resistance arose in the relationship with Gangaji. Inwardly, subtly, I could see that this resistance was actually a hiding from my own Self. But when one gets into relationship with one's Self as true teacher, all barriers must fall. There is a ruthless slashing of every level of hiding.

About this Gangaji has said:

> *The special, secret relationship of guru/student is not for the faint-of-heart! Any idea of what this relationship is, is outdated and always unrealistic.*
>
> *The essence of the relationship is in the meaning of the word guru—revealer of light (TRUTH). In the revelation of TRUTH the student's ego is recognized to be the only obstruction. Ego is the false identification with thoughts, images and experiences as WHO ONE IS. False identification must be destroyed. This destruction is the guru's gift, regardless whether that guru be in human form or formless presence.*
>
> *The true guru desires only the student's Self Realization. The mature student recognizes that the relationship with the guru mirrors the student's relationship with Life. When Life, or guru, is resisted or run from because it doesn't conform to preconceived ideals, Life withholds the secret. When Life, or guru, is met openly in surrender, the secret treasure of TRUTH is revealed. This treasure naturally dissolves all apparent limitations of both guru and student.**

In my past, I had not loved life. Life was full of things that disgusted me—violence, selfishness, abuse of all kinds. How could I embrace that? So I had held life as separate from myself. Most of it was something to be kept away, so that I would not be polluted by it. This perception of separation, this belief in separation, ironically, perpetuated the illusion. It perpetuated the identification with mind, which is in itself the essence of violence, selfishness, and abuse of all kinds.

I had perfected my ability to hide, and life had withheld its secret from me. When I met Gangaji she began to systematically destroy this illusion. My love and attachment for her were crucial, for she became the one reality I could not run from, could not hide from—even when "push came to shove."

One way she pushed me was to ask me to sing in satsang. She began to do this in mid-July, after I wrote another song for her called "Eternal Friend." It is an ode to the Self. I had written the music some years before, but had never been able to get the words quite right. Now, with Gangaji as inspiration, they tumbled out perfectly.

My Friend
Who is not in time
You always see me
With eyes Divine
And you
Reveal that joy
Which thrills the soul
And lies beyond what the senses know.

For you
Are the deepest light
Inside my soul
Behind my sight
And you
Are the door beyond
The burning sun
Where shadow dances never come.

My friend
Who never sleeps
Through stormy nights
Your watch does keep
Oh, it is for you
The heart expands
And drops this life
In your timeless hands.

My friend
I am at your feet
You fill my heart
My day, my sleep
Oh, and as I see
That you are me
It keeps unfolding
Endlessly
Keeps unfolding
Endlessly.

I wanted to sing this song for her in satsang, but every time I even thought about it I would feel so unbearably shy and exposed that my whole body would tense and become hot, and my heart would thud crazily. I felt it was the most intimate song I'd ever written, a love song to the True Self, to Gangaji, and it made all my intimacy-resistance arise.

Even so, one day I brought my guitar to satsang, at Toby's encouragement. He said, "Maybe if you just bring the guitar you'll feel like singing." Dubiously, I loaded it into the car. But about halfway to satsang I knew I wasn't going to be able to do it, and the tears started to fall. I felt so totally frustrated and discouraged with myself. "How can Gangaji even tolerate me hanging around as her student?" I sobbed, "I can't even sing the song I wrote for her."

Toby chided me for being so silly and dramatic. But part of my frustration was that it felt like I'd gone backwards. In Santa Fe, when the mind had dropped so completely, it had been so easy to sing. Now, I reasoned, surely I must have gone back into my mind.

As we stood outside the church, waiting for satsang to begin, our friend John approached and asked me what was wrong. As I tried to express to him my dilemma and discouragement, Maitri approached us and asked to speak with me in private. Grumpily, I followed her across the lawn, away from the crowd, and hoped she wasn't going to ask me to do anything that required any kind of clarity. When we were alone, she reached into the armload of notebooks and papers she carried and handed me a beautiful silk scarf. "Gangaji wants you to have this," said Maitri, adding, "she said, 'This will look great on Amber.'"

Instantly the frustration and pain vanished, as if a soothing balm had been applied to the open wound of my heart. I was floored. Flattened. Not just at the beautiful gift, but at the perfect timing of its delivery. Just at this most frustrating moment, Gangaji appeared like a beacon of love in this beautiful way. I couldn't say anything. I just stood there dumb, holding the scarf to my heart. But Maitri didn't need me to say anything. She knew.

Suddenly I realized that it didn't matter if I played the song or didn't play the song. All this judgment of myself was only in the mind. The gift from Gangaji had floored the mind, once again, so that I could see this. The personality was prostrate before Self, and before the perfection of how Self was manifesting in my life.

Another example of this unbelievable perfection occurred around the first time I brought a meal for Gangaji. Actually it was not a meal I myself had prepared. Terry had cooked that day and, because she had to go to the airport that afternoon to drop off her boyfriend, she decided to break me in by letting me deliver the meal. In this way, she told me, I could get used to taking the food over and setting it out in the kitchen.

I knew the house well because I'd been cleaning it every week. And I'd watched Terry set the food out sometimes when she'd come over while we were cleaning. Terry instructed me how to arrange everything—what went into the crockpot, what went into the refrigerator, and what stayed on the counter. But because I was still very shy around Gangaji, I asked nervously, "What if Gangaji is there?"

"Just don't bother her," said Terry, then added, "but she probably won't be there. And if she is, she'll be in the other room. I'm telling you, I hardly ever see her and I bring her meals every day."

Gangaji was still staying at Shivaya Ma's at that time, and so around 5:30 that evening I brought over the meal which I had picked up from Terry. As I walked down the steps to the house, Gangaji was standing by the front door, about to leave on an errand with Shivaya Ma. Gangaji greeted me warmly, opened the door for me, and asked me if I was cooking.

I was gripped by the most awful nervousness. My knees began shaking uncontrollably. I managed to explain to her that Terry had cooked the meal, and I was only delivering it, but I could hardly walk across the threshold. Somehow I managed to get the food into the kitchen without dropping anything, but I felt like such an idiot.

The next day when I saw Shivaya Ma, she said, "You were surprised to see her, weren't you?"

I said, "Terry said she wouldn't be there."

She laughed. "Well, Gangaji was happy to see you."

"*Why* am I so unbearably shy with her?" I moaned.

Shivaya Ma smiled, "Who isn't shy in the face of That?"

"Yes, but I have to be able to bring her a meal without dissolving into a total idiot. I'm going to start cooking soon."

Shivaya Ma was very soothing and sweet to me. She said, "You were fine. Gangaji doesn't notice that. She sees your heart."

I looked into my friend's eyes and saw Gangaji there. Into those eyes I said, "The last prayer of this life time is to just be *calm* in her presence."

Miraculously, that prayer was heard. Within two hours after uttering it, I stopped by the health food market to do some shopping. As I was rounding a corner in the store, I almost ran into someone. I looked up, and saw it was Gangaji!

She smiled and said, "Hello, Amber." Then she took hold of my wrist, and—I can't really describe what happened after that because it left no trail in memory. Truth leaves no tracks. I just know that we stood there together for some time. I was looking into her eyes and she was holding my wrist. And I was completely and totally *calm*. Then she let go of me and went on her way.

It was like a divine, timeless interlude, right there in the health food store. My desperate prayer must have been answered, not just in that moment, but for all time, for I was never so idiotically nervous in Gangaji's presence again—which turned out to be very helpful because I began cooking about once a week after that and, contrary to Terry's prediction, I nearly always saw Gangaji when I delivered the meals.

Shortly after this I got up my nerve to record the song "Eternal Friend" and give it to Gangaji on tape one day in satsang. That particular satsang was especially beautiful because a lot of people were expressing their love and gratitude, and Gangaji talked a lot about the importance of an open heart. When she opened the envelope with my tape in it, she looked up at me and asked if I had brought my guitar. I shook my head no. Then she asked if I could sing a cappella. Again, I shook my head.

She asked another musician present if he had brought his guitar. He said he hadn't. She frowned and said something like, *Hmm, the guitars are hiding today.*

At the end of the satsang, Maitri told me to go to the small meeting afterward. It was the first small satsang I had ever attended. I came in and sat down on the floor in front of Gangaji, who was already seated on a chair. She smiled at me and asked if I would sing there, in the small meeting. Again I refused and told her I couldn't sing without my guitar. I could tell she was not pleased with my stubbornness, but I just couldn't do it.

Finally she said, *From now on put the guitar in the car and have it available.* Then she told everyone that I had an etheric voice, adding, *It's not even of this realm.*

In that moment I felt my heart break open in love. Quietly I thanked her for the compliment. Yet inwardly I remember thinking to myself, "But God forgot to give me a 'performing personality' to go with it."

That satsang was about the shortest satsang I have ever been in. I believe it lasted about six minutes. But it was also one of the most powerful. The whole time I was sitting there, my heart was exploding more and more with an intense, uncontainable love. Others were experiencing the same thing. Many were expressing their deep love and gratitude—some verbally, some silently. Gangaji is not usually affected by expressions of love and devotion toward her, any more than she is affected by anger or animosity toward her. But it seemed she was very moved by the tidal waves of love in that small room that day, and at one point leaned back in her chair and put her hand on her heart, saying, *How much do you think I can take?* And this slight show of vulnerability made my heart melt even more.

Shortly after that she put her palms together and said, *Om Shanti.* As she got up to go, I moved over to make an aisle for her. She walked past me and my eyes met hers. All the love of my heart was pouring out to her, unabashedly, without restraint, and I felt that I was open and receiving her love more fully than ever before. She placed her hand on her heart and smiled at me, and in that smile was the brilliance of a thousand suns.

The very next satsang I obediently brought my guitar. I hid it in the back of the hall, secretly hoping that Gangaji would not remember. As the satsang began she read a couple of letters and then took some questions. About halfway through the satsang a lady from Arizona spoke about an experience she'd had on a boat trip with her husband and how he'd made her face the fear of being out on the water. "He brings up all my latent tendencies," said the woman. The hall roared with laughter. Gangaji commented on how beautiful it is to recognize that the latent tendencies are arising in oneself to be burned, not because of something wrong in the relationship.

After this lady was finished speaking, Gangaji's eyes suddenly fixed on me. I was sitting on the floor about eight rows back.

I hear you're going to sing today.

I was taken aback at first. Who had told her that? Instantly I suspected Gayatri. When I'd come to satsang that day I had seen Gayatri and Govind, who were in Boulder for a few days visiting from Santa Fe. Gayatri had asked me, "When are you ever going to bring your guitar to satsang?" I told her I would have to bring it from now on, because Gangaji had asked me to; but I never actually mentioned anything about singing.

"Do you want me to sing now?" I asked Gangaji, when I'd recovered from the shock of this unexpected attention. She said:

In a minute, but, just start getting nervous right away so it can be over.

The hall erupted in laughter again. A wave of embarrassment and a feeling of being naked and exposed seared through me. Gangaji added:

I bring up all of <u>her</u> latent tendencies.

158

Again laughter rang in the hall. For a moment I actually felt irritated with Gangaji for exposing me so ruthlessly in front of the group. But immediately I also felt the soothing balm of her love, and there was a realization of how unfathomably deeply she sees me, and a feeling of relief with that—that there was absolutely no possibility of hiding in her presence.

> *I bring them up in satsang. This is where latent tendencies belong—to be brought up in satsang. Then they can be set free. Then they can be realized to be nothing but tendencies—having to do with the body or the emotions or the intellect. Having nothing to do with who one is.*

As she spoke these words, I knew their truth. This nervousness, the latent tendencies of shyness and fear of exposure were not me. She was showing me this by making them arise in satsang. The mortification gave way to gratitude. Still I felt nervous about singing, but I didn't hate myself for it. I let it arise. I let it arise in satsang, so that I could see it had nothing to do with who I am.

Gangaji took a few more questions and left me to sit there and fry for a while. After about fifteen minutes or so, her eyes settled upon me again.

> *Okay. You want to sing now?*

I nodded. Then she asked me if I was going to sing the song I sent her on tape, saying that she hadn't had a chance to listen to it yet. She was referring to the "Eternal Friend" song. But I still wasn't ready to sing that one in public. It was too intimate. So I told her I'd sing the "River Ganga" song, and that seemed to be okay with her. As I went to get my guitar she said:

> *Yes, we all speak sutras in different ways and live sutras in different ways. From this beautiful Arizona way, this beautiful Amber way, this beautiful Mercy way. Just to surrender and let it be sung how it will through any particular form. This is the secret.**

I sang the song, and because some people knew it by then from when I'd sung in Santa Fe, many joined in on the chorus. I didn't feel I'd done a very good job with it, and I didn't feel I'd done what she had asked me to do: *Just to surrender and let it be sung how it will.* I didn't feel very surrendered. I felt exposed; I felt nervous. Much more nervous than I'd been in Santa Fe.

Gangaji was asking me to surrender and let the singing take place, and I couldn't quite. But what she had said about the latent tendencies being brought up in satsang started to sink in. From that day on I started to "get it" that I was not going backwards. That in the stopping, in the stillness, in the purity of satsang, deeper and deeper levels of hiding were being dredged up—dredged up in satsang to be freed.

And so I continued to bring my guitar to satsang every day. I would sit there squirming, nervous that she might ask me to play. Sometimes resistant thoughts would arise like, "It's ruining the satsang for me to have my guitar sitting back there and this specter hanging over me that I might have to play," or, "She doesn't know who this person is; I'm not a performer," or, "In Santa Fe I could do it only because she was helping me. I can't do it by myself." But I began to see that these were only thoughts and ultimately meant nothing. So I would just let them arise, burn, and fade away.

Meanwhile, I kept cooking and cleaning for Gangaji. Periodically I would get messages through Maitri or through Shivaya Ma about how much Gangaji liked my cooking. These messages always melted my heart. At first it surprised me that she liked my cooking so much because I did not feel my culinary talents were anything special. But I would put all my love into the food as I was preparing it for her and always took care not to have anything else going on—no conversation, no phone calls, no thought even—except my love for her.

In serving her like this, or in cleaning at her house, I would always feel a sense of "not doing"—that the action was taking place, but "I" wasn't doing it. There was an effortlessness with these actions, and a bliss and a freedom which I'd rarely experienced in my life. Though I sensed that this kind of domestic service was probably not the way Truth would ultimately use me—for a domestic goddess I most definitely was not—I felt irresistibly drawn to serve her in these ways throughout that summer. Looking back on this time it's clear how this devotional activity was helpful in melting the resistance and the shyness, which in turn opened me more and more to her love, and to the Truth and Grace that radiated from this lineage so purely through her.

I met a friend during this time named Jim who was crazy-in-love with Gangaji and had no inhibitions about sharing with me his devotional experiences as well as his outrageous love letters to her. He also shared a couple of her letters to him, because he felt they were meant for me also. He told me that she had once said to him, "The reason you feel this way is because you have no resistance to my love for you." These words affected me deeply, because they exposed the fact that I did still have resistance. Sometimes I could almost feel an intense, unbridled torrent of love being showered upon me, and yet a sense that I was unable to receive it fully. There were still subtle resistances that kept parts of me closed off. Looking back on that summer, I can see that Papaji played a vital role in removing these resistances and in keeping me open to Gangaji. Besides the time in Santa Fe, when his presence had filled my room the night before I sang for her the first time, there was another important dream/vision of Papaji which came to me that summer.

In the dream I was sitting on the floor beside Gangaji. Papaji was sitting in a chair in front of us. I couldn't see him very well, just his feet actually, because I was intently focused on Gangaji—and she was intently focused on him. After a while Gangaji turned and hugged me. I felt resistance arising at first and embarrassment. Then suddenly I found myself surrendering to that embrace, quite completely. And in that surrender, a gigantic wave of resistance departed.

When I awoke in the early morning, my heart was expanded as it never had been before. It felt open, physically open, and free. As I sat in silence for a while, it seemed my heart exploded like a supernova, exploding in love for all the universe. For several days after that I found I was in love with everything I saw—trees, squirrels, mountains, everything. I told Gangaji about the dream in a small satsang soon afterward and she confirmed that it was a true dream. When I thanked her for it she told me to thank Papaji. "This is *his* Grace," she said. So I wrote him a letter and told him of the dream and thanked him for keeping me open to my teacher's Love and Grace. For I could see now that this was the role he was playing in this Leela, and it is the role he continues to play.

More than a week went by without Gangaji asking me to sing again. Then, around the beginning of August, there was a special outdoor satsang up on Flagstaff mountain above Boulder. Gangaji was sitting in front of us on a futon chair atop an ancient slab of rock with a beautiful blue Colorado sky behind her and the jagged mountains looming all around. The evening was warm and clear with a light cool breeze wafting through the pines. There were only two letters on the futon that night. Mine was the second one she picked up. I had not signed my name to the letter, but had signed it "Nobody at all." Since I had typed it on my computer I felt certain, as Gangaji began reading it, that I was going to get away with remaining anonymous.

In the letter I reported to her what I'd been experiencing recently. I told her that I had become aware of a fulfillment, deep inside, which now seemed like it had always been there:

> . . . and that the so-called personal needs and wants that had structured my life for some time now had been sort of "made up"—not real at all.
>
> There is a sort of emptiness with this, but it is not an uncomfortable emptiness. It is a deep peace, an expanded-ness, and a feeling of being very relaxed. In this relaxed-ness, I feel "stuff" (that has been held in the body and mind) coming unhinged, but this does not overshadow the fulfillment and peace, even though it is quite strong sometimes. I simply watch it arise, burn, and fade.
>
> And it seems like there should be this question, "Well, my life is only half over and what is going to structure it now?"

She looked up at this point and breathed a deep sigh of contentment and joy.

> *Oh yes. Yes, lucky life, that at some point—half over or even the last breath before the life-form is finished—at SOME point this declaration of fulfillment can be realized. And then yes, the next, "Now, what to do with this life?" Very beautiful. Its personal lack of fulfillment is realized to be "made up." And in that realization, fulfillment overflows. Now, what about this life?*

As she continued reading, I was still pretty sure she had no idea who the letter was from. But I didn't mind her knowing any more. Some kind of nervousness about that was dropping away as I watched her, looking incredibly beautiful against the evening sky.

> But I don't really have a question. Not now anyway. A few weeks ago, you spoke about a "vigilance" which is necessary at a certain point in one's awakening—a vigilance with regard to the arising of desire; and the surrender, moment by moment of all desires, even the desire of not wanting the desire to arise. Just this vigilance of remaining totally unmoved in That which one is. Then you said all phenomena, all desires, all Leela arises to challenge this immovability, and if met fully, serves to drive the realization deeper. At the time you spoke about this, I wasn't quite ready to take it in fully. Now I see how profound it is. And how this is the challenge now.
>
> Since Estes Park, I have known that the rest of my life would be to serve this Truth. And there was a time when I was impatient to know how this Truth was going to use me. Now I realize I will *never* know how it is going to use me.

She looked over at me then and said:

> *That's right! You have to look backwards to see how.*

I realized then that she knew who the "nobody" was who had written the letter.

From moment to moment, I will never know. It is just this continual surrender to That which is unknown, unmeasured, uncaptured by time or by a "plan." The mind finds this a little scary. But it seems clear now that what will happen to my life is not my choice—or even the Truth's choice—but the choice of this Divine Play. And the challenge is to remain unmoving in that play. Is this right?

She looked up at the mountains, hesitating for just a fraction of a second, then said:

What happens, in terms of the circumstances of this life, this is somehow fore-ordained—by past desires, by present desires, by genetics, by what happens to the earth, by what happens to the person sitting next to you. But how you meet what happens—this is where choice is. And if you meet whatever happens in surrender to Truth, then realization can only be revealed to be deeper and deeper. And then this Divine Play is realized not to be separate from Truth. Then your life-form in this Divine Play is not separate from Truth—regardless of circumstances. Regardless of fame and fortune, or lack of fame, lack of fortune—regardless. This is the victory. This is the mastery—not over life. But as Life. Where no circumstance disturbs That.

She continued reading:

I used to wonder how you could answer every question in satsang so perfectly. Now I see—it's because you don't move. You absolutely don't move. And when I saw this immovable aspect of you, I loved it. It's so beautiful. And it became my resolve to be as absolutely unmoving as you are—to realize that in my Self.

She paused for a moment, and I thought she was pleased with my resolve. But I also became aware, with a slight tremor of apprehension, that once again I had made a declaration to her and to the universe which would surely be tested. She read on:

> It's been three months since meeting you, and the grace, the love, the gratitude just keeps deepening. Being in satsang with you is the most precious gift of this lifetime—of any lifetime. I have felt Ramana's hand in this gift, often seeing his face in meditation, or his whole form in vision, like some ancient friend calling me home. I believe now that it was he who answered my prayer to the universe for a teacher. I asked specifically for a *Westerner* . . .

Here she dissolved into laughter, then looked over at me, still laughing, and pointed accusingly:

So YOU'RE why I have to wear this western outfit, this western body.

Continuing with the letter again:

. . . who was *living the infinite,* and who was *nearby.*

She looked up at me and said:

Yes. Very close.

These were the most beautiful words she had ever spoken to me. Barriers that were still lurking around my heart shattered as she gave me the most loving, all-embracing glance. In that moment I felt, once again, no separation whatsoever. She continued reading:

> These were my three requests. It didn't take long to see that you were that teacher—even more perfectly manifested than I could have imagined or hoped for. I thank Ramana every day for this gift. Some weeks ago I wrote to Papaji and thanked him too—for sending the Ganges to flow in America.
>
> I never know how to thank you. Whatever I say or write or sing or do always seems so inadequate. There is a beautiful Sanskrit verse that goes . . .

She stopped and laughed again, and looked up at me playfully.

Oh, but you know, I can't pronounce these Sanskrit words. I'm a "Westerner".

She asked me if I could pronounce them. I nodded, yes. She asked me if I would sing them. Without hesitation I nodded again.

Oh, good. Let's have the microphone to this "nobody at all" wearing this name "Amber."

I sang the verse a cappella, with no guitar, like I'd told her a couple of weeks before I could never do. I was not nervous. Everything felt huge and one, without separation. I was drowning once again in the River Ganga. She had me sing the little verse three times. The third time I looked directly into her eyes while I sang it, which I'd never been able to do before. Then she read out the English translation:

The only gift I can give, my Lord, is this surrender.

She smiled and seemed pleased, then said:

This is the only thing required. The only thing asked for.

The sun had set by then and a deep blue twilight was glowing magnificently in the sky behind her and on the mountains above. She seemed ecstatic that night, and very happy with the radiance she saw glowing from each face. At one point she said:

What a beautiful time of day. Do you know why we like this time of day? Because we can see distinctions start to fade. And in that, distinctions are beautiful—as they are fading. And as distinctions fade, this Light shines even brighter. Trust this Light. It exists in the core of all Being. Recognize this Light as your own Self. And it is the same Self that exists in the core of all Being. From pine needle, insect, animal,

*human, planet, sun—same Light at the core. It's the Light of
peace.*

*First recognize this. Then you delight even in distinc-
tions. In the world we have recognized distinctions and overlooked this. And you know the result of that. You can discover the result of that a hundred times in your day. First—
this Light, that which makes no distinction. Then celebrate
distinctions—as coming from That.* **

A musician named Stephen raised his hand and said he'd
written a new song which was very relevant to what she'd been
speaking about that night. She said:

Oh good. Will you sing it? Did you bring your guitar?

Stephen said, "No, but Amber brought hers." He had
asked me before the satsang if he could use my guitar, in case
the impulse to sing arose, and I had told him he could.
Gangaji said:

Very good, because I wanted Amber to sing a song too.

After Stephen sang, Gangaji took a couple more questions
and then asked me to sing "Eternal Friend." The tape I'd made
for her hadn't come out, she told me, so she wanted me to play
that particular song. Without any nervousness, without any
hesitation, I sang the song which I had once felt was far too
intimate to ever sing in public. All my old hang-ups about it
were gone, melted into the hugeness and love that enfolded me,
Gangaji, everything. The surrender was to That, to her, not to
the mind-stuff that told me I couldn't do it. The intimacy issue
about that song dissolved away in the closeness I felt with her
that night, the absolute absence of any separation.

She'd drawn me deeper into her heart. At least, that's
what it felt like. Yet I sensed that wasn't quite the truth.
Gangaji had taken me completely into her heart the first
time we'd met. It was only my resistance and mind-created barriers that prevented me from opening fully to it—my

shyness, my fear of being vulnerable, my habit of hiding, my wanting to stay in control. But now it was clear—how can there be any fear of intimacy with one's own Self? It's absurd.

As I lay in bed that night, an ecstatic bliss and love pulsated through my being. Awareness was too huge all night to be overtaken by sleep. Around midnight Gangaji came to me in a vision. (I call it a vision rather than a dream because I wasn't actually asleep, but awareness was deeper than waking consciousness.) It was one of the most tender and intimate experiences I'd had with her. And I apologize that I cannot describe it in words. It was far too close. But I can say that it was clear to me that she was removing very specific resistances and blocks which I must have still been harboring. Some of this removing was physically painful, but the love and tenderness with which she did this filled me with awe and the most unspeakable gratitude, annihilating me even more thoroughly in this unfathomable Love.

These kinds of visions of her, where she would appear vividly in subtle physical form to remove resistance, happened periodically all through the summer. Sometimes she would even heal some physical problem. For example, I once developed a rash, which initially was caused by an insect bite. The rash began to spread, perhaps because of the heat of that summer, and eventually got worse and worse. I tried natural herbal medicine, I tried the harshest allopathic medicine, and still nothing seemed to help. It spread and got worse and became so uncomfortable that I thought I might have to see a doctor about it, which for me is a last-resort tactic. Then, one night, Gangaji came to me in a vision. It was mostly a teaching vision, but just as she dissolved back into the ethers, she reached out and lightly touched the troubled area—and that was the end of the rash.

This was not the most miraculous of the healings that took place. But the details of these experiences are not so important. The importance of the visions lay in their use by Self to clear away any obstacles to this deepening, to smooth the way for Its own unfolding, and to connect me ever more closely with my

Gangaji and Amber

Photo courtesy of Maitri Robbins

teacher. The form that the vision of her would take—as guru, as healer, as friend, as mother, as lover, or even once as a young Buddha—was always perfect for the particular resistance being dealt with at the time.

I knew, too, that the visions were my own Self appearing as Gangaji. Sometimes the vision of Gangaji's form would even fade into an appearance like my own. However, it became clear that there *is* no difference—Gangaji and my own Self are one.

Continually I was amazed and astounded by the mystery and magnitude of what was taking place. My resistance was being burned to ashes by this intense, "closer than breath" relationship with my own Self as Gangaji. Yet it took a long time, months, before I was able to relate any of this to her. Finally, in December, I wrote her a letter describing for the first time some of the visions I'd been having and expressing my awe and gratitude in this way:

> How mysterious and beautiful that one human being could do this for another—to appear as one's own infinite Self, giving form and personality to that which was too abstract for the person to recognize otherwise.

Regarding the healing aspect of the visions, I told her:

> I would never have *asked* you for anything like this.
> Not after all you have given me. Yet you are there for me,
> always, in every way.

And so, though initially I struggled with, and questioned the appropriateness of, this intense attachment to Gangaji, gradually it became apparent that the attachment was very important. It was being used by Self, in the most intimate and subtle ways to reveal Itself to Itself for Itself as Itself—deeper and deeper.

Attachment to the teacher is often misunderstood, especially in the West. It can be mistaken for something personal and, like anything else, taken into the mind as some "thing." At first, I constantly made this error. But a true teacher will not let you rest in such mistakes, will not let you rest in the mind anywhere. In a video of an early satsang in India, Gangaji gives a beautiful exposition of this attachment to the teacher and clarifies certain misunderstandings that can arise regarding it. During the satsang, which took place at Papaji's house in Lucknow, a man asked the question, "What do you do with your attachment to the physical form [of the guru]? It can be a trap."

Gangaji replied:

> *It seems to me there's no trap in the attachment to the physical form of Papaji—unless you expect that form to behave in a certain manner, like, "not die," or "look at you right now," then there's a problem. But the attachment to the form is blissful. It's only when there's an attachment to somehow controlling this form that problems arise.*
>
> *If you can just be attached in surrender to this form, then what can be wrong?*
>
> *People ask me this a lot about Papaji, and maybe other gurus they've had. They say, "Oh, I'm so attached to the guru," or "I'm attached to the Buddha . . . I need to kill the Buddha." And there's a very big misunderstanding that has come out of this. Of course, I understand this concept of, "If you meet the Buddha on the road, kill him." This means, if you*

170

meet a concept of the Buddha, kill it. You meet the Buddha, you prostrate—and let the Buddha kill you! [laughter]

So this attachment to his form is no problem. The attachment to your idea of what or how this form should be, this is the same old problem, isn't it?—that you've then brought to this meeting with truth.

I don't know if it's true for Asians or Indians, but in my experience it seems very true for Westerners to have a kind of struggle with this independence and dependence—this fear of dependence and this seeking independence—just out of a misunderstanding of the truth of oneself in aloneness.

So, if it's an emotional kind of dependence, this is still seeking for some kind of control. Control of the attachment. Some kind of relationship—"if I'm dependent enough, I'll have control." And this independence is some kind of "well, now I don't need anything. Now I've got it." Both of those are just traps of the mind.

But this attachment, with no possibility of severance, this has nothing to do with dependence or independence. And nothing to do with I am dependent or I am independent, or I need to be independent.

Be attached. Be totally attached. Be so attached there's no possibility of separation. Look at Sri Ramana, he was totally attached to Arunachala. He went there and never left. This is attachment. Has Poonjaji ever left his master? Never. This is attachment.

I'm very attached to his form. I'm very happily attached to his form. Therefore, I have to recognize his form everywhere. And to recognize his form in his form, hah! is double, triple bliss. *

Attachment to the master cannot be grasped by the mind. If the mind tries to grasp it, it will come up with the usual "pairs of opposites"—in this case dependence and independence. Or there will be a fear of losing one's power, of losing control. There is a certain terror, a maddening frustration, and an utter vulnerability that must be faced in the uncontrollableness of the guru, of a true teacher. People who loudly resist and even malign this attachment to a teacher are often those who cling instead to some image they can control, some "teacher" they can control. Ironically, their lives filled with attachment, they resist the one attachment that ends all attachment.

14

DEEPENING

*A*s the summer satsang sessions in Boulder were drawing to a close and fall was approaching, I realized that Gangaji would be leaving Boulder soon and that she was not scheduled to return for seven months. This prospect was terrifying. Since my meeting with her in late April, I had never been physically apart from her for more than a few days at a time. My husband was still in graduate school and we were on a tight financial budget, so it was unlikely that he would send me to California, and even more unlikely that he would send me to Hawaii, where Gangaji would be giving the winter series of satsangs. So I began steeling myself for the shock of separation.

After formal satsang ended in late August I attended another retreat with Gangaji in Crestone, Colorado, which was emotionally very turbulent for me. All my attachment to being near Gangaji in physical form, all my fear of being separated from her, kept arising. Intellectually I understood that the attachment I was hanging onto was unreal. I told myself that it was the *phenomenon* of Gangaji that I was clinging to, especially her form and my proximity to it. It was clear that this attachment was the same old clinging to phenomena, clinging to the changing aspects of experience. All forms come and go, and will one day be finished altogether. I might as well have been attached to a car or a lover or a sum of money. Clinging to *any* phenomenon is bondage.

In this way I spent much of the retreat trying to fully "meet" this desire to be near her; and there were a lot of tears. A beautiful little stream ran through the complex where we were staying, and I had found a secret spot on its banks, hidden in a grove of evergreens, where I would sit for hours giving everything to the stream. I was not sleeping much and would sit for long hours in the night alone in the living room of the townhouse I shared with Shivaya Ma and Jeanne and two others.

I had brought my guitar to the retreat, but because of my gloomy mood I didn't feel at all like singing, so I didn't bring it to satsang. I figured that because it was a silent retreat anyway, probably Gangaji wouldn't ask me to sing. But one evening I remembered a song I'd written long ago, which I had hardly ever shared with anyone. It was a private meditation, a secret sutra which I felt few people would appreciate. There had always been a sense that I'd written it for someone special, someone I hadn't even met yet. Now it was clear I'd written it for Gangaji.

That night I sat by the stream and wrote it out from memory on a piece of paper and enclosed a short note with it. The next morning in satsang I put it up on Gangaji's couch, carefully positioning it on the bottom of the stack of letters, in order to reduce the chances that she would actually read it in front of the group.

When Gangaji came into satsang that day, she was wearing an outfit I'd never seen before. It was a blue silk pants and vest outfit. I found myself admiring it—a lot. This was unusual, for I normally don't think much about clothes—hers, mine, or anyone else's. Actually I became mildly irritated with myself because I couldn't stop thinking about this cute outfit.

Early in the satsang, Gangaji picked up my letter from the bottom of the pile—so much for that tactic—and began to read:

> Dearest Beloved Perfect Teacher of my Heart:
>
> Enclosed is a song written for you. It arose from this question of why does the "One" play with Itself in this way—in the appearance of diversity? I don't know if it's all correct, but feel free to edit.

Gangaji laughed and said:

She knows my habits.

> I would be happy to sing it sometime, if it's appropriate on this silent retreat, (maybe at the end) if you . . .

She stopped and looked up.

Well, why not now? Where are you, Amber?

I swallowed hard as I raised my hand, for I had not brought my guitar. She then asked me if I'd brought it. I told her it was in my room. She asked me if I could sing it anyway. With surprisingly little hesitation I said I would. So I sang the whole thing a cappella; I made a few mistakes, but they didn't matter because I felt she was liking the song, which goes like this:

Still lies the sea of unbounded Pure Consciousness
Shining, abiding in silent repose
Rapt in the joy of its infinite only-ness
A motionless ocean entirely alone
But how can the One ever see
Its own boundlessness,
For the seen and the seer are two?

Hark, for a sound softly stirs in the silentness
Oh there is no sweetness as sweet as that sound
The spark and the seed and the source of createdness
With wholeness in motion creation is found
Moved by the longing to know its own knowingness
The known and the knower are born

Now It waits for a voice
That's awake to its timelessness
For thrilling and filling the stillness with sound
And it longs for a heart
That can move in its tenderness
For melting and sending the sweetness around
On the watch for an eye to perceive its pure goldenness
And an ear that can hear silence sing

The sound that began now is found as a symphony
Swinging and ringing in rhythm Divine
Measured in the rhymes of its radiant melody
Creation unfolds in the sequence of time
Yet hung in the heart of its boundless diversity
Pure Consciousness stays only ONE.

She sat with her eyes closed for a long time after I'd finished. When she finally opened her eyes, she immediately put her palms together and said *Om Shanti,* ending the satsang quite early. As she was getting up to go, she looked over at me. I held out the copy of the song, which she had passed to me to use while I sang, silently asking her if she wanted it back. She held out her hand, indicating that she did, so I passed it up to her and then she left.

That evening I found about twenty notes on the bulletin board for me, thanking me for the beautiful song and asking me if I had a tape or CD of my songs. It was shortly after this that the idea emerged to put together some of my songs in an album and donate the proceeds to the Foundation. This idea came to me when the possibility of purchasing a retreat center there in Crestone was being discussed. A piece of land had been located that Gangaji liked and some of us were invited to go up and see it one morning. Everyone was thinking of ways to help purchase it, and I felt this musical album was one way I could make a contribution.

I happened to mention the idea to Shivaya Ma. A couple of days later, Shivaya Ma told me she had inadvertently mentioned it to Gangaji and that Gangaji had really liked the idea. Encouraged by Gangaji's response, I made a resolve to work on the album as soon as I returned to Boulder.

Near the end of the retreat, Gangaji read a letter from a man named Foster which evoked a profound response:

> Dearest Gangaji,
> I do not know who I am, what I am doing, or where I am going. Most of the time I think I know all kinds of things. And that I am capable of doing so many kinds of things. But in truth, I know nothing. And I cannot even do the simplest thing like be silent, be still. I sometimes long to lay myself bare, to let go completely of all the illusions I cling to, to be free at last. Is it possible for me to do this when I don't have one hundred percent willingness?

Gangaji looked up at us with a seriousness that shook something deep inside me.

No, it is not possible. Without one hundred percent willingness, there's no possibility of recognizing one hundred percent of who you are. Of course, with ninety percent willingness you will have explosions of bliss and truth. But there will remain some fragmentation that will be a denial of that explosion, some attempt to cling to Self-denial.

I am happy to disillusion you of the idea that you can halfway wake up to who you are and be free. That you can ninety percent wake up. The tide of conditioning is very large, make no mistake about that. It is encoded in the genetic structure of your body. It informs every instinct, every impulse, every thought, every emotion. It is tremendous.

However, it is no match whatsoever for one hundred percent willingness to awaken. All momentum is leveled in that. One hundred percent is the ease. Anything less, and there's difficulty—ten percent difficulty, fifty percent difficulty, one hundred percent difficulty.

This may seem to be a rude truth. It is a glorious truth. At last you recognize—if I let go, I let go. And in that the mind stills, naturally.

Better to perceive or sense that you are not one hundred percent willing to awaken to the truth of who you are than to deny it, to walk around saying, "oh, I am, I am, I am, 'cause I'm supposed to be." Because somebody said you should be one hundred percent.

It is crucial to see where you withhold simple willingness to be. When you can state that possibly you aren't one hundred percent willing, then you can ask, "What am I holding onto? And what do I imagine that will give me, or has given me, or might give me?"

Many times in the coming weeks I would ask myself these questions. They were words of Self-inquiry, words that could stop the mind and throw the awareness back onto Itself, deeper into the stillness of my own Being, which needs *nothing*.

Gangaji went on to speak about the ruthless "letting go" that is required to wake up one hundred percent.

*One hundred percent lose everything, and then see—what
has been lost? You can never see this, you can never know this,
truly, with conviction, until you have lost everything—consciously lost everything. You do lose everything every night
when you drop into sleep, of course. But we're speaking of the
waking state. You know when you drop into sleep, you cannot
sleep unless you one hundred percent drop everything.*

*Of course people come to the spiritual search from some
egoic idea of what they will get. This is the way it starts. It's
the positive aspect of ego. "I'm tired of suffering. I want to
be happy. I hear there's happiness over there in the spiritual
camp." [laughter] "I'll go get some. Maybe I'll get a lot."
That's all right. That's the positive aspect of ego. That's
actually a very developed ego, a functioning, integrated ego—
"I want to be happy."*

*What a surprise to realize—to be happy, you let go of
everything. You don't take anything. What a surprise. To
receive true happiness, you stop trying to GET anything.*

*Well, of course, it's unbelievable at first, so you still try to
get. "Yeah, yeah, I know that's what they say, but . . . I know,
yeah." [laughter] You know these deals, don't you?*

There was a feeling in the room of stark recognition.
Everyone had started out on the spiritual quest thinking they
were going to get something. I searched within myself, "What
am I still trying to get?"

*Trying-to-get takes innumerable forms. "Well, I'll get
something by dressing like the Buddha dressed," or, "I'll get
something by wearing all white," or, "I'll get something by
smiling, or gazing, or serving." But you continually come right
into the dead end of, "Why haven't I gotten it? I've been good.
I did right. I donated." [laughter] "Why haven't I gotten happiness?" You cannot get happiness by getting anything. You
get moments of pleasure, obviously. You can have the experience of temporary happiness, certainly. But to recognize YOU
ARE THAT WHICH IS HAPPINESS you have to give up
everything. One hundred percent. I'm not speaking of giving*

up your car or giving up your hair. [laughter] Or your job, or your wife, or your husband. Those are nothing. I'm speaking of giving up EVERYTHING.

She was quiet for a moment, just looking around the room into the still faces as the truth of her words sank in.

You know how long it takes?

An intense silence followed for some moments. Then she said quietly:

Less than an instant.

Her words reverberated in the silence. Some people around me seemed to heave a sigh of deep, unimaginable relief.

I'm not speaking of some protracted struggle where each day you give up something else. In that protracted struggle, each day that you give up something else you also pick up something else. No, I mean less than an instant. Not taking on, "Oh yes, that sounds good, perhaps I will try that some day." Then you have just taken on something else. Even saying to yourself, "Gangaji says I should do that. I'll consider that," is taking on something else. Give up Gangaji, give up these words, give up any interpretation.

Again, there was a long silence in the room. I felt ancient impulses of grasping being dislodged, being exposed.

Less than an instant. Recognize your true face, one hundred percent, and more. Then it is quite clear when you begin to "pick up." Then it is quite obvious how simple giving up is, and how difficult and complicated and protracted picking up is. It's just obvious. It's nothing you have to learn, nothing you have to remember, nothing you have to affirm. It's simply obvious.

We have the choice to choose the truth or deny the truth. Unfortunately we have denied the truth for a very long time. And so we feel choiceless. We feel, "Well, it just happens." But I don't accept that. I know that to be a lie. Denial does not just happen. It may appear from past denyings, but in that instant of recognizing "give it up," then there is choice. True choice. The choice to surrender, or the choice to not surrender. The choice to attempt to control—by either rejecting or trying to get—or the choice to give it up.

Even if you are trying to get a still mind, this is the same old trying-to-get. And finally you recognize, it just doesn't work. Mind is further agitated by trying to get stillness.

Stillness is Presence of Being. You ARE Presence of Being. Receive your Self. Drink your Self. Be nourished by your Self—whether you find this within some sense of a center, or without in the mountains, the sky, the clouds, the grass. Be nourished by That. And then, begin your exploration of That. Explore your Self.

I'm not suggesting you explore your thoughts. You have explored your thoughts. They have taken you as far as they can take you. And it's that same circle, that wheel. Not your emotions, not your feelings, not your sensations, not your circumstances. Explore your SELF. That which is before, during, and after all objects of awareness, all phenomena, all emotions, all circumstances. THAT. That is the Presence of Being.

Some people have referred to it as emptiness. But if you imagine emptiness, it is not that. Some people have referred to it as fullness. If you think you know what fullness is, not that. Some people have walked around saying, "Not this, not that, not this, not that." It's also not that. [laughter] If you think it is some philosophy you must follow, no. If you think it is some philosophy you must not follow, no. Much closer. If you think it is personal, no. Much closer. If you think it is impersonal, no. Much more beyond.

So, yes, it takes one hundred percent. It takes everything you have collected. It takes everything you have.

> *It takes it <u>anyway</u>. You understand that? It takes it any-*
> *way! The opportunity is to give it consciously, now, before*
> *the body drops. This is the secret.* *

An important disillusionment took place during that satsang which is difficult to describe in words. In essence, it was
a deep recognition: nothing can give you who you already are.
Nothing!

In September, Gangaji stayed in Boulder the whole month.
There were a couple of small satsangs for volunteers, but mostly she rested during this time. I cooked for her a few times and
cleaned every week. But the prospect of her leaving Boulder
loomed heavily over my heart. I had no idea what it would be
like. I wanted to be mature about it and not act like a child
being ripped from its mother's arms, but as the time of her
departure drew near, that was exactly how I felt.

As the last satsang was approaching, the pain in my heart
became unbearable. It had been the most beautiful, the most
profound summer of my life, and I could not imagine what it
would be like in Boulder without Gangaji. Everything would
surely be meaningless, ordinary, mundane, absurd. On some
level, I believe I feared the loss of everything that had taken
place—the cutting of the identification with mind, the expansion of awareness, the bliss of serving her, the bliss of sitting in
satsang with her, the visions, everything.

Friends, seeing my depressed condition, tried to cheer me
up by offering to take me to the movies, for a walk, out to
lunch. But I was inconsolable. While I appreciated these offers
of help, I sensed that there was something important here to be
met, directly, without deflecting away from it with some pleas-
ant distraction. I didn't try to explain this to anyone—except
Shivaya Ma. I knew that here was one friend who would completely understand this longing. She had been with Gangaji for
four years, had lived and traveled with her, and had told me
stories of her own struggles with physical separation from her
beloved teacher. So, one night during the worst fire of this
pain, I had a long talk with Shivaya Ma. She verified what I

intuited to be true—this was not something to deflect away from. The challenge was not to try to "feel better," but to dive into the core of it and "let it have you."

That night, I sat alone with it all night long, and let it have me. It seemed like I would die from it. And I was willing to die. But the pain and fear would not subside. When finally I slept, in exhaustion and despair, Gangaji came to me in a vivid dream which flooded my awareness once again with the Truth that there is no possibility of separation. I wrote to her about this dream and gave her the letter during the last satsang before her departure—a small meeting at the Foundation for people who had helped put on satsang that summer in Boulder. The letter first described the intense longing and how it had begun in a small satsang the week before and then become unbearable:

> By the next day this pain had become very intense, physically intense, like a stake driven through my heart. I felt like I would die if I had to be separated from you in this way.
>
> Five different friends called me that day and wanted to cheer me up, wanted to take me out to lunch, for a hike, etc. Only one gave me the advice I took. She said, "Put your arms out like on a cross, and be crucified in it."

Gangaji looked up and smiled:

That's a true friend. A ruthless friend.

And I thought, yes, Shivaya Ma is definitely that—a true friend, a ruthless friend. She told me once, "I don't speak so strongly with most people. But somehow, with you, I find myself being as ruthless as I am with myself."

> So I sat with it all day and half the night, willing to die, wanting to die and be crucified, and still it continued horribly.
>
> Then, as I finally slept, you came to me in a dream. You were so loving, like a mother is with a young child— and I *was* a young child, being held and comforted. This image of you, as mother, is unusual for me, because I have mostly seen you as Guru, as Kali, usually ruthless, and always intense. But even in the dream I saw that this image

of you as loving mother was in truth my own Self appearing in this way.

The dream was filled with Grace, as though I was being bathed in it. Then, when I awoke, I still felt the Grace all around me and the love—and the intense pain in my heart was relieved.

I felt closer to you than I have ever felt, as if some great knot of separation had been untied in the Grace of that dream. And I knew more clearly than ever that you are my own True Self guiding me home in whatever ruthless or loving way I can best hear it.

Thank you, Dearest Beloved Gangaji, for reminding me that you are ever present, always *always* right here.

Gangaji looked up at me with a long loving glance that pierced deep into my soul. Then she held up the letter to the group and said:

<u>This</u> is the reality. The rest of it is the dream.

With a sweep of her hand, she took in the room and all of phenomenal existence, reminding us we are in truth *always* in the arms of the Beloved Self.

A few days later, the day before my birthday, Gangaji gave me the blue silk pants and vest outfit I had admired at the retreat. I had never told her or anyone else that I liked that outfit. But somehow, she knew. How could she not? She is my own Self.

15

THE BABY EAGLE

*G*angaji had one week left in Boulder, but there would be no more satsangs. Her husband, Eli Jaxon-Bear, was giving a workshop that week on the Enneagram System of Character Fixations. After the workshop he and Gangaji would both fly to Marin County, California, where the next session of satsangs would take place.

Originally I had no intention of taking the workshop. I do not particularly like workshops, especially those which deal with psychological/emotional subject matter. But I was curious enough to attend an introductory talk on the Wednesday night before the workshop was to begin. I knew nothing about the enneagram, except that I'd sometimes heard people around satsang discussing the different character fixations in the same way people discuss astrological signs. "Oh, I think he's a four." "No, he's definitely a nine." All I had been able to figure out from these conversations were that there were nine character types, called fixations, and it is important to find out which one you are. My friend Jim told me that when he was being considered as a possible roommate in a house the previous summer, he'd had to read a book on the enneagram and figure out what number he was before they would let him move into the house.

I was mildly familiar with Western astrology, Eastern jyotish astrology, and a few versions of numerology, and could not understand why another system of categorizing personalities would add any significant contribution to the quest for truth. Along these lines, I asked Eli during the introductory meeting, "What does learning which number you are have to do with awakening to the truth of your being?"

He answered by explaining that the character fixation is deeper than personality, and is actually a substratum of subtle strategies on which the personality is built. Even after a significant awakening, the character fixation can continue to arise, drawing one back into the mind and still coloring the expression of one's life, even coloring the relationship with the guru by the imagined needs of the fixation. He gave an example which uncannily described some of the neediness and attachment I was experiencing with Gangaji. I don't even remember what this example was; all I remember is that he nailed me so exactly that I began to laugh uncontrollably.

Seeing my breakthrough, Eli laughed delightedly and said, "Gotcha, huh?" I just kept laughing, and other people started to laugh too, and I couldn't stop. Something very deep that I'd been hanging onto was released in that laughing. I don't even know how to describe what it was. I just felt a letting go of something deep that had been held tightly before. And this experience impressed me enough to sign up for the five-day workshop.

Most of the participants were familiar faces from the group that had attended satsang all summer, and we began each session with a quiet sitting, just like in satsang. Eli began the workshop with a brief history of the enneagram. Its exact origins are unclear, but some adherents trace its beginnings to the Naqshbandi Brotherhood of the Sufis, and before that to a Mesopotamian brotherhood called the Sarmoun.*

Though the enneagram is often used superficially, simply to determine character types, much as Western astrology is used to determine personality types, Eli's presentation took it to a much deeper level—as a way of assisting in the awakening to Truth. In this light, the nine character fixations are seen as basic strategies a soul uses to hide from itself—by moving toward, moving away, or moving against. Each of the three basic strategies has three subsidiary versions—internal, external, and core—hence equalling nine fixations. Sitting in satsang with Gangaji over the previous five months, I had already seen the significance of "not moving." I could now understand the enneagram as delineating the three basic ways that this moving takes place. It didn't take long to see that "moving away" was the characteristic strategy I used. And it seemed to me that I was pretty "internal" about it, which translated into a "five" fixation on the enneagram.

As the workshop progressed, Eli went through all the nine fixations and plotted them on a chart with nine points. The strategy of "moving against" is called the anger point; characteristically, people on this point see problems as existing "out there," in the world or in others, and they have a tendency to try to fix things. The "moving away" strategy is called the fear point. People on this point are characteristically mental and spend a lot of energy keeping themselves safe from all kinds of imagined dangers. Their strategy is "protection," and in its most internal manifestation, even isolation. The "moving toward" strategy is called the image point; people on this point are characteristically emotional and have an insatiable need for love. Their strategy of life involves constantly seeking ways of getting love, keeping love, or lamenting its loss.

As Eli went through the nine fixations I saw how each one could be used to deflect the soul away from the true Self—by keeping oneself busily absorbed in the illusion that fulfillment was possible if one could just "fix enough problems," or "keep enough nasty stuff away," or "get enough love." I found all this very interesting and revealing, and enjoyed listening to Eli speak. He had a strong silent presence about him that remained very still, no matter what people threw at him during the session. I told him after one session, "I like watching the way you don't move."

Unlike Gangaji, however, who rarely let people go into long discussions about their problems, Eli patiently let everyone speak as long as they wanted—not only about their own problems, but their boyfriend's problems, and their ex-girlfriend's problems, and their ex-girlfriend's mother's problems, and on and on. It was the last thing in the world that interested me, and as the emoting revved up around day two, I began to tune out, began to wish I'd stuck to my accustomed habit of avoiding such workshops. I felt trapped there, listening to all these people going into the grisly details of their personal problems. My fixation was manifesting—I wanted to get away, isolate, protect myself from other people's emotional junk, as had been my habit throughout my life.

I complained to Eli after one of the sessions. "I hate this," I told him.

He said, "Hate what?"

I said, "All these people and their stupid problems."

He was quiet for a moment and just looked me in the eyes very deeply. Finally he asked, "How lovable are you?"

It was the last thing I expected him to say, and it stopped me for a moment. Finally I shrugged. "Pretty lovable, I guess."

He said, "Yes. You are love itself. Now, tomorrow, see if you can find that love in everyone's eyes as they are speaking."

Somehow this instruction shifted my attention. The next day, as people were speaking, no longer was I fixated on the unsavory problem they might be sharing. Behind that, deeper than that, I saw a profound love shining there in each person's eyes. Allowing my attention to be with the love, rather than on the stories they were telling, made the next few days of the workshop endurable.

But these were the last days before Gangaji's departure from Boulder, and as they ticked away the prospect of being separated from her hung over my heart like an ax, which made me whiny, emotionally volatile, and generally uninterested in everything. Eli was very patient with me, however, and simply smiled and patted me on the shoulder whenever I got into complaining about something.

At one point in the workshop Eli had us all close our eyes while he led us in a guided meditation. He told us to imagine a high mountaintop with an eagle's nest on top of a crag. Far below was a deep valley. In the nest lived a mother eagle with its baby. Each day the mother eagle would go off in search of food, and after a little while return to the nest to feed her baby.

One day, the mother didn't come back. As hours went by, alone and hungry the baby became anxious. Still the mother eagle didn't return. The baby's anxiety turned to fear. "Why hasn't she returned? I'll starve here, all by myself. Has she forgotten me?"

Just as the baby was becoming really terrified, the mother finally returned—with a mouse in her beak. But she didn't alight in the nest and push the food into the baby's mouth as she had always done before. Instead, she perched on the edge of the nest, just out of the baby's reach. From her beak the mouse dangled invitingly. The baby's hungry eyes fixed upon it; on wobbly legs, he lunged forward. The mother eagle suddenly flew up, just out of the baby's reach. The baby found himself standing on the edge of the nest as the mother circled around in the air.

The baby began squawking and complaining, confused and angry that his mother was being so cruel. Didn't she know how hungry he was? The mother swooped down close to the baby and he lunged again at the mouse dangling from her beak. Again, at the last moment, she glided out of his reach.

This time, the baby's lunge caused him to topple over the edge of the nest and he began to fall—down, down, down toward the valley below, squawking, crying, struggling. He was shocked that his mother could just let him drop like this. She had taken such good care of him all those weeks in the nest.

The mother eagle was circling above, but she did not interfere with the baby's fall. Down, down the baby eagle dropped, tumbling, squawking, screaming at his mother. The valley floor drew closer and closer. The baby became angrier and angrier with his mother. How could she do this to him?

Finally, anger turned to terror as the baby realized he was probably going to die. He glanced at the approaching valley floor. There was nothing to do but give in to his fate. At the last moment, he put his head into the fall and surrendered. As he did this, his wings relaxed and spontaneously stretched out. Miraculously, he began to glide. He was flying! He was free!

His mother now swooped down beside him. Together they soared up and up, high above the valley floor. Then she began to teach him how to ride the air currents and soar even higher.*

Eli asked us to open our eyes and then inquired what our experience had been. Immediately I began to laugh. He looked over at me and asked me to share my experience. I said, "I was the baby eagle. Gangaji was the mother eagle." Contracting my face into a pout I added, "And she's going to Marin and dropping me!"

188

The room erupted in laughter. Everyone probably thought I was real stupid and attached. But I didn't care what people thought. And besides, it was true. I felt like the baby eagle.

After Eli stopped laughing, he told a story from when he and Gangaji had first met Papaji. In this particular instance they were trying to convince Papaji to come back to Maui with them and live there and give satsang. They told Papaji that it would be much more comfortable in Maui, and being in the middle of the Pacific he would be accessible to both his Asian and American students.

Eli turned to me and said, "Papaji's reply to this was, 'The young tree can't grow very well in the shade of the big tree.'"

I took that in for a moment and realized, yes, it must have been necessary for Gangaji to be away from Papaji, surrounded by her own students, to blossom into the teacher she had now become. But I couldn't figure out why Eli was saying this to me. I was only a little sapling. Little saplings have to be protected by the shade of the big tree. Otherwise they might get scorched by the sun or eaten up by insects.

Somehow this little interchange caused me to feel even more hopeless than before about whether Gangaji was ever going to indulge me in this desire to be near her. Looking back on this time I can see that I had always held certain images in my mind of what it should look like to "be with one's master," what it should look like to be "totally accepted by one's teacher." And it looked like this: you are at her feet night and day, you meditate beside her, you sleep on her porch, you are available to serve her in every moment, you live with her, travel with her, etc.

I was extremely attached to these romantic images. Every time the outer relationship with Gangaji didn't seem like it was going to fit these images, I was tempted to feel I wasn't accepted, or that I was doing something wrong, or that she was not pleased with me, or that I was not progressing fast enough. Now I can see that all this anxiety was caused by holding onto these images in my mind. A true teacher will not indulge your mental images. A true teacher burns all images to ashes—the sublime ones along with the horrific ones. And this is exactly what Gangaji did.

On a video I later heard her say:

If it has a word, if it has an image, if it has a sensation, go deeper. *

And so, as Gangaji prepared to depart for Marin, I put my head into the fall and went deeper.

16

NON-ABIDANCE
IN THE MIND ANYWHERE

*I*n early October I experienced for the first time being physically apart from Gangaji and formal satsang. In spite of the fears I'd had of her physical absence, I was amazed at how close I felt to her in every moment, at how intensely the deepening still kept unfolding. About a week after Gangaji left for Marin, I wrote the following report to her in a letter:

> I see that you have not gone anywhere. You are right here, more present than ever, closer than ever. So strongly present that in the night sometimes, even though my body sleeps, my awareness remains awake—awake in this Presence of you. How ridiculous that I could have ever doubted this, given the experiences of the past five months. I guess I was just freaking out because since meeting you I have never been physically apart from you for more than a few days at a time. Thank you for letting me go through that awful longing while you were still physically present. By Tuesday when your form left [Boulder], I was feeling no separation at all.

In this letter I also told her for the first time about some of the visions that had taken place during and since Estes Park. I don't know why I couldn't tell her about these before. I suppose I was still trying to maintain some aloofness, some sense of privacy. But I could see now that there was no place for hiding in this relationship. With the teacher who has appeared as one's own Self, the intimacy is absolutely *unknown* in its depth. It is an ever-deepening closeness that cannot be understood by any mental, personal, or human concept. It is the revelation of Self to Self.

So I told her everything in that letter. As some of it has already been described in previous chapters, I won't reproduce the whole text. But the last few paragraphs were as follows:

> Twice you showed me the universe dissolving before my eyes. At least, that is how it seemed. The first time this happened, sometime in June, I drew back from it. But a couple of nights ago, it happened again and this time I could say, "Okay, let it dissolve," and there was the recognition, "I am not that which dissolves, but this awareness that it dissolves *in*." It was sort of like a kaleidoscope picture, breaking apart, and a feeling of everything dissolving. My awareness was huge and everywhere, one with this vast Presence which is you.
>
> Still, I miss you. Not a longing, but a sweet missing. It's such a mystery, this relationship where there are not really two to be related. The mind stops, just trying to think about it—this amazing Grace, this Love. I'm seeing now that you have given me everything, *everything*. And still it keeps unfolding, deepening. I can't help but give this to everyone I meet; whether spoken or unspoken, whether they can receive it or not—it is given, spontaneously it is given.
>
> Gangaji, precious Self, I am at your feet. No, that's too far away. I *am* your feet—and your hands and voice and eyes.
>
> Yours endlessly,
> *Amber*

Within a few days of sending this letter, in spite of my original assumption that traveling to Marin was out of the question, various circumstances conspired to make the trip possible. One of my sisters, who lives in the San Francisco Bay area, invited me to stay with her; air fares from Denver to San Francisco were at an all time low; and Toby agreed that if I wanted a chance to see Gangaji before she sequestered in Maui for the rest of the winter, I should go now.

The trip was effortless and perfect. I noticed that my mind remained very still, even in the midst of Bay Area traffic, which had grown infinitely worse since the time I had lived there nearly twenty years before. From the time I was twelve, my family had lived in the small suburban town of Orinda, nestled in the hills about ten miles east of Berkeley. Out of six children only one sister, Susan, still lived in that area with her own family.

The small college where satsang was being held was on the other side of the Bay, in San Rafael. The daily commute was a nightmare of intertwining freeways, tunnels, and bridges. But none of this affected me as I drove through it, making my way across the Bay every day. Inwardly, my experience was of no movement at all.

Because I used to live in the Bay Area, I naturally ran into a number of old friends at satsang, some of whom were from the previous spiritual group I'd been with. Even though I am not in general a particularly social being, I found myself effortlessly attending many gatherings of these old acquaintances. During these interactions satsang was usually being discussed, questioned, and compared with other kinds of spiritual teachings. I often found myself in the position of speaking with a confidence and authority that surprised people who had known me as a shy and quiet person. It even surprised me.

At one luncheon some old friends were discussing the teachings of a particular master they had been studying with. The discussion quickly turned esoteric, with questions arising regarding various levels of existence in the astral realms, what levels a person goes to if they die before enlightenment, and what levels they go to if they reach enlightenment prior to physical death, and so on. I listened without much interest in this discussion, until one man turned to me and asked what Gangaji had to say about where one goes after death.

Without even having to think about it I said, "'Where do you go after death?' This is the kind of question that leads into the mind. Now the question, 'Who dies?' that is the kind of question that stops the mind. That is the kind of question Gangaji is interested in." Everyone just stared at me for a moment. I don't know whether it stopped their minds, but it certainly stopped the conversation.

In this way I began to notice that satsang was coming out of my mouth, quite spontaneously; and also that I was being placed in situations where questions like these were being directed to me. There was an effortlessness in action and a surrender in each moment which seemed to miraculously deposit me in the right place at the right time.

During my stay in Marin I tried to express this new relationship with action to Gangaji in a letter, which she read in satsang at Dominican College on November 1, 1995.

> Beloved Gangaji, Precious Self:
>
> Something has been happening for the past week and a half which is difficult to describe in words. It is a shift in awareness of some kind. Action doesn't come from the same place anymore. There is not such a need to figure things out, but instead this deep trust that the next moment will reveal the next step. It's like walking on stepping stones that don't even exist until the next foot is set down. And there is less of a need to make decisions with the mind.
>
> Each moment is met freshly, freely, without "agenda" from the mind. And this gives each moment a quality of effortlessness, preciousness.
>
> Sometimes there is this sense of not moving, even though the body moves, and also of not being identified with this particular form so strongly—as though my awareness is not located just in this form.
>
> Sometimes anxious thoughts will arise like, "How can I keep this?" or "Is this going to last?"

Gangaji looked up at this point and said to the group:

> *Does this sound familiar? Everyone can relate to this, right?*

She continued reading.

> But then they are seen as only thoughts, and in this seeing are burned up.

> *Yes! That's seeing.*

> Constantly, hundreds of times a day, awareness is thrown back onto Itself, surrendering to this presence which loves me and is Love, and is you. I feel so totally immersed in your love, every second. And your love is not separate from my love anymore. So it is effortless to be

194

true to That, to be in service to That. And I feel 'That'
(you) using 'this' (me) all the time now.
    Is this which I'm experiencing now the ceasing of the
identification with the mind?

She just laughed softly here, and did not answer the question.
At first I was miffed because she had skipped over my question.
I wanted her to confirm it. But then I remembered that in sat-
sang the day before she had said:

*The answer comes first. The question is the doubt of the
answer.*

And I saw that this was true about this question. As I was writing that letter, wondering what these experiences pointed to,
the answer came to me: "The ceasing of the identification with
the mind." But it just seemed so fantastic, so profound that
such a thing could be happening to me, that instead of writing
it as a realization, I wrote it as a question! She was not about
to give this doubt any credence by even acknowledging it, so
she just went right on reading.

You have my heart, dearest Gangaji, and my head and
voice and eyes—everything. I *is* yours completely.

She looked up at me and asked if I would sing. I said yes
and got up to get my guitar which was in the back of the room.
I was sitting right in front that day and so I had to get up in
front of everyone and traverse the whole length of the hall to
get my guitar. Normally this circumstance would have caused
me a lot of anxiety and self-consciousness, especially since
Gangaji was talking about me as I was walking to the back.

See if you can hear this in her voice . . .

But I felt none of that. In fact, as I walked back to get my
guitar, I felt huge, like my awareness filled the hall, and that I
was not moving, or perhaps I could say "moving within
myself," and therefore it didn't feel like movement. There was

no longer any identification with myself as myself, but as a bigger Self that included everyone in that room.

She had me sing three songs that day. I didn't feel I played very well, because I couldn't quite get my guitar in proper tune; it was having a reaction to the very moist ocean air of San Rafael. But it didn't seem to matter. People cried and laughed and were very moved. After satsang many people asked me if I had a tape or CD of my music. I told them I was working on one and if they would leave me their names I'd get back in touch with them when it was available.

Around this time another one of my sisters, who lives in Oregon, decided to fly down to San Francisco because she wanted to meet Gangaji. Elaine is my closest sibling in age, and she had always been interested in all my spiritual pursuits—which most of the family viewed as unnecessary, crazy, and totally un-Christian. I had previously sent her the *River of Freedom* video and a few other videos and audios of satsang, which she had felt touched by. So she flew down for a long weekend and sat with me in several satsangs. She was very quiet and I wondered how she was receiving all this, but did not want to press her for a reaction. Eventually, as she was leaving to go back to Portland, she surprised me by saying, "I'm happy to have met Gangaji. She's so beautiful. But I feel that *you* are my teacher."

At first I thought this was an unfortunate choice, since I couldn't see myself ever being anywhere close to the perfect teacher that Gangaji is. But I remembered friends from Boulder who are Papaji devotees who can't understand why everyone isn't in love with Papaji like they are. It is a mystery who appears in your life as your own Self and reflects that so purely back at you. It is not the same for each person, and it cannot be understood or predicted by another. It is all a dance of Self anyway. All things, all beings are a reflection of one's own Self. But that first time you see this so powerfully, that first complete reflection in another, *that* is honored as teacher. Just like a baby duck at birth—whatever it first sees, human, dog, or mother duck, that image gets imprinted and that is what the baby follows from then on. For me a kind of imprinting, mysterious and divine, had happened when I first met Gangaji. I wrote her once:

> I found that this transcendent, undifferentiated ocean of Being took on a kind of "flavor"—which is you. This doesn't make sense, I know, because "That" is supposed to be without attributes, but I now experience "That" as sort of colored with you, with Gangaji—because you were my door into it.

Maybe for some it is a mountain, or for some a vision or a dream. For me it had to be a Westerner, one who was living the infinite and who was just like me. Who can say for another?

Before my sister flew back to Portland, I told her that I honored her choice of teacher, and assured her I would be there for her always, as her own Self.

One day after satsang I was surprised to see my friends from Santa Fe, Steven and Tanya. They had just returned from a trip to India, where they had gone to visit Papaji in Lucknow, and were passing through San Francisco on their way home. Enthusiastically, I asked them, "How was India?" As they responded, I could see that their faces were drawn and tired, and everything inside them seemed shattered. They informed me that they hadn't liked India at all, and that the whole trip had been pure hell. Papaji and Lucknow had not been remotely like what they had expected or hoped for. Papaji had mostly read out of a book while they were there; the readings being about sin and levels of hell. And some of Papaji's devotees had said things about Gangaji that were disrespectful.

As I stood there talking to them, listening to the grisly details of their trip, a strange thing happened. Some of this hell they'd experienced transmitted to me. I could feel vividly what they'd experienced. I found anger arising, and fear, and confusion, and hopelessness, and judgment—as if every awful thing still lurking in the depths of my consciousness was being dredged up by this conversation with them. Then something totally unexpected occurred. It was as though all this hell that was being experienced had no place to stick. The words that my friends were relating went deep into my brain, made all this mind-stuff arise, and then started taking everything apart. I felt a strong heat, which burned terribly—not just physically, but mentally—as if incinerating subtle habits of mind stored in the very cells of my brain and body. I saw the habitual tendency arise to try to take refuge in the mind, to try to analyze and evaluate this information, to compare it with things I'd heard before, with opinions, etc. But there was *nothing* it could cling to. Nowhere it could alight. Everything that arose in mind burned instantly; everything that arose was seen as only thought—meaningless shadows boxing with themselves, empty impressions, worthless images. And for the first time I understood directly what Papaji means by "non-abidance in the mind anywhere."

This intense burning and the shattering of mind lasted several days. After I returned to Boulder I wrote to Gangaji about the unusual way this particular experience of mind-annihilation had taken place:

> . . . You know like that kind of poison you put out for cockroaches that gets on their feet and then they track it back to their nest and it destroys the whole nest. It was like that with these words from Lucknow. They just penetrated into my mind and took it apart, every shelf of reality shattered. I found fear arising at first and confusion. Then, I watched the burning of this, and a deep letting go took place; then a disintegration of mind more complete than ever before. Then there was nowhere to abide, *anywhere*.
>
> The people who brought me these words from Lucknow had no idea what effect they were having. (They didn't even like Lucknow, and left after two days.) Then I saw how you, as Satguru, had taken this circumstance of words spoken in a brief conversation, and used it to drive me deeper, to shatter some remaining shelves of identification my mind was unconsciously clinging to. And in that seeing, surrender and trust deepened again.
>
> So I bow to these people who brought me these words, and to Papaji for his ruthlessness, and to you for pushing me deeper—from every direction. I used to cling to this subtle hope that you would not be as ruthless with me as Papaji is with you, because I didn't perceive myself to be as strong as you. But after this experience, somehow, I have

abandoned that hope of easiness and that perception of weakness. For I see that my relationship with you is not different from your relationship with him. It's the same relationship—Self to Self, Guru to disciple, lover to Beloved. It is the most precious, the most special, the most intimate relationship in creation, and the greatest blessing any life can hope for. Beyond hope, actually, beyond deserving—it is Divine Grace alone.

What had taken place was absolutely unfathomable. And it seemed like a test of some kind, because this hell that got transmitted was the sort of thing my mind might have gotten all caught up in analyzing and agitating over, maybe even six months before. But somehow, I couldn't follow that. I could no longer trust that. Trust had shifted to a deeper reality, beyond the world created by the mind. This shift in trust affected my life in ways that are difficult to describe. It became clear that what appeared to be happening, was not what was really happening. What appeared to be happening was only in mind. And when one does not abide in the mind, a deeper reality reveals itself to be that which all of appearance arises in.

But if it was a test, it was clear that "I" had not passed it. I had not done anything. I was simply, mysteriously, caught up in a rushing current, a raging river of Grace.

⁐

17

DIVINE LONGING

*S*oon after returning home from California I realized I was being called upon to speak satsang more and more often. Friends from many years before who had been seeking desperately, longing for the Truth, practicing for the Truth, had heard that I had "stopped" and began to come and inquire, either by phone or in person, about what had taken place for me.

Often people would begin their inquiry by saying, "I heard you're with a new master." At first I wasn't sure how to respond to this question. My experience was that there is only one master—Self. And this Self appears in many different forms at different times in one's life, according to how one can best open to it. Superficially it might have appeared that I was "with a new teacher," but I knew this appearance was only in mind. I knew that what I was at the feet of was the True Teacher, the Satguru, beyond all form, all mind, all appearance.

Though I'd had the great privilege and blessing to sit at the feet of several awakened beings in my life, beings who were obviously living examples of Truth, and though the desire had always been strong to surrender, to give my life completely to That, somehow, true surrender did not happen until I met Gangaji. The profound connection that took place then, which stopped the mind and triggered an explosion of Self-recognition, did not occur by individual will or choice. It was a surprise. It was Grace.

The particular form Self takes as final teacher, as the one who stops the search at last, who severs the identification with mind, is naturally honored above all other forms Self has taken. As mentioned earlier, the Infinite can actually take on the "flavor" of the personality who takes you through the door, such that there is perceived to be no difference between the teacher and That.* And so, yes, I am at Gangaji's feet. How could I be otherwise? For me she is the embodiment and totality of Truth. The Satguru.

Whether the form be human or divine or, as in Ramana's case, a holy mountain, the heart naturally explodes in gratitude for the form Satguru has mysteriously chosen. This gratitude can be found expressed in the ecstatic hymns of devotion recorded in the mystical literature of every age and every tradition around the world.

The mind will struggle mightily to resist the surrender of itself to Self. And that is all the guru/disciple relationship is about—mind surrendering to Self, illusion falling before Truth. It is not about persons "giving over their power" to other persons. It is the surrender of all that is personal to That which is before the person, after the person, beyond any person. During the enneagram workshop Eli said something that rang very true in this regard: "If you see the guru as separate, as other than Self, you have not seen the guru. You have seen a thought, an image in mind."

Gangaji clarifies this very beautifully in the following passage from her book, *You Are That!* Someone asks, "Are you a guru to us?" She replies:

> *I am your own Self. I am perceived as whatever you project onto me. You may see sister or mother or friend or guru. Someone even told me once that I was like a big food truck. A letter in satsang yesterday called me the mass murderer of the false self. And of course there are those who see me as the enemy.*
>
> *Whatever is projected onto me, I know to be just a projection. I am steady at the present knowing that I am your own Self.*
>
> *Project whatever you want as long as you hear what I am saying. If you have to call me guru to hear what I am saying, fine. So listen. The guru says, "I am your own Self. I am not separate." ***

Seeing that many of my friends were still caught up in a mental concept of "guru" as a separate person, and of "enlightenment" as something you attain, I would often feel frustrated, not knowing how to express to them what had been realized. For a while I felt a certain pressure. What should I say to them? How can I transmit this? How can I possibly describe what has happened? It's unspeakable. But as more of these satsang interactions took place I realized that there was no need to figure out the "right" thing to say. There was no need to say anything. Just being present, empty and present with no thought, was enough. If words came to me in that, then fine. They were the perfect words. But I let go of the idea that it had to look like something or sound any particular way. Satsang doesn't look like *anything*. Satsang is no "thing" at all. Satsang is stopping—stopping the following of the mind and resting in the Truth of one's Being.

In December I finally wrote to Gangaji and told her of one of these satsang experiences.

> Last Saturday I went for this job interview (because my husband said I have to get a job if I want to go to Maui). The lady is an acupuncturist in Boulder who also teaches some kind of classes on "taking control of your life." She needed a secretary. As we sat down together, I saw she was very stressed and tense. I thought, "This is a very disagreeable sort of person and I don't think I'd like working for her." She asked me what I could do. I said I'd been a freelance writer for the past twelve years.
>
> After some more job-related questions she asked me again, "What do you *really* do?" I thought she wanted a deeper answer so I said, "I like to speak about the Truth." She said she needed some Truth in her life right now and asked who is my teacher. I said "Gangaji." She had heard of you, and had seen a Papaji tape recently. I told her how you had stopped me and awakened me to who I am. As soon as I said this, she started to cry. She told me her life was a disaster. She didn't know if she wanted to be an acupuncturist anymore. She didn't want to do anything. Everything in her life was a lie—what she had tried to be, to do, to have.
>
> I just let her cry and speak. I didn't know what to say. She went on about how horrible everything was, how mean she had been lately—to everyone. She had thought about suicide (which was what her father had done).

I began to feel this was over my head. She needed help. She needed Satsang, but I didn't feel qualified. The thought arose, "I haven't been with Gangaji long enough." But immediately I heard your voice: "You've been with me always."

Finally she said, "I'm nobody, that's the problem. I *know* there's nobody in here, and it's so painful. I've tried to pretend there's somebody in here."

She was speaking Satsang. I found myself saying to her, "This is beautiful. This is Grace. You can't look for who you are in all these things anymore." She said, "But it's so empty. I feel like nothing." For a moment I saw my own Self in her, covered up with all this stuff, struggling to get free, and I felt love for her. I realized too that the room was filled with your Grace—this form was filled with your Grace.

I spent over an hour with her, having her go into the nothingness, encouraging her to let the story go. She kept trying to go back into the story, but when finally she seemed quiet, I asked her what was there. She said "It's God. It's just Spirit." And I asked her if there was any separation between herself and that Spirit. And she couldn't find any. Then I saw she was brighter. Her whole face and presence had changed.

Then she told me she had been praying all day for some kind of help, and couldn't believe it had come like this, so quickly, so unexpectedly. She called it a miracle. She said, "I don't know who you are, or where you came from, but I feel so grateful. No one has ever given me a gift like this."

I told her someone had given me a gift like this, and so I'm just passing it on. Figuring the interview was over, I gave her a tape of yours to listen to, and left her.

She called me that night to tell me her whole life was transformed and that she was closing her business down for a while and going to Maui in January to see you. A few days later she called to tell me she had reconciled with her fiance and that they have both committed themselves to this Truth. Her sixteen year-old son has caught fire too. A couple of days ago I dropped off some videos of you for them to see, and they were really glowing, transformed. It's so beautiful.

I felt transformed too. Floored, actually, because I saw how Self seeks itself out and draws itself to itself at just the right moment. This is what happened when I met you; at the exact right moment, Self penetrated time and shattered the illusion forever.

Satsang is all Self. Self hunting itself out and finding itself and calling itself home. And I am happy to live this life in surrender to That, in love with That, happy to be one of your field workers.

With ever deepening love and awe,

Amber

In spite of the fact that I did not get the job, Toby began to lean favorably toward the idea of my going to Maui. This took me by surprise, for by December I actually had given up on the idea of going. Truthfully, I felt a slight foreboding about it, similar to what I'd felt just prior to the Estes Park retreat. Analyzing this foreboding I found an intuitive sense that another level of "death" awaited me on Maui. And in seeing that, there was a letting go of the resistance and a willingness to embrace whatever awaited me; for as January drew near, Toby's sense of the rightness of my going grew stronger. He felt, from somewhere deep within, that it was important for me to go, even though the trip seemed financially irresponsible at the time.

This particular incident, of my going to Maui, marked a great shift in his perception of and connection to all that was taking place, and again shows the depth of his commitment to Truth. After I had departed for Maui, he wrote to Gangaji:

When Amber met you last Spring, her surrender was immediate and total. Not that this was produced by her desire or intention—it just happened. The rest of the summer was spent coming to terms with what had happened and letting go of any subconscious remnants of resistance. The totality of her surrender and of the re-orientation of her attention was so complete, one hundred percent, that it naturally had its effect on our marriage, in the form of some initial discomfort on my part. But over the course of 2-3 months as I came to understand that Amber had absolutely no choice in the matter, that her meeting with you and its consequences had grabbed her and borne her irresistibly along like some swift, rushing, all-powerful torrent, I realized that the only sensible option for me was to also stop resisting what had happened, and to "surrender to her surrender."

It has been my joy and privilege since then to support her in whatever ways I can. One small recent incident comes to mind. As Amber was preparing to leave for Maui, I found myself in the position of disbursing what are for us right now fairly large sums of money. Interestingly, I felt no resistance to this. My sense was that this was the intention of the universe, and that my role was merely that of a small conduit through which that unlimited ocean of abundance chose to flow in support of Amber. It was wonderful to just let go and let it happen, to be in tune with universal intent.

Thank you, Gangaji, for Amber. For all that she is now is due to your Grace and is a reflection of you. Thank you for your Grace in our lives. What great luck—to have been touched by That so magnificently, to have Amber in my life. I am blessed.

I thank you with all my heart.

Love always,

Toby

The trip to Maui was smooth and effortless. Although Toby was not able to attend because of his academic commitments, our friend John was going, and so we scheduled our flights together, rented a three bedroom house in Haiku with one other person, and shared a rental car.

The duration of the trip was to be three and a half weeks. As John and I planned the dates of our departure and return, we took care to schedule it so that we'd be able to attend the maximum number of satsangs. However, in spite of all our planning, we learned just before departing that the first three of the scheduled Maui satsangs would be cancelled. Gangaji's father had passed away, and she had flown back to Mississippi to be with her family for the funeral. It was too late to change our travel plans. So we arrived in Maui on a Friday, knowing that Gangaji was not due back on the Island until Monday or Tuesday.

I had never actually been to Hawaii, except for a couple of two-hour stop-overs in the Honolulu airport on my way to Thailand and the Philippines many years before. Maui was delightfully more rural than I'd imagined, and its beautiful shorelines and majestic mountains reminded me of the beauty of the Oregon coast where I had spent the summers of my childhood.

Shortly after arriving, John and I found out there was a get-together planned on Saturday at the satsang hall to celebrate Ramana's birthday. In spite of Gangaji's absence the celebration would go on as planned. So, the next afternoon we drove up to St. John's Church in Kula, where the satsangs would be held. I had brought my guitar because we had heard that the celebration would be mostly music, and I no longer felt so shy about sharing my songs.

When we arrived at the church a number of musicians were already assembled, tuning up their instruments, and songsheets were being passed out so that people could follow along with the singing. One of the songs on the sheet was one that Shivaya Ma had taught me last summer. It had a verse about Ramana and a verse about Papaji. The song was like a chant, with each verse being repeated many times so it was easy for a group to follow. Shivaya Ma had once told me that several musicians had attempted to write a verse for Gangaji, but as far as she knew, no one had come up with anything yet. During the Crestone retreat last summer I'd played around with the melody a little and the following words came to me which seemed to fit perfectly with the other verses of the song:

> Gangaji, River of Light,
> Ramana's silence
> Shines from your sight
> On me,
> Letting me see
> That I am free.

I felt the verse would be an appropriate addition to the celebration, because it included Gangaji in the song and also brought it back to Ramana in a nice way for the occasion. I approached the man who seemed to be in charge of the music and asked about adding this verse to the song. But he was not very interested in adding any verses to the song at this late stage. I shrugged and dropped the idea. I had also written another song about Ramana's awakening at age sixteen and his life in silence on the holy mountain Arunachala. It would have been perfect for the occasion—but, again, there was a strong feeling that the program had been set and there was not an openness to any changes or to any new musicians being added.

I settled into the role of spectator and into enjoying the music and the celebration, reflecting how ironic it was that when finally I'd gotten over my fear of singing in front of a group, I was met with a situation where my contribution was not welcomed. The mind gives up trying to figure out what the right course of action is. And that was exactly the lesson that Maui had in store for me.

After the festivities ended, John and I connected with the volunteers who were in charge of the satsang set-up crew and asked how we could help. Some of them knew that I had cooked for Gangaji, and although I was told she didn't need any cooks right then, the volunteer meals which were provided after every satsang did need a cook. At first I resisted this job, because I had never cooked for such a large number of people (about thirty) and also because I had not brought any of my recipes or cooking supplies. In addition, the place where John and I were staying had a tiny little kitchen and very limited culinary equipment. Eventually I agreed to bring the salad each day.

In the course of our interactions that first day with the Maui volunteers, we both picked up a subtle sense that we were not quite welcome. This puzzled us at first, and we decided to ignore it. Later we learned that there had been for some years a subtle rivalry between the Boulder group and the Maui group, having something to do with the fact that Maui had been the first place Gangaji had ever held satsang, in her living room, six years before. Because Satsang Foundation & Press, which now organized all Gangaji's activities, happened to be located in Boulder, there was some perception of competition with the Boulder contingency. This particular circumstance, however, turned out to be the perfect backdrop for the burning of mind-identification I was to experience on Maui.

The next few days passed slowly. Formal satsang was not scheduled to begin until Wednesday. I spent my time playing my guitar, checking out the local shops, and reading Gangaji's book, *You Are THAT!* On Sunday I joined a cleaning crew at Gangaji's house to help prepare for her return. It had been over two months since I'd seen Gangaji, the longest I'd been away from her physical presence, and so I looked forward to her return with a joy not unlike that of a lover too long separated. Before leaving her house that day, I left a poem on her desk as a welcome home:

Beloved Satguru:

I used to chase your butterflies
Impound your frogs and dragonflies
Such fascination unexplained
Yet I ran after them again, and again
Through the fields, under summer skies
I chased you in your bright disguise
Oh, if I had only known
The song of the crickets was really your own

You were the innocence in the animals' faces
You, the silence in my secret places
In family warmth and mother's care
I didn't see you hiding there

You are the lover, the love, and the loving
You are the goal of every kind of longing
And if but once a heart sees your Love
That heart becomes blind to any other love
And it sets the soul on a journey sublime
That ends in the ocean of Love Divine
Oh, if I had only known
Your voice has always been calling me home.

The next day we heard that Gangaji had returned to Maui and would take a few days rest before resuming the satsangs in Kula. Satsang would be cancelled until Saturday. My first reaction to this news arose only from a sense of protection for my teacher—happy and relieved that she was taking care of herself in this way and taking the time to rest. My second reaction, occurring about fifteen minutes later, was of devastating longing. I had only three and a half weeks to spend with her before another long three-month separation, for she was not scheduled to return to Boulder until late April. Now one of those precious weeks must be spent apart from her.

Tears burned in my eyes. A fiery heat singed my insides. It felt like I was being thrown against a wall, and I was absolutely inconsolable. John tried to encourage me to see some of the sights, get some exercise, relax. But I was not interested in anything. I had not come for anything but to sit at the feet of my Master. Even in the midst of my pain, the irony of it occurred to me—most people probably come to this beautiful place to enjoy the world, and yet there was a sense that I had come for the end of the world. And Gangaji was obliging, by throwing me into the hottest volcano on Maui—her own fire.

I sat in my room for several days, unable to eat, unable to sleep, unable to do anything but meet this torrent of longing that seemed like it would crush me. There were moments during that time when I thought, "How can she possibly love me and be this ruthless?" And yet I remembered words I'd written to her in a letter just a few weeks before:

> Precious Self, you are a ruthless and divine lover. And I accept this divine love affair, with all that it entails—the ecstasy and the longing, the kiss and the slap, the many deaths that must be died. I accept everything. I welcome everything as your Grace.

It was a fact of my experience that, from the very first letter I wrote to Gangaji in Estes Park, every time I declared some realization or another in a letter to her, that realization would be tested, often severely, shortly thereafter. It happened with such predictable regularity that I wondered why, by now, I hadn't learned to keep my mouth shut. Often when I'd sit in satsang, watching with anxiety while she opened one of my letters, I would think, "*Why* do I keep doing this to myself?" This question now arose once more. But the answer was clear: this is the reason I am at her feet; this is the reason I was born into this life; this is exactly what the relationship with her is for—to expose myself completely, to root out every corner of separation, to push me endlessly deeper into the Truth of my Being.

Looking for some guidance I opened Gangaji's book, *You Are THAT!,* and my eyes fell upon a passage where she speaks about her own teacher, Papaji:

> He is <u>absolutely</u> loving. *Still wanting nothing from you, he will search out the last little corner of hidden identification with ego and rip it out by the heart.*
>
> *This is what I call a teacher. Anything else is just child's play . . . playing a game of awakening, while always trying to maintain control.* *

Yes. That's what I was doing, saying, "I am willing to accept anything, to welcome everything as your Grace." And yet all the while there was this hidden agenda, this wanting to maintain control—"I'm here in Maui, I've spent all this money and time to come and see you, so I should be able to see you!"

But there was no controlling her. We had heard stories about the year before in Maui when Gangaji had actually cancelled *all* the Maui satsangs because of some organizational problems. I realized she could easily do that again now.

The powerful, habitual impulse arose once again to bolt, to distance myself from this attachment that was causing so much pain. The tendency was strong to turn away from the longing, to get rid of it. For some people I'm sure this turning away might have taken the form of trying to find some other object of longing that was more controllable, that was more attainable. And in a beautiful place like Maui, certainly opportunities for that abounded. But for me, the strategy was the same one I had used since age five: to escape, to try to convince myself I didn't need anything. "Why do I persist in loving her so much? I don't need this. I would be so much happier if I could just leave." How very deeply etched into my psyche was this tendency to run!

But the bond with Gangaji was already too deeply sealed. There was no question—I could not run. The realization that had already dawned was too deep and clear to allow such an indulgence. This habit of running had already been seen as illusion, the illusion of separation perpetuating itself by retreating into more separation! The opportunity once again was to stay still. To not move. To meet this longing. To allow all separation to be ripped out by the heart.

So I gave up the idea of running. I gave up the idea of control and surrendered fully to the longing, met it head on. I'm sure on the outside this looked very much like a six-year-old having a colossal tantrum. To some it may have seemed like an overly dramatic display, unwarranted by the simple circumstance of enduring a few more days without seeing my teacher. But there was more to it than just this simple circumstance. The circumstance had triggered another death-experience to be met. And inside, I was meeting this death, this unimaginable, crushing longing, face to face in each moment.

A passage from *You Are THAT!* again brought understanding and confirmation:

> *Longing for the true Beloved is not content with even the last moment's realization. The Beloved's embrace must be always fresh, always alive, always new.*
>
> *Whenever longing arises, it may trigger habitual responses of attempting to satisfy the longing with some object, some experience, or something other than itself. These responses are latent tendencies of mind. These tendencies reflect the way we have been taught to deal with longing.*
>
> *Divine longing is for deeper realization of the fullness of Self. It is very useful. Don't put it aside. Don't move into mental agitation around it. It exposes even the slightest misidentification of yourself as separate from the Beloved.*
>
> *This longing is a great gift. It is God's gift. It is the longing of the soul, and it will continue until without a shadow of a doubt you are submerged in the Beloved.**

In the months ahead I would experience this longing many more times, at deeper and deeper levels, but for now, as I surrendered deeply and fully, some Grace broke through. I experienced the longing as my own Self in the form of Gangaji, drawing me closer. I began to perceive her, tangibly present right there in my room. Finally she appeared to me in a vision, which was very loving and close, and melted, for the time being anyway, all experience of separation.

By the end of that week, the longing and the separation had burned up. And I saw the truth of her words—what a blessing this longing is! When it is not turned from, when it is met fully and completely, it is seen for what it is—Self, calling Itself home.

I saw the perfection of everything, and the Grace of it, and felt closer to Gangaji than ever before, fully accepting not being able to see her at all on this trip to Maui, if that was what was to be.

18

BEYOND THE PAIRS OF OPPOSITES

*S*aturday finally arrived. I sat quietly in the satsang hall about six or seven rows back. When Gangaji walked into the room, she moved regally and gracefully toward the couch. It was like Silence moving. My heart thrilled at the sight of her, yet there was also a calmness present that came from the deep knowing that I'd never really been apart from her.

The first letter Gangaji read that day was from the acupuncturist who had awakened so dramatically during my "unsuccessful" job interview in Boulder. The letter described our interview, the woman's desperate state of mind, the way she had been relentlessly pointed deeper into herself, and her subsequent awakening to the Truth. Her description of the incident was slightly different from the way I had remembered it, but it was beautiful and Gangaji was very pleased. In that letter the woman gave me the most precious compliment anyone could ever give me. She wrote to Gangaji:

> [Amber] had a way of speaking, a tone of voice, and a way of simplifying everything down to the minimum of words that touched me to the core of my Being. It was only upon hearing your audio tape later that day, and your videos later that week also, that I realized that whatever it is that speaks you was also speaking her on that day.

A deep fulfillment permeated my soul. This was all I wanted in the world—to speak the Truth that Gangaji speaks. The reading of that letter in satsang that day served as a deep confirmation that the Truth of this lineage could be transmitted through this life-stream. I knew this to be true already, but this confirmation in satsang removed all possibility of denying it.

After Gangaji finished reading the letter, she held it up and said:

This is God's answer to the question, "Are you your brother's keeper?" I'm not saying that you should immediately go speak to everybody in a particular way. Being taught how to be your brother's keeper has been tried throughout time. I'm saying to be who you are. And in that, you are "the keeper"—of all that arises in who you are. You are the keeper, you are the releaser, you are the freer.

You know, when the spiritual search begins it seems that what is wanted and cried for is personal joy and personal release, personal enlightenment. But personal enlightenment is a myth. What enlightenment is, is a realization that there is no person separate from any other person—except by appearance. The inseparableness of every person with every other person is permanent and unchanging. To be the "keeper" is to be true to that.*

How well I remembered the beginnings of my own search and the personal fulfillment I imagined it would give me—happiness, power, brilliance, freedom from the vulgarities of the world. Even when I finally met Gangaji and saw the true person-less Self reflected in her eyes, there was a tendency to try to make *that* personal—my personal guru, my fulfillment, my beloved. Even after seeing this trap of the mind again and again, deeper layers of the illusion kept surfacing. It is the identification with "me" which is the problem and which must be dropped. In the next two weeks, this identification was to be exposed and burned.

The next day I had begun to feel extremely hot, as if a fever had developed. I hoped that I was not getting sick. I had been careful not to drink the tap water, as I always am when I travel, due to a very sensitive physiology. But as satsang began that day, this heat increased. At one point, just as I felt that I might faint, Gangaji looked over at me and asked if I had brought my guitar. I shook my head no. Then she asked me to bring it Wednesday to satsang. I nodded, grateful that I would not have to sing just then.

I had signed up for the small meeting that day, so after satsang I waited on the steps outside the chapel where the small satsang would be held. Gangaji was meeting privately with some staff people, so we all waited quietly for the signal to go in. Shanti sat on the steps near me and I noticed that she was watching me closely. She asked if I was okay. I said, "I feel so hot. Maybe I'm sick." She smiled and said, "You're not sick, Amber. Ramana's got you." Later on she gave me some electrolyte packets to put in water and drink. She told me this had helped her when she was traveling with Gangaji in India and experiencing a similar burning.

When they finally let us into the small satsang room I somehow ended up right in front, and so sat next to Gangaji. She smiled at me and told me how happy she was with the reports she was receiving. As I sat there looking into the radiance of her eyes all I could say was, "I feel so hot."

She looked at me seriously for a moment, said "good," and then went on to say that she had received another satsang letter of awakening from someone else I had spoken with. I tried to figure out who this could be, but Gangaji didn't remember the name. As others were filing into the room Gangaji said she wanted to speak to me about something else, but would talk to me afterward.

After the satsang, when Gangaji got up and left, a brief fight took place within me as to whether to follow her out or not. We had all been told, as usual, to sit quietly until Gangaji had a chance to leave. But she had said she wanted to speak to me. So, in spite of the rule, I finally got up and followed her out to the parking lot. She turned when she saw me coming up behind her and, taking me firmly by the hand, walked with me toward the car where her husband was waiting.

She told me she liked the poem I'd left on her desk, and also the new song I'd sent from Boulder entitled, "I Started Out In Sunday School." She had written to me at Christmas-time and told me that Eli had really liked that particular song, but she hadn't said anything about how she'd liked it, so I was happy to hear this. Then she asked me to cook a meal for her while I was there. I said I'd be happy to. She added, "Just let me know when you'd like to cook."

She let go of my hand then and left me standing there in the driveway of the church in ecstasy. John came up to me and said in his humorous way, "Holding hands now, huh?" I shrugged, smiled shyly, and then quickly hurried inside to oversee the set-up of the volunteer meal.

Initially I had agreed to just bring a salad each time, then eventually also took on the responsibility of overseeing the coordination of the meals—their preparation, the setting up of the tables, and the cleaning-up afterward. At first this seemed like a big job, but I found as I surrendered to this task that it didn't feel like I was "doing" anything, except being present.

By the next satsang, which was Wednesday, the intense burning had eased and I was feeling much better. I brought my guitar to satsang, ready to sing, yet fully aware that Gangaji might not remember she'd asked me. I was feeling perfectly at ease singing in satsang by then, but I was still not at a point where I would *ask* to sing. When I was sitting in satsang with Gangaji, her transmission of Silence usually captivated me so completely that the thought of singing a song did not arise.

This day, however, something different happened. Near the beginning of the satsang Gangaji looked over at me and asked:

Did you bring your guitar?

When I nodded, she said:

Good. We'll have a song later.

During the satsang I began to think of which song I would sing, which one would fit in with the satsang. I began to think, "I can help her with satsang by playing just the right song," or "Yes, this song would be perfect, or maybe that song." In this way my mind got real active around the playing of the perfect song and the contribution I would make to the satsang by playing a song in line with the types of questions being asked.

As the satsang continued and Gangaji had not asked me to sing yet, I started wondering, "when is she going to ask me to play?" Or thinking, "now would be perfect." But the satsang went on and on, and she didn't look over at me again. I thought, maybe she wants me to remind her. Maybe she forgot.

Gangaji took question after question, answering them perfectly, beautifully. Finally she put her palms together and said, *Om Shanti*. The satsang was over. As she stood up to go, I thought, "She forgot. I should have reminded her." But, just as she was about to step down from the platform, she glanced over at me with a stern look. So much was transmitted in that look. She had not forgotten. She didn't want me to sing. And it was only then I realized what had happened—I had gone into my mind with it. In the last satsangs in Boulder and in Marin I had been singing with an emptiness of ego and mind. But today my mind had arisen blatantly. That's why she didn't want me to sing.

I felt horrible, like I'd failed and disappointed her, and the fire of this raged through my body and soul like an inferno. I went to the room in the back of the hall where the small satsang was being held and tried to get in, but the woman in charge must have been having a bad day herself for she was not very welcoming to me. I walked away in tears.

Feeling numb I went into the kitchen to check on how the meal was going, but could not focus on it. I felt irresistibly drawn back to the room where the small satsang was taking place. As I approached the small meeting room again, I saw the door had been closed. The satsang had already begun, and so I waited outside with Shanti and a few others.

The small meeting lasted a long time, but finally Gangaji emerged. When she saw several of us waiting out there, lining the walkway, she said, "What's this? The coterie?" I felt embarrassed to be standing there like that because it was clear she didn't particularly like it. I was so embarrassed, in fact, that when she walked right by me without appearing to notice me, I felt relieved. However, at the last moment she turned and took hold of the scarf I was wearing. "This is so perfect on you, Amber," she said causally. It was the scarf she had given me the previous summer. Before walking on, she looked into my eyes briefly and said, "So, you'll sing tomorrow."

I nodded.

The rest of that day the sting of my mistake kept me in misery. I wanted to just stay in my room and cry my eyes out. But John suggested it might help if I got some exercise for a change. So after our satsang duties were finished we drove to a broad beach near Haiku with nearly a mile of sandy shoreline. John says it was a beautiful beach we walked on that day, but I can't remember much of it. I felt like I was being consumed in a blistering fire. Up and down the long sandy shore we walked, me sobbing, John wading in the water and skipping stones. He was the perfect satsang buddy. My misery did not affect him or fool him in the least. He knew what this was and did not indulge it with any sweet consoling words, nor deny it by wishing I would cheer up and shut up. He just let me cry, undisturbed. About that day, John wrote:

> The temperature was perfect, the sky was deep blue. There were the appropriate number of white puffy clouds hanging around, and the waves were big and in abundance. It was late afternoon, when most of the surfers had finished for the day, so there wasn't much activity on the beach. It couldn't have been better, except for one thing—Amber, although there in form, was lost behind an unending torrent of tears.
>
> I considered it great luck to have become friends with Amber and Toby, and over the months I had become accustomed to being with Amber when she was burning so intensely that the tears could not be stopped. This was one of those times and quite possibly the most intense of all times that I had seen. We walked for quite some time. Whenever I would stop for more than a few seconds, Amber would find a place to sit and the tears would flow even harder.
>
> She didn't talk very much on that walk, and it was clear that this form called Amber was quite distraught. But in spite of all this apparent suffering going on, I could not help experiencing the great silence and love emanating from her. She was deeply in love with her Beloved and I was blessed just to be in her company.

When we returned to our house, I shut myself in my room and continued crying—into the night. Around midnight our other roommate, Ariel, came home and struck up a loud, heated phone conversation with her husband, who was in California. Her room was right next to mine and the walls were very thin. I could hear every word. I hesitated to say anything because I had complained about her loud nocturnal capers a couple of nights before when she'd had a boyfriend over. Ariel was young and wild, and both John and I had been unsuccessful in our attempts to encourage her to come to satsang. She kept saying she "wanted" to come but there were so many other things going on—a tantra workshop, new friends she'd made, the sights and excitements of Maui. Yet I sensed a deep spiritual yearning in her.

Finally the noise level was intolerable. I went next door and asked her to talk somewhere else. She apologized for disturbing my sleep. I confessed that I had not been sleeping, but I did not relish hearing every word of her conversation. "Besides," I said, "you should have more privacy when you speak to your husband." She complained that if she went into the living room to talk, she would disturb John, whose room was right next to it. But the phone was a mobile phone, so I suggested she might use the front porch.

"Well, I'm almost done," she replied. "I'm not getting anywhere with him anyway."

I went back into my room. She continued to argue with her husband for at least another five minutes. When finally she hung up I heard a knock at my door. It was Ariel. She came into my room and sat on the edge of my futon. She had seen I'd been crying and wanted to apologize again for disturbing me. She told me about the situation with her husband, and how he was not open to the spiritual quest that was unfolding for her right now. We talked for a while and gave each other satsang. In the course of that conversation something Ariel said clicked, and I realized that the mind-stuff which had arisen in satsang that day had not been a mistake. It was a gift. The gift of satsang.

This is where latent tendencies belong, in satsang, so they can be seen to have nothing to do with WHO ONE IS.

Suddenly I saw that what had arisen in satsang that day had arisen purposefully, to be burned, to be freed. The arising and the burning was necessary; the flogging of myself was not necessary. That was the "unnecessary" suffering. A deep letting go took place then and I thanked my young friend for her satsang and slept peacefully the rest of the night.

The next day in satsang I sat right up in front. By then the mental stuff that had been dredged up surrounding the whole incident of the day before had burned away. I felt very empty, and once again awareness was expanded beyond this individual form. I wasn't concerned about whether I sang or didn't sing. At one point during the satsang, someone raised their hand and said, "I'm happy to be here."
Gangaji replied:

Oh, that's beautiful. Happy to be here.

Then she looked at me and said:

We should have a song, "Happy To Be Here."

I found myself wishing I had a song like that to sing for her, but I didn't. Then she asked me to sing something, so I sang the song about Ramana as a boy of sixteen, the song I had wanted to sing for Ramana's birthday celebration. Gangaji had never heard it before. She seemed pleased, and many people were moved to tears.

After satsang, at the volunteer meal that evening, I sat with Lee, the man who used to drive Gangaji in Santa Fe and whose luggage I'd once brought from Boulder. Lee said I looked different, more open. I said he looked different too—his face was radiant and joyous, with none of the troubled currents that I'd picked up from him in Santa Fe. He told me that he'd been cleaning Gangaji's car the other day and had found a tape of my songs in the cassette player. I thanked him for sharing that with me. He grinned and said, "I thought you'd like to know that." We talked about Gangaji, about how intense it was to be with her. And he gave me this advice, "You have to ask her for what you want. *Tell* her."

I said, "I have. I told her I want to be as unmoving as she is." As I heard myself saying this to Lee, I realized what an awesome thing that was to say to her. My God, no wonder I'm burning up. In order to be as unmoving as she is, every tendency to move into the mind, every impulse to follow thought as reality (mental thought, emotional thought, physical thought or circumstantial thought) must be consumed.

In the next few days I worked on writing a song about "happy to be here." At first I wasn't sure I'd be able to do it. Songs usually come to me very spontaneously and I'd rarely written a song "on command" like that. But the words and melody tumbled out quite naturally and when it was finished I wrote it out on a piece of paper and took it to satsang.

I placed the song up on the couch with the other letters that day, feeling a certain sense of pride at having written a song that Gangaji had asked me to write. It was a special gift to her. What I didn't realize at the time was that there was a sense of personal accomplishment and attachment—a sense that "I" had done it. How tenacious and subtle the mind is! But the true Self doesn't miss a thing. When Gangaji picked up my paper with the song written on it she looked at me and asked casually:

Is this a new song?

I nodded, noticing that she didn't seem to have any recollection that it was the song she'd asked me to write. She asked me if I'd like to sing it. As I got up to go and get my guitar she said:

While Amber's getting ready I'll take another question.

An older man in the back of the hall raised his hand and asked if he could look into her eyes. She motioned for him to come up to the front. As he approached the couch to sit down with her, Gangaji told me to start singing. She said:

You can be the troubadour—serenade us.

I didn't particularly want to sing while she was talking to this man, but I had no choice. That's what she'd asked me to do. So, I began to sing this song:

> I used to wander ceaselessly
> Looking for what was true
> Hoping to find some future time
> When all the light breaks through
> Now I'm happy to be right here
> Happy to be here now
> Happy to be right here
> Stopped in time somehow

As I sang, Gangaji began talking to this man, looking into his eyes, laughing with him, interacting with him. It seemed that she was absolutely unaware of the song I was so proud of. I sang the second verse with less pride.

> In all the things I pushed away
> And things I wanted near
> I didn't know what I was looking for
> All this time was here
> Now I'm happy to be right here
> Happy to be here now
> Happy to be right here
> Stopped in time somehow

As I finished singing, the man and Gangaji were just finishing too. She said a few more words to him, then sent him back to his seat. Immediately, Gangaji took another question. Nothing was said about the song I'd sung. She didn't look at me or smile at me the way she usually does when I sing. It was as though I hadn't sung at all. It was as though I didn't even exist.

I sat there stunned, my guitar in my lap, shocked to the core that she would treat me like this. Just when I had finally gotten over my fear of singing in front of people, just when I had opened so trustingly to her, she'd slapped me harder than ever.

Deep feelings of rejection and worthlessness began to arise, more extreme than I'd experienced before. Thoughts came up like, "I shouldn't have given her the words to the song. I shouldn't have sung the song. I shouldn't have even *written* the song. It's a stupid song anyway. I should never sing again!" And worst of all, "Get away from this teacher; she's hurting you."

Briefly, I felt the impulse to run, felt my heart start to withdraw from hers. And then, miraculously, *it all collapsed*. All these thoughts and feelings just vanished, melted into Self. The mind surrendered, was flattened, prostrate before Truth. And with that came the vivid perception that all these thoughts and emotions were *nothing*, were based on the past—past memories of rejection and worthlessness. They had nothing to do with this moment. They had nothing to do with who I am. They were absolutely meaningless.

After satsang I got up to put my guitar away, still feeling a little stunned and strange. My body and brain seemed on fire with intense heat—as I interpreted it at the time—from the incredible flattening I'd just experienced. I didn't particularly feel like going into the kitchen to oversee the meal. My impulse was to be alone, to sit on a rock somewhere in the forest. Then I realized I *was* alone, alone with mySelf. In spite of the appearance of surroundings, with people bustling to and fro, taking down the stage set-up and handling the sales tables, there was a sense that nothing was happening, and that no one was there for it to happen to. Though I felt a definite sting from Gangaji's slap, as my mind kept trying to evaluate and react to the events that had just transpired in satsang, each thought was immediately consumed by the fire.

As I began making my way to the kitchen, which was in the back of the hall, Maitri came up to me with a radiant smile and said, "Gangaji really, *really* liked the meals you cooked for her." I had been wondering how Gangaji liked the two meals I'd brought her that week. I had not brought any of my recipes with me to Maui and so had to be inventive. Maitri relieved me of all concern by sharing with me something Gangaji had said: "Those two meals from Amber were pure nectar." I marveled at this exquisite dance with Satguru, marveled at the way the sword was always balanced with roses, the slap followed by a kiss.

It wasn't until a few days later that I fully recognized the significance of the collapse into Self that had occurred that day. Eventually I wrote to Gangaji and reported what had taken place during and after that satsang.

> I watched as the mind began to interpret this and then react to it emotionally and construct a story, all based on the past. Then, in an instant of Grace, the mind surrendered all this to Self; it was floored, flattened. And in this surrender, all that interpretation and reaction which was being constructed by the mind and which seemed so real a moment before just disappeared—like on Star Trek when the holodeck gets turned off and the scene vanishes, leaving nothing but a meaningless grid.
>
> From this surrender, an intense burning arose in the physiology which lasted a couple of days. I understood this to be the latent tendencies being consumed by Self. What a relief it is to see this mirage, this play of mind, and to understand this intense burning—which I always experience when I'm with you in form. I know I have struggled against it sometimes. But I relax into it now, after this flattening.
>
> A few nights after this realization I woke in the middle of the night (or rather, awareness woke up while the body still slept) and there was this clear seeing of how the whole world is this same mirage, is nothing but *mind* in an endless cycle of pairs of opposites—pleasure/pain, arrogance/worthlessness, success/failure, acceptance/rejection, exposure/hiding—and how much imaginary suffering this causes. The image that came to me at the time was "mental wasteland." It was a stark realization, shocking in a way. And there was some impulse at first not to believe it, but there was also a deep knowing that this is the Truth. And in surrendering to this knowing a laughter welled up from deep inside, and a profound relaxation occurred—which can not be described in words.

I saw so clearly how the mind creates interpretations of experience, all based on past memory, and how these interpretations create the "pairs of opposites" which are then used to find meaning in circumstance, and to evaluate one's self, either with worth or with worthlessness; this then plunges one into suffering and bondage. These pairs of opposites are like the two sides of a coin—you take a coin, you get both sides. You take, "Oh, I am great!" What follows on its heels, sooner or later, is "My God, I am worthless!" Whole lives are spent trying to keep the side of the coin that says "worthless" from coming up, and trying to keep the side that says "great" to the fore.

Finally I understood directly one of Papaji's sayings: "If you touch it, it will bite you." It is with the mind that things are "touched." And it is the mind alone which deals in this double-sided currency. Freedom is revealed when the coin is not touched at all, either side of it. When one ceases to identify with mind as who one is, one is freed from the suffering of these incessant polarities, this constant tug of war, this wheel of samsara.*

I saw the whole quest to find "meaning in life" as absurd. There *is* no meaning in phenomenal life. There is no connection between circumstances and who one is. This apparent link is an illusion created in mind only. It's just like in a play when two guys are fighting and one stabs the other and kills him. The stabbing has a certain meaning within the content of the play, but in reality, outside the play, it has no meaning, no connection to *who these people really are*. The two guys may be the best of friends and go out to lunch afterward and have a good laugh over it.

Upon seeing the meaninglessness of events and circumstances I experienced directly how Maya becomes Leela, how the suffering vanishes and the world of phenomena is then seen as a Divine play, sometimes delightful, sometimes horrible, but having nothing to do with *who one is*.

A few days later the musical tape I had recorded arrived from Boulder. Toby had sent about twenty copies because Gangaji had said she wanted the tape to be put out on the satsang sales table. Somehow the arrival of that tape caused a whole new level of "exposure-fear" to arise. As I sat there on the living room floor, gazing at all those tapes with my picture on them and "Awakened From A Dream" printed across the top, I experienced an intense constriction and heat in my chest. I didn't particularly like the way the album cover had turned out. It had been created quickly, just before my departure from Boulder. I had wanted the cover to indicate that the music was acoustic, not synthesized as so much New Age music is these days. We didn't have the time or the funds for a professional design, so Toby had simply taken a photo of me with my guitar. At the time, I imagined the tape would probably go onto the shelves of New Age bookstores and be bought mostly by people who didn't know me. I was actually quite surprised, even shocked, when Gangaji had said she wanted it on the sales table at satsang. She had never allowed any music tapes on the sales table before. Now, here was my tape, going on the table in front of all these people who *did* know me—many of whom, as far as I could tell, didn't really like me all that much, for a decidedly critical scrutiny of the way I was managing the volunteer meals had emerged.

John was enthusiastic about taking the tapes to satsang that morning and giving them to the sales people, for he had promised Toby that he would oversee the marketing aspect of the tapes while we were in Maui. But I wasn't quite ready to do that. I needed time to get used to this. I stalled, telling John I wanted to give Gangaji her copy first before anyone else saw them.

The next day in satsang I enclosed a copy of the tape in an envelope with a short note of gratitude and put it up on Gangaji's couch with her mail. Again I felt some sense of pride at having completed the benefit album which I'd told her the previous August, I'd do.

Perfectly, Gangaji didn't even open the envelope with my tape in it. In fact, when she left satsang that day she didn't even take it with her. I was never quite sure whether she ever reconnected with it, or whether she even liked it, for she never mentioned anything about it to me.

The following day John could not be put off any longer. The tapes went out on the sales table. The sense of excruciating exposure heightened and yet it seemed to be taking place at some distance. I was definitely "experiencing" it, but there was also a strange sense that "I" was not being touched by it.

During satsang that day a girl asked a question about an experience of "awakeness" she'd had at the Crestone retreat the previous summer. She claimed she had since "lost the experience" and wanted to get it back, adding that the part of her that seemed awake was so "little."

Gangaji replied:

> So, this that sees parts—that sees awake parts, asleep parts, enlightened parts, unenlightened parts, good parts, bad parts, this—is this little?

The girl sighed, laughed slightly and said, "No."

> So, why identify yourself with some part that you see? Why not identify with the seeing itself? Why not rest in awareness, rather than in some object that has appeared in awareness and is evaluated as "asleep?"—some objective experience where you can say, "Oh, that's asleepness. Oh, that's wrong-headedness." "Asleep" is not a gross object, but it's still an object in mind, isn't it? Yes. But the seeing of this object, this that the object arises in, can you measure this?
>
> What can you do with a measuring stick here? Can an object, a measuring device, measure that which is aware of all measuring? Can a part be bigger than the whole?

The girl said, "It is the whole."

> If you know that, then the question of awake and asleep is solved. You are awake. You know that, you know everything. Because of the identification with parts, and seeing many parts—some good, some bad, some that give you pleasure, some that give you pain—because of this identification and then the conclusion, "I don't want these parts, but I want those parts. Oh no! I've got some of these parts I don't want; where are those that I want?"—there is mis-identification, to one degree or another. Sometimes, of course, there is extreme suffering. Some lives are lost in extreme suffering.

But in your life you say you have glimpsed awakeness. Now that which glimpsed awakeness, has it ever been asleep?

There is a point in a very blessed lifetime, where the reflection is empty—where there is nothing to identify with; where you look into the mirror and the mirror is transparent, it's clear, and no object can be seen. And in that instant, Truth is realized.

Then, perhaps, objects begin to appear again. And there is the conceptualization of "objectlessness" as a small part. When this event occurred, did you do anything for it?

The girl replied, "No."

Okay. That's the secret. Stop doing something to get it back. Stop doing something to fight the experience that is occurring right now. And then you will see the emptiness of this experience also. And when you see the emptiness of this experience, then you will say, "Yes, the part is the whole... Emptiness is empty. Consciousness is everywhere."

Questions of awake and asleep, then, are absolutely absurd.

As I sat there listening to this discourse, a fear arose that people would think I was arrogant for naming the tape "Awakened From A Dream." Who is it that awakens anyway? There isn't really anyone who awakens. I began wishing, once again, that I hadn't put my picture on the front, that Toby hadn't sent the tapes to Maui at all. More exposure-feelings accompanied these thoughts, as if my whole soul lay naked and vulnerable out there on the sales table in the form of the tape. I could feel the feeling of wanting to bolt arising and yet there was also a sense that that was not an option any more. There was no way out of this. A rock and roll band was playing that day in the park outside the church. They began singing an old 70's song, "Nowhere to run, nowhere to hide . . ." How perfect. Nowhere to run. Hiding was over. I was in the presence of the Satguru. This exposure had to be met. Again my body felt inflamed with the burning of it. At one point I raised my hand with the idea of asking Gangaji about this feeling of being exposed—to expose the exposure. She saw my hand but didn't call on me. I waited for an opportunity to raise my hand again, but after taking a few more questions, Gangaji put her palms together and said, *Om Shanti,* ending the satsang. The burning intensified then because of being passed over by her.

After satsang I wandered out to the parking lot, feeling numb and very hot. One of the Maui volunteers came up to me and said accusingly, "How come *your* tape is out on the sales table? We have a lot of great musicians here in Maui and none of their tapes are on the table." I wanted to explain to him that it was just part of the Leela. Ironically, I was probably the one musician present who didn't particularly want their tape on the sales table just then. But I said nothing and just shrugged.

I saw Eli standing in the parking lot waiting for the small satsang to get out so he could drive Gangaji home. I had brought a tape for Eli that day because I had heard from some of his students that he had been playing my songs during his Enneagram retreats and workshops. The recording he had was an earlier version, from before the final mixing was completed, and I wanted him to have a good copy. As he was standing there speaking to someone, his hands clasped behind his back, I approached him from behind and quietly slipped a copy of the tape into his hands. He turned when he felt it in his hands, looked at it for a moment, then put his arm around me, giving me a warm hug of thanks. I admitted to him that I felt exposed about the tape being out. He just smiled and hugged me tighter. Though there was always a feeling of deep friendship with Eli, he rarely said anything to me. Our communication seemed to be more on a silent level.

Gangaji then emerged from the small meeting and descended the steps into the parking lot. Eli let go of me and immediately went to her side to guide her through the hordes of people toward the car. Unintentionally, I happened to be standing in the pathway between her and the car. As I realized she was coming toward me, I put my hands together in a *namasté.* She walked by, apparently without noticing me. It was a situation that even a few days before might have caused some sense of rejection to arise. But there was so much fire already burning inside that if anything arose, it went unnoticed, probably being immediately consumed along with everything else. Then, from about ten feet away, Gangaji turned around and looked at me. She said, "Did you want to speak in satsang?"

I shrugged, "It wasn't important."

She took a few steps toward me and said, "What is it?"

I said, "I just feel so exposed . . . with the tape being out and everything."

She said firmly, "Stand in the core of it. Don't fight it." I checked within myself and responded truthfully, "I believe I'm doing that. I'm not fighting it."

"Good." She spoke with someone else, then glanced at me again before she got into the car. A wave of intense, universal love swept over me with that glance. I had felt this love before after close interactions with her, but had often mistaken it for personal love—for that is the kind of love the mind understands. Now I sensed that what I was experiencing was not personal, and the "person" felt some disappointment at this. I had heard Gangaji say many times, "This love is not personal and not impersonal." And though I thought I had a mental understanding of what this meant, I had not yet really "gotten" it until that moment.

As the car drove off a woman came up to me and started to tell me what she'd experienced when I'd played a song a few days before. She admitted that she had been jealous at first, because she also was a songwriter. As she started expressing this she began to cry and her words were choked. I felt her sincerity and a deep wave of love for her arose in my heart. I put my arm around her and encouraged her to continue trying to relate her experience. This was unusual for me, for I am not a touchy/feely sort of person, but this action arose totally spontaneously. She went on to say how she had realized, as I sang, that it was her own Self singing and her own song being sung. I smiled at her and said, "Yes, same song, same Self." The words felt like Gangaji's words; the love felt like Gangaji's love. For in that smile a tremendous wave of love went out to this person. Yet it was not personal. It may have *looked* personal—if someone had seen me standing there with my arm around this woman—but it was completely not personal. I didn't even need to know her name or ever see her again—just this love, in that moment, love for that which was expressing through her, love for that which is my own Self, love that has nothing to do with anything in phenomena at all, love that is closer than personal and bigger than impersonal. And I knew finally, not by mental understanding but by *seeing*, that this is the love Gangaji speaks of and lives. It is with this Love that she loves me, loves everyone.

That night I sat in the living room after dinner, reflecting on this not personal/not impersonal Love that was seen, and realizing how great is the tendency of the mind to try to bring this Love into a personal, graspable, holdable context. Especially with Gangaji, this tendency would arise quite strongly, for I still clung to a deep personal attachment to her. The mind did not want to let go of this personal love, and there was a feeling of loss associated with seeing this.

I sat there meeting it, realizing that I was still holding onto romantic ideas about this guru/disciple relationship and how I wanted it to look.

After a while John came in and asked if I'd like him to read something from a book he'd brought with him called *I Am That*, by Nisargadatta. I had also received a copy of this book for Christmas, but I hadn't had a chance to read any of it yet, so I told him to go ahead.

John opened the book at random and read this passage:

> Nisargadatta: You as the person imagine that the Guru is interested in you as a person. Not at all. To him you are a nuisance and a hindrance to be done away with. He actually aims at your elimination as a factor in consciousness.
>
> Questioner: If I am eliminated, what will remain?
>
> Nisargadatta: Nothing will remain, all will remain. The sense of identity will remain, but no longer identification with a particular body. Being—awareness—love will shine in full splendor. Liberation is never of the person, it is always from the person.*

231

How perfectly Self appears at every moment with the exact right instruction. Hearing these words I felt the characteristic burning I had come to associate with the surrender of mind to Self.

Gangaji continued to play with me using the music—telling me I would sing on a particular day, then not having me sing; telling me I would sing and then having someone else sing instead. The mind could not figure it out. Did she want me to sing or was she tired of my singing, or what? Finally, there was nowhere for the mind to get a foothold, no ledge to grasp onto, no way to "know" anything. And in that, I could feel the mind, once again, simply giving up.

Meanwhile, I was still managing the volunteer meals. Many cheerful volunteers were pitching in every day to help in the kitchen, and these many hands made the work light. Sometimes I even had to turn people away, there was so much help offered. It seemed to me that it was all going quite well, that everything was getting done effortlessly and perfectly. But this was not always the perception of those "in charge." Whether the meal got out too soon or too late or there wasn't enough salad or someone had burned the soup, it was all carefully and assiduously pointed out and laid at my feet. The situation was one that, at any other time in my life, I would have removed myself from in an instant. I had never stayed voluntarily in a situation where criticism was being leveled at me like this. I just didn't need any circumstance badly enough to stick around if it got unpleasant.

But again, there was a sense that what appeared to be happening was not what was really happening, that the *awareness* of the circumstance was more real than the circumstance itself. I recognized, once again, an opportunity to stay still, an opportunity to not move. And in this recognition, the circumstances were seen as not real. Awareness alone is what is real. What seemed to be coming "at me" from these people had no meaning with regard to who I am, and in this sense it was perfect, an opportunity to meet it head on and watch it burn to ashes. It was an opportunity to see that other people's mind-stuff is as meaningless as my own, is the same mind-stuff! Whether it is "phenomenal" mind-stuff, or "circumstantial" mind-stuff or "internal" mind-stuff—it's all the same. Nothing. Meaningless. Having not the slightest connection with the Truth of my Being.

Ultimately I watched the mind, once again, surrender all this to Self. It was becoming more and more obvious: *nothing* that arises in mind means anything. There was no longer anywhere to abide, except in Self. There was nothing to do but surrender, continually, every*thing*, in every moment, twenty-four hours a day.

On my last day of satsang in Maui, Gangaji asked, "Is this your last formal satsang?" I nodded. She said, "Then you should sing." I nodded again, indicating I'd be happy to. But before I got the signal from her that it was time to sing, another musician, who was sitting behind me raised his hand and asked if he could sing. His song was so beautiful and expressed so much of what I was experiencing in that moment that I couldn't have sung anything after that. The refrain went:

> Just one look into your eyes
> Now I'm forever falling
> Into the silence inside.

Thankfully, right after he finished, Gangaji put her palms together and ended the satsang.

I realized all this that had taken place on Maui was a deep burning of that which I had identified with as myself. I saw how false and how fragile is this entity called "me," how it is constructed in mind and falsely identified with as oneself. With this identification arises the need to defend and protect this false self by developing strategies and fabricating elaborate stories and masks. And all this is simply a house of cards. Like in the man's song, one glance from the true teacher is enough— the house of cards begins to topple. One penetrating look into the eyes of Self, and all that was fabricated and false begins burning to ashes. It does not take place in time and yet it penetrates time. About this burning I wrote to Gangaji:

Yesterday it seemed everything that happened was specifically designed to throw what is left of my 'personality' into this fire. It felt really strange, watching this consuming of identification with individuality—like watching my own funeral pyre being torched. But there was no attempt to resist. Just watching it go up in smoke. Actually, there was no *one* to resist.

After this most recent death, a kind of 'dissociated' feeling has been present, and with that an expansion and a freedom. I believe it is the freedom of not having to protect 'this' any longer. What a relief! What a lot of work it has been.

In the past few days a profound willingness has been present to really let everything arise, in a deeper way than before. Just a complete willingness to see everything that has not been seen, and a realization of how necessary this willingness is for surrender to deepen—because the surrender, the stopping, makes stuff arise, and if there is unwillingness to see, then the surrender is subtly resisted. I see how the slightest unwillingness is like a string that pulls one back into the dance of mind.

Then comes more stopping, more surrender, more willingness. And a flood of all that which I have held deep inside, held away, rushing to be met—to be freed. It is a deep washing.

By the time I left Maui the strong habits of mind that had once driven this personality had been permanently loosed. I began to see clearly the thoughts and ideas that held it all together, that held "me" together, and also to see the key thoughts on which the rest were hanging, including the most central thought of all—the "I-thought." When I would wake in the morning, there would be a moment when it was clear that the I-thought had not yet arisen. For some moments there would be no identification with "person" or "body" as myself, just a huge expanse of blissful Presence. Then I would watch the "I" arise. This arising would often be accompanied by a burning sensation in the body. This experience each morning allowed me to see the effect of this I-thought arising and to glimpse how all other types of mind activity—such as judgments, emotions, fears, and desires—are created and identified as oneself, how they all collect around and hang on the

"I-thought" like branches and leaves on a tree. I could sometimes see how even time and space are created by the mind
and identified with. Finally I was able to experience directly
the truth of Ramana's words—in the little book *Who Am I?*
—which had made no sense to me only a few months before:

> Of all the thoughts that arise in the mind, the "I"
> thought is first. It is only after the rise of this, that the
> other thoughts arise. It is after the appearance of the first
> personal pronoun that the second and third personal pro-
> nouns appear; without the first personal pronoun there
> will not be a second and a third.
>
> The thought "Who am I?" will destroy all other
> thoughts, and like the stick used for stirring the burning
> pyre, it will itself in the end get destroyed. Then, there will
> arise Self-realization.*

It was not long before whole days would go by without the
I-thought arising at all. I began to notice an effortlessness in
action which seemed almost magical—things were getting done
without the sense that "I" was doing anything. Circumstances
that would have caused me to "react" in some habitual way
before, now were met with a stillness and presence which
allowed me instead to simply "respond" to the situation. I had
heard Gangaji speak about "true responsibility" in connection
with this ability to "respond" but had not clearly understood it
before.

> *You cannot respond as long as you are weighted down
> with some formula of what truth is. It's impossible. You can
> only react.*
>
> *The ability to respond must be free, spontaneous, and
> totally intuitive, or it is burdened by this weight of past con-
> cepts—what it should look like, what it should feel like, how
> it should be received. This is all from the past. This is not
> responsibility. This is some imitation of responsibility, and it
> is a burden.*
>
> *True responsibility is not a burden at all. It is a joy. It is
> a willingness to surrender, to be who you are without having
> any concept of what that is.*

When circumstances are met with an agenda based on emotional and mental baggage, the meeting gets colored by this baggage and one's response is as if filtered through a darkly tinted lens. When there is no agenda, no personal baggage, the response to a situation is free, spontaneous, and true.

The tendency to look to the mind as a reference point of being was dissolving, and deeper and deeper levels of that tendency and of that dissolving kept being revealed by Satguru. With this dissolving, a sense of freedom was dawning beyond what can be captured in words, beyond the "pairs of opposites"—beyond arrogance and worthlessness, beyond independence and dependence, beyond personal and impersonal, even beyond enlightenment and ignorance. True Freedom, true Self, not abiding in the mind anywhere.

Gangaji didn't return to Boulder until April 26th—exactly one year after our first meeting. The morning of her return I left a bouquet of roses in her house with a note, reminding her that this was the anniversary of our meeting and thanking her for the most precious year of my life. Later she wrote me a note in response to some chapters of this book I'd given her to review; at the end of the note, which contained some editing of satsang transcriptions, she wrote: *Beloved Self, the depth of this meeting is endless.*

What a beautiful promise this is. In all that has taken place, in all that has been revealed, the most amazing Grace of all is this unknowable, mysterious endlessness. In Papaji's words:

> Freedom is the start of something
> that Nobody knows:
> there is no end to Satsang,
> it is always new fathomless Bliss.
> The firm conviction
> that One is Existence-Consciousness-Bliss
> is the end of the Teaching.
> Yet there is a sacred Secret beyond even this.
> This sacred secret must be asked for in Secret
> and followed sacredly.*

Gangaji will never take credit for anything that has been revealed for me or for anyone else who awakens in her presence. "I haven't done anything," she always says. "You are already, always, completely, fully THAT." This is the truth of my experience, and yet, mysteriously, it was this "meeting," this meeting with Satguru, this meeting with Grace *as her,* that revealed the ever-present Truth, revealed what is so simple, so utterly, utterly simple that it is overlooked. How exquisite that Its very simplicity has held It as the deepest secret.

END OF THE SEARCHER

*W*hat I have written down in these chapters is an account of the meeting with my Satguru, in form, and the experiences and revelations that took place in the first year of that meeting. Though I have ended the story here, the unfolding of Self to Self has not ended. After my return from Maui, the identification with mind continued to burn at increasingly subtle levels. The tendency to look to *anything* in outer circumstances for who I am continued to be cut. The love, the visions, the bliss and peace of being "held" in each moment by True Self continues to deepen and become more vivid. However, I am finding that the "story" of it becomes harder and harder to tell.

When I first met Gangaji, the explosion of love, the fire, the resistance, the fear, the excruciating "letting go," all made for a very dramatic story. Now, as the surrender continues to deepen, the resistance and dramatic ripping away of identification with mind melts more and more into nothingness, melts into an effortless, undramatic, very ordinary moment by moment surrender of mind to Self.

When I say ordinary I do not mean dull or uninteresting or even usual. In this every-day surrender, ordinary moments become sublime and filled with the joy of eternal Self-discovery. As Gangaji once described it:

> It is just blissful, eternal surrender—this prostration of mind to Self. True Self. Not image of Self, not thought of Self. True Self. That which cannot be imaged or thought.*

So in this sense, every moment of life has become extraordinary. However, it is not "dramatic" in the way the mind perceives the drama of events. That drama, I realize now, was created by the sense of a "me" who was letting go, who was dying, who was exploding in love. Now this "me" is not experienced in the same way any more, for the identification no longer has the same power. And I find it difficult, at least at this point, to put the months which have transpired since Maui into "story" form, or even into words.

Looking back, I would have to say that when I set out on the spiritual quest I was not really looking for enlightenment. I was looking for personal improvement, personal fulfillment. I wanted to improve my mind, my personality, my body, my circumstances, and to fulfill the personal destiny of this life. In my search I was led to very powerful and profound ways of doing this. But the true longing, longing for the eternal Self, longing for real freedom, remained unfulfilled—until this "me" who was longing dropped away.

This is the irony, the great cosmic joke, the great secret of "enlightenment." When the person who searches for enlightenment dissolves, then and only then is the object of the search revealed—having been obscured all along by the "me" who wanted it.

The discovery that "personal enlightenment" is a myth can be received as quite a shock. From my own experience I can verify that the mind and personality does not happily embrace this discovery when it is first glimpsed, for it makes one look somewhat ridiculous. All the searching, all the practicing, all the trying to "get" it, is seen as worthless, is seen as having perpetuated the illusion of "me," as having obscured what was and is already here, what all this striving and practicing is occurring *in*—one's own limitless Self.

This invitation that Ramana, who speaks from the core of your being, calls you to with the simple phrase, "Be still," is the invitation to Truth. Not your truth. It is the invitation to Life. Not your life. Invitation to Freedom. Not your freedom. It has nothing to do with YOU.*

How amazing that the personless Self had to appear in my life in the form of "person" in order for me to drop the identification with "person." This is the great mystery of the Satguru—that at some point in the journey of individuality the timeless penetrates time, the personless appears in person, the formless manifests in form, and reveals Itself to Itself in time, in person, in form. This mystery is not separate from the Beloved. This mystery is what the great seers of all spiritual traditions have written their ecstatic poetry to, have sung their divine hymns to, and yet have never quite found adequate words for.

So much of what has been revealed in the meeting with Gangaji has not been revealed through words—cannot be revealed through words. When the Satguru is met in form there is a mysterious transmission that takes place from heart to heart, from Self to Self. This cannot be spoken. Words can sometimes point to it, but only if the pointing words are not clung to, are not taken into the mind as some "thing."

How do you know that you have met the Satguru? You just *know*. It is unmistakable. It is Grace.

This Grace is a Divine and Sacred Mystery. It comes in the most mysterious and unexpected ways. It cannot be deserved, it cannot be bought, it cannot be demanded or searched for or even hoped for. It is where all deserving, all striving, all hoping ends. It is where the *searcher* ends.

> *Be Still. Let the tiger come to you. You can't go hunting It. It's a very big, wise tiger. It waits for YOU. It likes to capture—by surprise.* *

Though all that I have written is the experience of this particular life-stream, many who have read these chapters have told me that what I have written is their experience too. This is not surprising, for the journey of Self awakening to Itself is a universal one. Often I have heard Gangaji say that the Buddha's awakening is your awakening, Christ's awakening is your awakening, Ramana's awakening is not separate from your awakening. At first I did not understand this. Now the truth of these words have become clear. It is only one Self, eternally awakening to Itself in different forms.

Finally, there is no one who gets enlightened, no one who awakens. Who one truly is, has always been awake. The one seeking is found to be an illusion, created by the mistaken identification with mind as who one is. As the mind surrenders to its Source, the illusion of the person, the illusion of the journey, the illusion of separation, collapses into Self. Then Self-discovery unfolds endlessly.

The door to the Infinite that opened in my meeting with Gangaji continues to open, continues to deepen, continues to reveal more profound, more subtle openings. I haven't yet found an end to it. Gangaji says she hasn't found an end. And Papaji says he hasn't found any end to it either. From my own experience I would have to say that this meeting with Satguru *in form* is the most powerful, most subtle, most ruthless, most sacred meeting of any lifetime. It is a secret and a mystery. I bow to this mystery. I serve this mystery, the mystery of this Grace, the mystery of this meeting—which has no end and no beginning.

NOTES AND REFERENCES

*Note: Some of the satsang transcriptions in this book
have been slightly edited for clarity in the written form.*

Page 1:
— SIDDHIS: yogic powers, described in
Chapter II of Patanjali's Yoga Sutras,
and attained by certain practices. These
powers include invisibility, levitation,
clairvoyance, clairaudience, ability to
understand all languages, ability to still
hunger and thirst, immortality of the
body, and others. They are considered a
trap by many spiritual teachers as they
distract the aspirant away from true
freedom and back into mind and ego.

Page 5:
— From chapter VI, verse 19 of the
Bhagavad Gita. Translated from the
Sanskrit text by Martin Wolff.

— PAIRS OF OPPOSITES, refered to in
the *Bhagavad Gita*, chapter IV, verse 22.

Page 10:
—"Satsang With Gangaji," audio tape,
(Satsang Foundation & Press) Boulder,
CO, April 26, 1995.

Page 21:
—"Satsang With Gangaji," audio tape,
(Satsang Foundation & Press) Estes
Park Retreat, May 1, 1995 AM.

Page 22:
—H.W.L Poonja, *Wake Up And Roar*, vol
2, (Maui: Pacific Center Press, 1993), p. 2.

Page 26:
—SAMSARA: the illusion of the world.

Page 27:
— BRAHMAN: the Infinite, wholeness,
the totality of universal essence.

Page 33
— NAMASTE´: a traditional greeting
of India, with palms placed flat together and the head bowed, signifying "the
God in me salutes the God in you."

Page 34:
—"Love Is All That Matters," Satsang
with Gangaji audio tape, (Satsang
Foundation & Press) Estes Park
Retreat, May 2, 1995, AM.

—THE UPANISHADS: sometimes
translated, "Breath of the Eternal," or
literally as, "sitting near devotedly."
Considered among the most mystical
and esoteric writings of Indian scripture.

Page 39:
— SHIVA: pronounced "Sheeva", and
sometimes transliterated "S´iva"; one of
the three gods in the Hindu trinity, the
others being Brahma and Vishnu. It
wasn't until several weeks later that I
discovered Ramana's master was the
sacred mountain Arunachala, which is
said to be an incarnation of Shiva.

Page 44:
—"Satsang With Gangaji" audio tape
(Satsang Foundation & Press) Estes
Park Retreat, May 3, 1995 PM.

Page 48:
— SAMADHI: a state of deep inner absorption into the bliss of pure consciousness, alone without thoughts or any object of perception.

— KUNDALINI: the subtle energy that travels up the center of the spine. Oriental traditions often depict the kundalini as a serpent that lies sleeping, coiled at the base of the spine. The serpent is supposedly awakened by spiritual practice to travel upward through a subtle nerve channel in the center of the spine, enlivening the seven spiritual centers (chakras) as it rises.

Page 54:
— GANGA: the Holy Ganges River, originating in the Himalayan mountains, and flowing south and east across northern India, emptying into the Bay of Bengal. According to legend, the goddess Ganga was asked to descend to earth to help purify mankind. However, she was so wild and tempestuous that she had to be caught in Shiva's hair in order to be tamed before she could safely be allowed to tumble onto the rocks high in the Himalayas and begin her purifying journey down through the mountains and across India.

Page 62:
—"Satsang With Gangaji" audio tape, (Satsang Foundation & Press) Estes Park Retreat, May 6, 1995 AM.

Page 70:
— *Satsang With Gangaji,* newsletter, March 1995 (Satsang Foundation & Press), pp. 14-15.

Page 73:
—HALF-LOTUS position: sitting cross-legged with one foot on the opposite thigh. "Full" lotus is both feet on the thighs.

Page 81:
—*Who AM I? The teachings of Bhagavan Sri Ramana Maharshi,* 7th ed. (Tiruvannamalai, India: Sri Ramanasramam, 1995), p. 6.

Page 85:
— SUTRA: a potent, succinct expression of Truth, an aphorism.

Page 86:
—"What Do You Really Want?" Satsang with Gangaji audio tape, (Satsang Foundation & Press) Santa Fe, May 20, 1995.

— Months later I would come to realize the truth of this behest, through direct experience of the eternal nature of Self, which is totally unrestricted by the separation of time and space—and is in truth what all time and all space arise in.

Page 101:
—"The Myth of Enlightenment," Satsang with Gangaji audio tape, (Satsang Foundation & Press) Santa Fe, May 28, 1995.

Page 104:
— LEELA: the play of God. Gangaji once said that when one is identified with the mind, the world is experienced as "Maya," as illusion and suffering; when this identification has been cut, Maya becomes Leela—a joyous play.

Page 110:
—By this time I was beginning to wonder where all these Indian names had come from, for I had no desire whatsoever to replace "Amber" with some Sanskrit epithet. Shortly after that I was relieved to learn that Gangaji herself gave no Indian names. Such names had either been given to people by Papaji, usually upon request, or by some other teacher.

Page 123:
— Discussion about Papaji's *japa* disappearing paraphrased from *Papaji: Interviews,* edited by David Godman, (Avadhuta Foundation, Boulder, CO, 1993), pp. 37-40.

Page 126:
—"At Her Master's Feet," Satsang with Gangaji video, (Satsang Foundation & Press) Lucknow, India, January 31, 1993.

Page 134:
—"A True Marriage to Truth," Satsang with Gangaji audio tape, (Satsang Foundation & Press) Boulder, June 22, 1995.

Page 138:
—"Satsang with Gangaji," audio tape, (Satsang Foundation & Press) Boulder, June 25, 1995.

Page 149:
—"Surrender To Stillness," Satsang with Gangaji audio tape, (Satsang Foundation & Press) Boulder, July 9, 1995.

Page 152:
— Gangaji's response to a request from a Swedish magazine to write something regarding the teacher/student relationship.

Page 159:
—"Invitation To Truth," Satsang with Gangaji audio tape, (Satsang Foundation & Press) Boulder, July 23, 1995.

Page 167:
—"Let Yourself In," Satsang with Gangaji audio tape, (Satsang Foundation & Press) Boulder, August 3, 1995.

Page 171:
—"At Her Master's Feet," Satsang with Gangaji video, (Satsang Foundation & Press) Lucknow, India, January 31, 1993.

Page 181:
—"One Hundred Percent Willingness," Satsang with Gangaji audio tape, (Satsang Foundation & Press) Crestone Retreat, September, 1995, PM.

Page 185:
— Eli Jaxon-Bear, *Healing the Heart of Suffering: The Enneagram and Spiritual Growth*, p 14; manuscript available in English from The Leela Foundation; published in German under the title: *Die Neun Zahlen des Lebens*, (Munich: Droemer Knauer, 1989).

Page 188:
— The Baby Eagle Story, (paraphrased from memory) as told by Eli Jaxon-Bear during his Enneagram workshop in Boulder, CO, September, 1995

Page 190:
—"Zen Daughter," Satsang with Gangaji video, (Satsang Foundation & Press) San Diego, August 8, 1994.

Page 200:
—When I first discovered that the Infinite had actually taken on the character of my teacher, I asked Gangaji in a small satsang one day, "Will the Infinite always be for me endlessly you?" Her reply was that this is too deep; it cannot be spoken about. "But," she said, pointing to me, "you can *know* it. And you *do* know it."

Page 201:
—Gangaji, *You Are THAT!* Vol. 1 (Boulder: Satsang Foundation & Press, 1995), p. 13.

Page 210:
—Gangaji, *You Are THAT!* Vol. 1 (Boulder: Satsang Foundation & Press, 1995), p. 18.

Page 211:
—Gangaji, *You Are THAT!* Vol 1 (Boulder: Satsang Foundation & Press, 1995), p. 87

Page 214:
—"Are You Your Brother's Keeper?," Satsang with Gangaji audio tape, (Satsang Foundation & Press) Maui, January 13, 1996.

Page 225:
—SAMSARA: The illusion of the world.

Page 231:
—Sri Nisargadatta Maharaj, *I Am That*, *Talks with Sri Nisargadatta Maharaj;* translated by Maurice Frydman. Paperback ed. (Durham, NC: The Acorn Press, 9th printing, 1996), p. 343.

Page 235:
—Sri Ramana, *Who AM I? The Teachings of Bhagavan Sri Ramana Maharshi,* 7th ed. (Tiruvannamalai, India: Sri Ramanasramam, 1995), pp. 7 – 8.

—"Beyond Obedience and Rebellion," Satsang with Gangaji audio tape, (Satsang Foundation & Press) Marin, July 4, 1994.

—"The Spin Into Hell," Satsang with Gangaji video, (Satsang Foundation & Press) Santa Fe, October 6, 1994.

Page 236:
— H. W. L. Poonja, *The Truth Is,* (Lucknow Satsangs edited by Yudhishtara, 1995), p. 498.

Page 238:
—"Surrender To Stillness," Satsang with Gangaji audio tape, (Satsang Foundation & Press) Boulder, July 9, 1995.

Page 239:
—"The Three Manifestations of Mind," Satsang With Gangaji audio tape, (Satsang Foundation & Press) Boulder, Sept. 6, 1996.

Page 240:
—"Love Is All That Matters," Satsang with Gangaji audio tape, (Satsang Foundation & Press) Estes Park Retreat, May 2, 1995 AM.

ADDITIONAL RESOURCES

Audio and video recordings of Satsang with Gangaji referred to in the book are available from:

Satsang Foundation & Press
4855 Riverbend Road
Boulder, CO 80301
Ph: (303) 415-1000, Fax: (303) 449-6633

Other materials available from Satsang Foundation & Press:

River of Freedom, documentary video of Gangaji
You Are THAT! Satsang With Gangaji, Vol. 1 & 2; (books)
Who Are You? The Path of Self-Inquiry, audio set, Gangaji
The Sage of Arunachala, video of Sri Ramana Maharshi
Wake Up And Roar, Vol 1 & 2, H.W.L. Poonja (books)
Awakened From A Dream, audio tape, songs by Amber

For information about Enneagram Retreats with Eli Jaxon-Bear, please contact:

The Leela Foundation
P.O. Box 936
Stinson Beach, CA 94970
Ph: (415) 868-9800, Fax: (415) 868-0900

ORDERING INFORMATION

Additional copies of *Surprised By Grace*
$14.50 plus $2.50 shipping & handling
Colorado residents please add 5% sales tax.

also available: *Awakened From A Dream*
audio tape, songs by Amber
$11.00 plus $1.50 shipping & handling
Colorado residents please add 5% sales tax.

> **TRUE LIGHT PUBLISHING**
> P.O. Box 17734
> Boulder, CO 80308 - 0734
>
> phone: (303) 447-2547
> fax: (303) 443-4373
> e mail: TLpub@ecentral.com